THE PLEASURES OF
COOKING

Fruits & Vegetables

Also by Carl Sontheimer

Classic Cakes and Other Great Cuisinart® Desserts
 (with Cecily Brownstone)

THE PLEASURES OF
COOKING

Fruits & Vegetables

EDITED BY MARIA KOUREBANAS

WITH CARL SONTHEIMER

ILLUSTRATIONS BY AGNI SAUCIER

THE ECCO PRESS

THE ECCO PRESS
100 West Broad Street
Hopewell, New Jersey 08525

Published simultaneously in Canada by
Penguin Books Canada Ltd., Ontario
Printed in the United States of America

Library of Congress Cataloging-in-Publication Data

The pleasures of cooking fruits and vegetables / edited by Maria Kourebanas with Carl Sontheimer;
illustrations by Agni Saucier. — 1st ed.
    p.   cm.
  Includes index.
  ISBN 0-88001-525-X
  1. Cookery (Fruit) 2. Cookery (Vegetables) I. Kourebanas, Maria II. Sontheimer, Carl G.
  TX811.P56   1998
  641.6'5—dc21   97-18009

Back issues of *The Pleasures of Cooking* are available from CHC of Connecticut, Inc., P.O. Box 4780,
Greenwich, CT 06831.

Designed by The Typeworks
The text of this book is set in Electra

9 8 7 6 5 4 3 2 1

FIRST EDITION 1998

Contents

Vegetables

Fruit

Acknowledgments

With warm thanks to Cecily Brownstone, our indispensable consultant, to Chris Goulet, Sue Jones, Pamela Murtaugh, Elizabeth Pearce, Sarah Reynolds, Susan Smith, Barbara Somers, and all the others of our dedicated staff, and to each of our contributors:

Michi Ambrosi
Elizabeth Andoh
Sally Olmstead Barnes
Naomi Barry
James Beard
Simone Beck
Jehane Benoit
Jules Bond
Giuliano Bugialli
Fay Carpenter
Hugh Carpenter
John Clancy
Marion Cunningham
Sally Darr
Deidre Davis
Lorenza de Medici
Jim Dodge
Jane Salzfass Freiman
Jean-Louis Gerin
Frédy Girardet
Joyce Goldstein
Anne Lindsay Greer
Marcella Hazan
Nika Hazelton
Mary Moon Hemingway
Solange Hess

Mary Hyman
Philip Hyman
Madhur Jaffrey
Carl Jerome
Jean-Jacques Jouteux
Madeleine Kamman
Elene Margot Kolb
Jeanne Lesem
Bernard Loiseau
Nick Malgieri
Abby Mandel
Copeland Marks
Lydie Marshall
Helen McCully
Jacques Menda
Perla Meyers
Beatrice Ojakangas
Jean-Louis Palladin
Ada Parasiliti
Angela Parlingieri
Gloria Pépin
Jacques Pépin
Jeanette Pépin
Joanna Pruess
Susan Purdy
Stephan Pyles

Elaine Ratner
Elizabeth Riely
G. Franco Romagnoli
Margaret Romagnoli
Julie Sahni
Gladys Sanders
Shirley Sarvis
Michele Scicolone
Richard Secare
Dinah Shore
Nina Simonds
Marlene Sorosky
Ruth Spear
Lyn Stallworth
Katie Stapleton
Sally Tager
Barbara Tropp
Roger Vergé
Giuliana Vicinanza
Lucy Wang
William Woys Weaver
Jan Weimer
Gayle Henderson Wilson
Marys Wright
Gloria Zimmerman

—Carl Sontheimer

Preface

It has been more than ten years since *The Pleasures of Cooking* ceased publication, but my wife Shirley and I still get requests for back issues almost every month. Former subscribers, food editors, professional chefs, and cooking enthusiasts all know the quality of the recipes that we chose, perfected, and published in a magazine that was a pleasure to read and enjoy.

When Shirley and I decided to start *Pleasures*, we had one success on our hands, the Cuisinart® food processor. That was a kitchen appliance, revolutionary in its way, but a far cry from a cooking magazine. But in one way, the Cuisinart® food processor exemplifies our philosophy: it was the result of innovative thinking and a commitment to excellence. We wanted our cooking magazine to have these same qualities.

A primary responsibility of producers to their customers is to provide products that perform as described in the instructions. Recipe writers have the same responsibility. We wanted well-tested recipes, clear instructions, and as few typographical errors as humanly possible, so that our readers could offer family and friends wonderful meals from many different cuisines without fear of failure.

To that end, we engaged established top chefs and talented newcomers to create examples of their most innovative dishes. One of our four professional test cooks, each at his or her own stove, tested every recipe at least three times. Once accepted, our editorial staff scrutinized each write-up, and our graphics team produced a magazine that was indeed a work of art.

The country's food tastes have changed in the twenty-five years since our first issue. Gone are the pâtés, the Crêpes Suzette and the Fondues au Fromage of that era; today our preferences are for lighter fare. This collection of delicious fruit and vegetable recipes culled from *The Pleasures of Cooking* responds to those preferences. We want to bring back pleasant memories for those who received our magazine in the past and introduce new friends to its pleasures—in a new setting.

—Carl Sontheimer

Introduction

In 1978, Carl G. Sontheimer, founder of Cuisinart® Inc., had a vision of creating a magazine dedicated solely to the art of cooking. Perhaps his initial motivation was to educate cooks about the convenience of the food processor, although *The Pleasures of Cooking* achieved so much more. For nearly a decade the magazine brought exotic cuisines from around the world into everyday home kitchens. It also introduced us to a host of famous cooks, including James Beard, Jacques Pépin, and Craig Claiborne, and not-so-famous ones who went on to become award-winning cookbook authors. Among them are Paula Wolfert, America's most knowledgeable person on the foods of the Mediterranean; Barbara Tropp, a Chinese scholar and acclaimed restaurateur; Stephan Pyles, a restaurateur known for his modern southwestern cuisine; and Nina Simonds, an authority on Asian cooking. The magazine was indeed ahead of its time. It presented a variety of outstanding recipes drawing from a wide range of traditions and techniques. With a solid balance of simple and celebratory recipes, familiar and exotic, classic and contemporary, *The Pleasures of Cooking* had something for every kind of cook.

A look through back issues of the magazine revealed just how modern and timeless the recipes are, and it seemed natural to collect the best of them in this cookbook. The focus is on fruits and vegetables because of their healthful appeal and versatility. More than twenty-five fruits and thirty vegetables, from apples to zucchini, are represented by over two hundred and fifty recipes—and all developed by prestigious cooks and chefs.

This book features the fruits and vegetables we find at the market and eat most commonly. Raspberries and potatoes, for example, have more recipes than kiwi and sorrel. The sections are organized alphabetically by fruit or vegetable, so you can quickly determine what to do with specific produce you have on hand, whether you want to make a starter, an entrée, or a dessert. Each fruit and vegetable is introduced by a brief headnote that covers a variety of relevant information, such as harvesting, how to choose the best, storing tips, and preparation techniques. While the recipes highlight fruits and vegetables, they are not all vegetarian or meatless dishes.

One note of guidance for the cook about to take advantage of the harvest: Prepare fruits and vegetables when they are in season. If the tomatoes at your market are pale and hard, don't buy them. Wait to make that tomato salad in August, when tomatoes are at their peak. There is an ample variety of fruits and vegetables available all year round, and in the recipes that follow the cook will find a rich source of possibilities and inspirations. There are uncomplicated recipes for every day, and then there are some for those times you want to prepare something extraordinary for friends and family. We hope these recipes inspire you and provide happy moments in your kitchen.

—Maria Kourebanas

THE PLEASURES OF
COOKING

Fruits & Vegetables

Vegetables

There is such astounding variety in the world of vegetables—represented by all sorts of shapes, colors, and sizes. The vast cornucopia of fresh vegetables at the market today is extraordinary—from lush boutique salad greens to a stunning assortment of exotic mushrooms, fresh herbs, and a rainbow of different-colored chilies. We've never had so many—and such fresh—vegetables at our disposal.

The healthful appeal of vegetables has led them to become the main focus of a meal and not mere side dishes and salads. Some provide protein, others carbohydrates or fiber, but almost all are rich sources of vitamins and minerals—from vitamin A found in carrots and sweet potatoes, to vitamin C in tomatoes, and calcium in leafy green vegetables. And because vitamins are water soluble—meaning they will leach out in water when cooked—it's best to use as little water as possible when cooking. Vegetables take well to essentially every method of cooking, including steaming, sautéing, roasting, frying, grilling, and baking. The key is to avoid overcooking them.

Overall, when buying vegetables, select those that look fresh and good enough to eat raw. Leafy vegetables should be vibrant, with no indications of yellowing or wilting. Root vegetables ought to be firm. To find vegetables that are at their best, select them according to their seasons and, if possible, buy local vegetables at farmers markets—these will be freshly harvested. When it comes to storing, harder ones last longer than soft. Hard vegetables, such as root vegetables, keep well in cool, airy places and soft ones, in general, will last for a couple of days in the refrigerator. For the sake of nutrition and flavor, consume vegetables soon after buying and wash them just before using.

Artichokes

Artichokes are one of the most beautiful vegetables — as members of the thistle family they would become flowers if left long enough on the stem. Globe artichokes come mainly from California and have a long growing season, from September to June with a peak in April and May. Artichokes ought to be deep green, heavy, and firm, with tightly overlapping leaves. They have a unique, delicate flavor and are delicious steamed. The soft, fleshy portion at the bottom of each leaf, the heart, and the base are the only edible parts of the artichoke — the prickly "choke" in the center is always scraped away and discarded. (Baby artichokes, however, can be eaten whole.) Eat artichokes as fresh as possible, ideally the day of purchase. For cleaning and preparing instructions, consult the recipe for Artichokes Vinaigrette (page 3).

Artichokes Vinaigrette

The use of anchovies in this sauce, or *salsa*, is an echo of the old Roman *liquamen* or *garum* sauce. Laboriously produced of fermented fish—mostly anchovies—this was used indiscriminately, it seems, to flavor any sort of food. Today, we skip the fermentation and use anchovies preserved in salt or out of tins. The strong fish flavor disappears once the anchovies are blended with the other ingredients, but their presence adds a special taste and saltiness to the sauce.

>   2 large globe artichokes
>   3 flat anchovy fillets, drained of
>   preserving oil
>   3 small cocktail onions, chopped
>   1 teaspoon Dijon mustard
>   3 tablespoons olive oil
>   2 tablespoons red wine vinegar
>   Salt, if needed
>   Freshly ground white pepper

Clean and trim the artichokes: Snap off the outside green leaves until the layer that is pale yellow at the base to green at the top fourth of the leaf is reached. With a sharp knife, cut off this top fourth.

Do not cut off the stem, but peel it and remove the dark outer layer, leaving the inner, almost-white stem. Cut off about ⅛ inch from the bottom of the stem.

With a knife, pare down the base where the tough leaves were snapped off and save as much of the white as possible. The artichoke should now look like a truncated rosebud.

NOTE: As you work, rub the exposed edges of the artichokes with halved lemon and take them in and out of cold water to which the juice of the lemon has been added. (Cut artichokes may stand in water to which the juice of a lemon has been added for up to an hour. If they remain longer they become flaccid.)

Cut the trimmed artichoke into halves, then into quarters. Cut out the fuzzy "chokes" with a paring knife.

In a stainless-steel or enameled saucepan, cook the artichokes in abundant boiling water with a teaspoon of salt per quart of water and the rind, in strips, of a lemon.

The artichokes are cooked when the hearts feel tender if pierced with a fork or cake tester—usually about 10 to 12 minutes for the average size.

In a mortar, mash the anchovies and onions to a paste. Stir in the mustard, oil, and vinegar and work with the pestle until the sauce is smooth and homogeneous.

Taste for salt (the anchovies should have added just the right amount) and add only if needed. Add a sprinkling of white pepper to taste and mix again.

Arrange the cooked artichoke quarters on a small plate. Pour the sauce over them and serve.

Serves 2 as a starter

[MARGARET AND
G. FRANCO ROMAGNOLI]

Golden-Fried Artichokes

4 medium globe artichokes
2 lemons
¾ cup all-purpose flour (see note below)
½ teaspoon salt
4 large eggs
Vegetable oil, for frying
Salt and freshly ground black pepper

Clean and trim the artichokes as directed on page 3. Cut them into thin wedges; remove the "chokes." Put the wedges in cold water with the juice and squeezed halves of one of the lemons.

Mix the flour and salt in a small bowl. Beat the eggs in a second small bowl.

Pour enough vegetable oil into a deep pot to reach a depth of 2 inches. Heat the oil to 375°F, hot enough to make a drop of egg sizzle instantly on contact.

Drain the artichoke wedges and pat them dry. Dredge in the flour mixture and dip in the beaten egg. Deep fry, in batches, until the artichokes are golden brown, about 3 minutes. Remove them from the oil and let them drain on paper towels. Season with salt and pepper to taste. Serve hot, with the second lemon cut into wedges.

Serves 6 as a side dish

NOTE: A cupful of all-purpose or bread flour can weigh less than 4 ounces or more than 5 ounces, depending on how the cup is filled. The flour in the recipes throughout this book has been measured by the "SSS" method: First, "stir" the flour in the canister. Then, using a dry measure as a "scoop," dip it into the flour and fill it to overflowing. Then "sweep" the straight edge of a knife or spatula across the top of the dry measure. A cupful of flour measured with this method weighs 5 ounces.

[MARGARET AND
G. FRANCO ROMAGNOLI]

Artichoke and Parmesan Salad

1 medium lemon (4 ounces)
4 medium globe artichokes (1½ pounds total)
Salt and freshly ground black pepper
¼ cup fruity olive oil
4 ounces Parmesan cheese, at room temperature

Squeeze the lemon and reserve 4 teaspoons juice. Add the remaining juice and the squeezed lemon halves to a large bowl of water.

Snap off the outer artichoke leaves starting at the base, leaving a central core of pale, tender leaves. Cut 1 inch off the top and trim the base where the tough leaf ends were snapped off and the tough outer layer from the stem. Cut off the stem ¼ inch from the base and drop the artichoke into the lemon water. Repeat with the remaining artichokes, adding them to the lemon water.

Cook the artichokes in a large saucepan of lightly salted boiling water over moderate heat, covered, until tender, about 25 minutes. Drain and cool.

Halve the artichokes lengthwise and scoop out the "chokes." Cut each half lengthwise into thin slices.

Combine the reserved 4 teaspoons lemon juice and salt and pepper to taste in a bowl. Slowly whisk in the olive oil. Gently stir in the artichoke slices and divide among 4 salad plates.

Shave the Parmesan cheese into thin slices with a vegetable peeler and arrange the slices over the artichokes.

Serves 4

[MICHELE SCICOLONE]

Artichoke Bottoms Stuffed with Crabmeat

- 3 medium lemons (about 15 ounces total)
- 6 large globe artichokes (about 4 pounds total)
- 1 tablespoon vegetable oil
- 2 tablespoons unbleached all-purpose flour
- 36 small radishes (8 ounces total), washed
- ¼ cup white wine vinegar
- 1 tablespoon plus 1 teaspoon Dijon mustard
     Pinch salt and freshly ground white pepper
- ½ cup walnut oil
- 2 tablespoons chopped fresh chives
- 1½ pounds lump crabmeat, picked over
- 2 strips pimiento, diced, for garnish
- 1 small head radicchio (about 3 ounces)

Squeeze the juice of 1 lemon into 1 quart cold water in a large bowl. Cut the stems of the ar-

tichokes even with the bottoms. Pull off and discard all the leaves. Remove and discard the "chokes," using a melon baller. Trim the bottoms where the tough leaf ends were snapped off and put them in the lemon water.

Squeeze the juice from the remaining 2 lemons into 2 quarts cold water in a large pot. Add the vegetable oil and whisk in the flour. Bring the liquid to a boil and add the artichoke bottoms; reduce the heat and simmer until the point of a knife penetrates them easily, about 12 minutes.

Meanwhile, trim the radishes and make thin parallel cuts from the root end almost to the stem end without cutting through. Press down lightly on each radish to make a fan shape. Reserve.

To make a vinaigrette, in a bowl whisk together the vinegar, mustard, salt, and pepper. Add the walnut oil in a steady stream, whisking, and whisk the dressing until emulsified.

Place each artichoke bottom on an individual serving plate. Spoon 1 tablespoon vinaigrette into each and sprinkle with ½ teaspoon chives. Divide the crabmeat into 6 equal portions and mound it onto the artichoke bottoms, drizzling with additional vinaigrette. Sprinkle each with another ½ teaspoon chives and a few pieces of pimiento. Surround each filled artichoke with radicchio leaves and radish fans. Pass any remaining vinaigrette separately.

Serves 6

[J A C Q U E S   M E N D A]

Asparagus

This popular harbinger of spring can be white, green, or purple, thin or fat. White asparagus—more common in France than in the United States—is "blanched," meaning that the stalks are banked with dirt as they grow to prevent them from seeing the sun and turning green. They are generally thicker and smoother than green asparagus and have a tinge of purple at the tip. Choose asparagus that are firm and bright colored with tight, compact tips. They should be eaten soon after purchase. Keep asparagus, tips up, in a wide-mouthed jar of water in the refrigerator until ready to use. To prepare, cut off about 1 inch, or more depending on the thickness, from the woody base of the stalk. Also, peel the skin from the bottom portion of fat asparagus, as this tends to be too fibrous to eat. Peel them with a vegetable peeler from just below the tip to the cut end.

Asparagus on Red Beet Purée

12 small fresh beets
2   tablespoons olive oil
    Juice of ½ lemon
2½ teaspoons coarse (kosher) salt
½   teaspoon freshly ground black pepper
36 asparagus spears, washed
¼   cup chopped washed, fresh basil leaves

Wash the beets under cold running water. Cut off the leaves, leaving about an inch of the stem attached to the beets.

Bring a large pot of water to a boil. Add the beets, reduce the heat, and simmer until the beets are tender, about 30 to 45 minutes.

Drain the beets in a sieve lined with paper towels and set over a bowl. Reserve about 1 cup of the beet liquid. Cool the beets under cold running water until they can be handled easily. Cut off the tops and bottoms of the cooked beets and slip off the skins. Place the beets in the workbowl of a food processor fitted with the steel blade. Process until smooth. Add the olive oil, lemon juice, salt, and pepper. Process until well combined.

Thin the beet purée with about 6 to 8 tablespoons reserved beet liquid so the purée can be spooned onto a plate.

Place the beet purée in a saucepan, cover, and set aside while preparing the asparagus. The purée can be made ahead and refrigerated for up to 2 days, if you wish.

Cut off the tough, fibrous ends of the asparagus, making each spear about the same length. Bring a large pot of salted water to a boil. Place the asparagus in the pot. When the water returns to a boil, reduce the heat and cook until the asparagus are just barely tender, about 6 to 8 minutes.

Reheat the beet purée, if necessary. Spoon the purée onto 6 plates, forming an even film on the bottom of each. Arrange 6 asparagus spears on each plate. Sprinkle with the chopped basil and serve immediately.

Serves 6 as a side dish

[JEAN-JACQUES JOUTEUX AND NAOMI BARRY]

Warm Asparagus Soup

20 thin asparagus spears (8 ounces), unpeeled
½   small potato (about 2 ounces), peeled and halved
1   medium leek, trimmed of all but

    2 inches of green, washed well, and cut into 1-inch pieces
1   medium onion (about 3 ounces)
4   tablespoons unsalted butter
    Salt and freshly ground white pepper

3 cups water
  Pinch dried thyme
  Small piece bay leaf (¼ inch square)
8 medium raw shrimp, shelled, cut into
  quarters, and seasoned with salt and
  pepper
  Chopped chives or chervil, for garnish

Cut off a 2-inch piece from the tip end of each asparagus. Reserve. Cut off the tough stem ends and discard them. Cut the remaining stems into 1-inch pieces. Process the stem pieces, potato, leek, and onion in a food processor with the metal blade until coarsely chopped; pulse 3 times, then process continu-
A cupful of all-purpose or bread flour can weigh less than 4 ounces or more than 5 ounces, depending on how the cup is filled. The flour in the recipes throughout this book has been measured by the "SSS" method: First, "stir" the flour in the canister. Then, using a dry measure as a "scoop," dip it into the flour and fill it to overflowing. Then "sweep" the straight edge of a knife or spatula across the top of the dry measure. A cupful of flour measured with this method weighs 5 ounces.ously for 5 seconds. Scrape down the workbowl as necessary.

Melt 2 tablespoons of the butter in a large saucepan and sauté the chopped vegetables, seasoned with salt and pepper, over moderate heat for about 2 minutes. (This reduces the vegetables' acidity.) Add the water, thyme, and bay leaf and bring to a boil. Reduce the heat and simmer, uncovered, until the vegetables are tender, about 10 minutes.

Drain the vegetables and return the liquid to the saucepan. Process the solids and ¼ cup of the cooking liquid in the processor with the metal blade until smooth, about 1 minute. Whisk the purée back into the remaining liquid in the saucepan. Season with salt and pepper.

Bring slowly to a boil. Add the reserved asparagus tips and boil, uncovered, for 1½ minutes. Add the shrimp and the remaining 2 tablespoons of butter and simmer, whisking, just until the shrimp are cooked through, about 1 minute.

Divide among 4 warmed shallow soup dishes and garnish with chives.

Serves 4

[J E A N - L O U I S G E R I N]

Salad of Shrimp and Asparagus Sauté

1 small sweet red pepper

2 ounces arugula leaves, washed and dried

2 tablespoons olive oil
  Salt and freshly ground black pepper

16 large asparagus spears (about 10 ounces), peeled and cooked, with ½ cup asparagus cooking liquid reserved

4 tablespoons unsalted butter

12 raw medium shrimp (about 8 ounces), shelled, cut crosswise into thirds, patted dry, and seasoned with salt and pepper

2 teaspoons fresh lemon juice

To roast the pepper, spear the stem end with a long-tined kitchen fork. Hold it over a gas flame on the stove, turning to char the skin on all sides. Or place a cake rack directly on top of an electric burner over high heat and put the pepper on the rack. Turn it with tongs to char the skin on all sides. Put the pepper into a plastic food storage bag and put in the freezer until cool enough to handle, about 15 minutes. Peel off and discard the charred skin. Core and seed the pepper and cut it into ½-inch dice. Reserve.

Toss the arugula with 1 tablespoon of the olive oil and salt and pepper to taste and divide among 4 individual serving plates.

Cut off about 1½ inches from the tip ends of the asparagus. Cut the remaining spears into ½-inch pieces. Reserve.

Melt 2 tablespoons of the butter in a large skillet over high heat. Add the shrimp and stir-fry until just cooked through, about 45 seconds, shaking the pan occasionally and turning the shrimp with a fork. Add the reserved red pepper and the asparagus and cook, stirring, until the vegetables are hot, about 1 minute more.

Divide the mixture over the arugula leaves on the serving plates. Set aside.

Add the asparagus cooking liquid and remaining 1 tablespoon oil to the skillet and reduce to about ⅓ cup. Whisk in the remaining 2 tablespoons butter. Remove from the heat and whisk in the lemon juice. Season to taste. Pour sauce over each salad and serve.

Serves 4

[JEAN-LOUIS GERIN]

Lobster Asparagus Soufflé

1 pound thin asparagus spears, unpeeled, cooked
3 large eggs, separated
  Freshly ground black pepper
1 large egg white
¼ teaspoon salt
1 teaspoon fresh lemon juice
6 ounces cooked, shelled lobster tail, cut into ¼-inch dice

Cut off about 1½ inches from the tip ends of 20 of the asparagus spears. Set aside.

Cut the remaining asparagus into 1-inch pieces. Process them in a food processor with the metal blade until smooth, about 30 seconds, scraping down the workbowl as necessary.

Preheat the oven to 400°F. Lightly butter 4 round 7-inch gratin dishes (see note below).

Add the egg yolks and pepper to the workbowl. Pulse 5 times to mix, scrape down the workbowl and pulse once more.

Beat the 4 egg whites with an electric mixer on low speed until foamy. Add the salt and lemon juice and continue beating on high speed until the egg whites are firm but not dry. Fold in the asparagus purée, then the diced lobster. Divide the mixture among the prepared dishes and bake in the center of the oven until the tops are firm and lightly browned, about 12 minutes. Arrange 5 tips spoke-fashion on each soufflé and serve immediately.

Serves 4

NOTE: The soufflés can also be baked in six 1-cup soufflé dishes. Butter each one and divide the mixture evenly among them. Bake for about 10 minutes.

[JEAN-LOUIS GERIN]

Spaghettini with Asparagus

1 pound asparagus, trimmed and cut on the diagonal into ⅛-inch pieces
8 ounces packaged spaghettini
2 large garlic cloves, peeled
2 tablespoons fresh lemon juice
1 tablespoon Worcestershire sauce
½ teaspoon freshly ground black pepper
  Salt to taste
4 tablespoons unsalted butter
4 tablespoons grated Parmesan cheese

Bring 2 quarts water to a boil in a large saucepot. Add the asparagus pieces and cook for 2 minutes. Drain the asparagus in a colander and cool under cold running water. Set aside.

In a kettle of boiling salted water boil the spaghettini until it is *al dente*. Drain and set aside.

Drop the garlic through the feed tube of a food processor with the metal blade in place and the motor running. Process about 10 seconds or until finely chopped. Add the lemon juice, Worcestershire sauce, pepper, and salt and process for 5 seconds more.

Melt the butter in a large skillet over moderately low heat. Add the asparagus and the garlic mixture and toss to combine. Add the spaghettini and 1 tablespoon of the Parmesan cheese and toss until well combined and just heated through.

Transfer the spaghettini to a large serving bowl. Sprinkle with the remaining Parmesan cheese, or pass the remaining cheese separately.

Serves 4

[JAMES BEARD]

Avocados

Botanically the avocado is a fruit, but is eaten as a vegetable. Avocados are loved for their buttery texture and can be added to just about everything—dips, salads, soups, quesadillas, or simply eaten with a drizzle of fresh lemon juice. The two most common kinds of avocados are the Hass and the Fuerte. The Hass has a black pebbly skin and a high oil content and the Fuerte has a smoother, greener skin and tends to be watery. Avocados ripen off the tree and are usually sold underripe. Look for those that yield to gentle pressure, have unblemished skin, and are heavy for their size. To ripen them at home, place them in a paper bag at room temperature for a couple of days. Ripe avocados are best stored in the refrigerator. Cut the avocado just before using, as it discolors once cut. Tossing the avocado with lemon juice will retard discoloration. If you are using just half of an avocado, leave the pit in the unused half, cover with plastic wrap, and refrigerate. This will help prevent discoloration.

Avocado Butter

1 very ripe medium avocado (about 8 ounces), quartered, peeled, and pitted
½ cup unsalted butter, at room temperature, cut into 8 pieces
1 tablespoon fresh lime juice
¼ teaspoon salt
⅛ teaspoon freshly ground white pepper
⅛ teaspoon hot pepper sauce

Process the avocado and butter in a food processor with the metal blade until smooth, about 1 minute, scraping down the workbowl as necessary. Add the remaining ingredients and process until combined, about 5 seconds.

Pack the butter in a dish or crock, cover, and refrigerate. If necessary, remove any discolored butter from the top before serving. The butter keeps up to 2 hours in the refrigerator.

Makes about 1¼ cups

[GAYLE HENDERSON WILSON]

Guacamole

1 large garlic clove, peeled
2 pickled jalapeño peppers (about ½ ounce total), cut into 1-inch pieces
2 small tomatoes (about 8 ounces total), quartered and seeded
2 very ripe medium avocados (1 pound total), halved, pitted, peeled, and cut into eighths
3 medium scallions (about 2 ounces total), trimmed and coarsely chopped
1 can (4 ounces) chopped mild green chili peppers, drained
1 teaspoon salt
½ teaspoon ground cumin
½ teaspoon freshly ground black pepper
½ teaspoon hot pepper sauce

Drop the garlic through the feed tube of a food processor with the motor running and process with the metal blade until finely chopped, about 10 seconds. Add the jalapeños and finely chop, about 10 seconds. Add the tomatoes and pulse 4 times. Add the avocados and pulse 6 times. Chunks of avocado should still be visible. Add the scallions and remaining ingredients and pulse just to combine, about 4 times.

Makes about 2¾ cups

[GAYLE HENDERSON WILSON]

Smoked Salmon and Avocado Canapés

8 ounces thinly sliced smoked salmon, cut into 4 × 3-inch pieces

½ very ripe medium avocado, halved, peeled, and pitted

4 tablespoons unsalted butter, cut into 4 pieces

8 ounces cream cheese, cut into 8 pieces

1 tablespoon fresh lemon juice

1 teaspoon grated lemon zest
Salt and freshly ground white pepper

24 slices cocktail-size pumpernickel bread, trimmed and halved
Chopped red onion and dill sprigs, for garnish

Refrigerate the salmon pieces on a baking sheet, covered with plastic wrap, until ready to use.

Process the avocado and butter in a food processor with the metal blade until blended but not completely smooth, about 30 seconds. Add the cream cheese, lemon juice, lemon zest, and salt and pepper to taste and process until smooth, about 1 minute, scraping down the workbowl as necessary.

Spread a generous tablespoon of the avocado mixture on each salmon piece. Roll up the pieces and refrigerate, covered with plastic wrap, until firm, at least 1 hour. Refrigerate the remaining avocado mixture.

To assemble the canapés, spread each pumpernickel piece with a generous teaspoon of the remaining avocado mixture. Cut the salmon rolls into ½-inch slices and place 2 slices on each piece of pumpernickel. Garnish with the red onion and dill.

Makes 4 dozen hors d'oeuvres

Orange, Avocado, and Jerusalem Artichoke Salad

1 pound flat spinach leaves, stems removed

1 small red onion, peeled

1 small wedge red cabbage, cored

3 large Jerusalem artichokes, peeled and well scrubbed

5 small seedless oranges

1 large avocado, firm but ripe, halved vertically, pitted, and peeled

2 teaspoons fresh lemon juice
Honey Dressing (recipe follows)

Wash the spinach and pat dry with a paper towel. Line a 5-quart salad bowl with enough leaves to cover. Tear any remaining leaves into bite-size pieces and place in a large bowl.

Insert the medium slicing disc in the food processor workbowl. Place the onion in the feed tube. Process, using medium pressure. Remove the medium slicing disc and insert the thin slicing disc. Place the cabbage in the feed tube and process, using firm pressure. Add the cabbage and onion to the spinach in the large bowl.

With the julienne disc in place, position the artichokes horizontally in feed tube. Process, using firm pressure. Add artichokes to the bowl and toss with the spinach, onion and cabbage. Transfer the mixture to the spinach-lined salad bowl.

Cut the ends of the oranges flat. Holding each orange in place on a cutting board, remove the rind with a sharp knife, cutting from top to bottom, conforming to the shape of the orange. Rotate the orange as the rind is removed. Carefully cut away the white pith.

With the medium slicing disc in place, position each orange vertically in the feed tube. Process, using light pressure. Arrange the slices in an overlapping circle on the spinach leaves, allowing 1 inch of green to show at the edge of the bowl.

With the medium slicing disc still in place, position the avocado in the feed tube. Process, using light pressure. Remove the processor cover and add the lemon juice to the avocado slices. Toss gently. Arrange the avocado slices in the center of the salad bowl, making an attractive design.

Serve the Honey Dressing separately.

Serves 8

[ABBY MANDEL]

Honey Dressing

　2　tablespoons parsley leaves
　1　small onion (1 ounce), peeled
　½　teaspoon dry mustard
　½　teaspoon Hungarian paprika
　¾　teaspoon salt
　½　teaspoon celery seed
　3　tablespoons honey
　3　tablespoons cider vinegar
　1　tablespoon fresh lemon juice
　⅓　cup light vegetable oil

With the metal blade in place, add the parsley and onion to the food processor. Process, turning the machine on and off 6 times. Add the remaining ingredients and process 10 seconds. Remove to a serving bowl.

Makes about ¾ cup

[ABBY MANDEL]

Beans

Economic and full of vitamins, beans are an indispensable ingredient in several cuisines. They can be cooked in so many different ways and are a mainstay of menus year-round. There are basically two types of beans, fresh and dried (a few varieties are available both ways). Sold freshly harvested, some fresh beans are eaten with their pods, such as green beans, and others are shelled, like lima and fava beans. Fresh beans should be stored in the refrigerator, where they will last for 3 to 4 days. Dried beans are a great source of protein and are also a pantry staple because they keep so well—up to a year at room temperature. They generally need to be soaked in water for some hours to rehydrate before cooking.

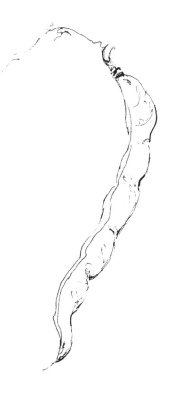

Black Bean Soup

1 pound dried black beans
¼ pound salt pork
3¼ cups beef broth, as needed
3 cups water
4 ounces lean smoked slab bacon
1 ham bone (optional)
2 tablespoons unsalted butter
1 medium onion, peeled and chopped
2 small leeks, trimmed, thoroughly
   cleaned, and chopped
1 carrot, peeled and chopped
¼ cup chopped celery tops
½ teaspoon freshly ground black pepper
¼ teaspoon dried thyme
1 bay leaf
¼ teaspoon salt (optional)
2 to 4 tablespoons dry sherry
2 hard-cooked eggs, minced
1 tablespoon minced parsley

Wash the beans very well in cold water, picking out irregular beans and discarding any foreign matter. Soak the beans overnight in a 3-quart bowl, with enough cold water to come 2 inches above the beans.

Drain the beans and put them in a 6-quart saucepot. Put the salt pork in a 1-quart saucepan with water to cover and bring to a boil. Continue to boil for 1 minute; drain and rinse under cold running water. Add to the beans. Add 3 cups broth, the water, bacon, and ham bone, if used, and bring to a boil. Reduce the heat and simmer, covered, while preparing the vegetables.

In a medium skillet, melt the butter over moderate heat; add the onion and sauté, stirring often, until soft, about 5 minutes. Do not let the onion brown. Add the leeks, carrot, and celery tops and continue to sauté until the vegetables are soft, about 3 minutes.

Stir the vegetables into the soup; add the pepper, thyme, and bay leaf and continue to simmer, covered, for 3 hours or until the beans are very soft, stirring occasionally to prevent sticking.

Remove the salt pork and bacon and set aside. Remove the ham bone and bay leaf and discard. Use the food processor fitted with the metal blade to purée the soup, 2 cups at a time, turning the machine on and off 3 or 4 times and then letting it run for 45 seconds. Return the puréed soup to the saucepot.

Dice the reserved bacon and salt pork into ¼-inch pieces and return to the soup. Heat the soup through over low heat; if the soup is too thick, stir in up to ¼ cup of beef broth.

Just before serving, adjust the seasoning, adding the salt, if needed, and stir in sherry to taste. In a small bowl stir together the minced egg and parsley; sprinkle some of the mixture on each serving.

Serves 6

[JULES BOND]

Sweet and Sour Green Beans

Salt
2½ pounds fresh green beans, with ends
    snipped
4 slices bacon
2 medium onions, peeled and chopped
1½ cups cider vinegar
4 tablespoons sugar

In a large saucepan, bring to a boil at least 4 quarts of water seasoned with 1 teaspoon salt per quart. Drop in the beans, a handful at a time, without letting the water stop boiling. Cook, uncovered, for 10 to 15 minutes or until just tender. Drain the beans immediately and refresh them in cold water to stop the cooking. You may complete the recipe to this point ahead of time and finish it later.

In a skillet over moderate heat cook the bacon until crisp, saving the fat. Crumble the bacon and set it aside. Sauté the onions in the hot bacon fat over moderate heat until they are transparent but not browned, about 3 minutes. Add the vinegar and sugar and stir to mix. Add the beans to this mixture and stir until heated through. Before serving, toss the crumbled bacon with the beans.

Serves 8 to 10

[M A R Y   M O O N   H E M I N G W A Y]

Cuban Homestyle Beans with Pork

Though Americans are fond of heaping sauced foods on top of their rice, the authentic Cuban way of serving this dish is with the rice on the side. When dining Cuban-style, only one forkful of beans and rice is mixed together at a time.

1 pound dried red kidney beans
2 bay leaves
1 large carrot, peeled and cut into 1-inch
    chunks
3 medium onions, peeled and coarsely
    chopped (about 1½ cups)
2 pounds spareribs or pork chops, or a
    combination of both
3 tablespoons vegetable oil
1 tablespoon salt
1 teaspoon freshly ground black pepper
1 can (8 ounces) tomato sauce
1 tablespoon fresh lemon juice
1 tablespoon minced garlic
¼ teaspoon dried rosemary
10 sprigs fresh cilantro, leaves only,
    chopped
    Cooked white rice, for serving

Rinse the beans in a colander and pick them over to remove any pebbles or grit. Place them in a 6- to 8-quart pot. Add 7 cups of cold water, the bay leaves, carrot, and ¾ cup of the chopped onions. Bring to a boil, lower the heat, and simmer, covered, for 1¼ hours, or until the beans are tender.

While the beans are cooking, prepare the

pork. Trim all excess fat from the spareribs or chops. Cut spareribs into individual ribs. The chops can be cooked whole or with the meat separated from the bones and cut into 1-inch chunks (but be sure you include the bones).

Heat the oil in a large skillet. Add the pork and brown on both sides over moderate heat, about 10 minutes in all.

Add the remaining ¾ cup chopped onions and the salt and pepper. With a wooden spoon, stir and scrape the bottom of the skillet to mix in any flavorful bits that adhere to the pan. Continue to cook until the onions are pale yellow and translucent. Add the tomato sauce, lemon juice, garlic, rosemary, and cilantro. Stir to mix all the ingredients. Add the beans with their cooking liquid. Stir gently to distribute the beans, being careful not to break them open.

Bring the beans and pork with the sauce to a boil. Lower the heat and simmer, covered, for 20 minutes or until the pork is tender.

Serve accompanied by white rice.

Serves 8 to 10

[GLORIA PÉPIN]

Maccù
Purée of Fava Beans

This is a rural southern Sicilian dish that goes back to Greek times. It is made with dried, peeled fava beans and flavored with oil and wild fennel. In different localities, chopped vegetables and a little bacon fat may be added to the purée; at times, it is made more substantial with the addition of cooked ditalini or other small pasta. Since wild fennel is not available here, use cut whole bulb fennel (finocchio) and add it to the *maccù* as it cooks. *Maccù* may be diluted into a soup with hot water or dry white wine. Cold, the peasants eat it as is or slice and fry it in hot oil.

1 pound dried, peeled fava beans (see note below)
1 large fennel bulb, trimmed and sliced
⅓ cup olive oil
1 medium onion, peeled and chopped
1 large garlic clove, chopped
  Salt and freshly ground black pepper
  Dry white wine (optional)
2 tablespoons olive oil (optional)

Soak the beans overnight in plenty of cold water. Rinse and put them in a large saucepan. Add cold water to cover the beans by about 2 inches. Add the fennel. Simmer, covered, over low heat for about 1 hour, or until the beans are semisoft. Check the water from time to time; if the beans run dry, add hot water.

Heat the oil in a small skillet over moderate heat and sauté the onion and garlic until soft but not browned. Stir into the beans and season with salt and pepper. Simmer, covered, until the beans are very soft. Crush them with a fork. Throughout the cooking time, check the water. To achieve proper consistency as a purée or as a soup, add more hot water or dry white wine. Sprinkle with the olive oil before serving.

Serves 4 to 6

NOTE: If the fava beans you buy are brownish and have a black spot at one end, they still have their peels. The peels can be easily removed after they have soaked overnight and before cooking. If the beans are an even pale color, and are slightly open at one end, they have already been peeled.

If you cannot find dried fava beans, you can use canned. Four 20-ounce cans equal 1 pound of dried. Rinse off the beans and remove the skins (they should come right off). The result, however, will not be as good as with dried beans.

[NIKA HAZELTON]

White Beans with Fresh Tomato

1⅓ cups dried white beans, preferably Great
     Northern
  2 whole cloves
  1 medium onion (5 ounces), peeled
  1 medium carrot (4 ounces), peeled
  4 large garlic cloves, unpeeled
  1 bouquet garni (see note below)
  1 teaspoon salt
 ⅛ teaspoon freshly ground black pepper
  1 tablespoon olive oil
  1 medium tomato (7 ounces), peeled and
     sceded
 ¾ ounce truffles, thinly sliced (optional)
  2 tablespoons unsalted butter

Soak the beans overnight covered with 1 quart of cold water in a large bowl (see note below).

The next day, drain the beans and discard the liquid. Put the beans in a large saucepan and add 2 quarts of cold water.

Stick the whole cloves in the onion and add to the saucepan along with the carrot, garlic, and bouquet garni. Bring to a boil, skimming off any foam that rises to the surface. Stir in the salt, pepper, and olive oil and skim again. Cook, uncovered, at a gentle boil for 1 to 1½ hours, or until the beans are tender.

Remove and discard the carrot, onion, and bouquet garni. Remove and reserve the garlic cloves. Drain the beans, reserving the liquid. Rinse the cooking pan and place the drained beans in it.

Chop the tomato coarsely in a food processor with the metal blade, 4 to 6 pulses. Add to the beans.

Remove the garlic skins and process the pulp with ½ cup of the reserved cooking liquid until smooth, about 15 seconds. Discard the remaining liquid.

Place the saucepan with the beans over low heat and stir in the garlic purée, truffles (if used), and the butter. Adjust the seasoning and serve.

Serves 4

NOTE: Instead of soaking the beans overnight, you can place the beans in a large saucepan with enough water to cover by 2 inches. Bring to a boil and cook for 2 minutes. Remove from the heat, and let stand for 1 hour, after which the beans can be drained and cooked as above.

Make a bouquet garni by tying together 3 sprigs fresh parsley, 1 medium bay leaf, and 1 sprig fresh thyme (if dried thyme is used, enclose ½ teaspoon in a small piece of cheesecloth and tie it to the bay leaf and parsley).

[PHILIP AND MARY HYMAN]

Vegetarian Mock Beef Broth
Pot-au-Feu du Vendredi

This recipe for vegetable stock, found in a forgotten French food magazine, tastes remarkably like beef stock. Coincidentally, its title was "Le Pot-au-Feu" and the publisher, editor and author was Madame St. Ange, an outstanding cook and teacher of cooking. Her book, *La Cuisine de Madame St. Ange,* is the best textbook for home cooks ever published in French. It has never been translated.

At the turn of the century, when this recipe was published, Friday was a meatless day for most Frenchmen, and that is why the French title is "Friday's Pot-au-Feu."

2½ cups dry white beans (small pea beans are good)
 1 medium onion, peeled
 3 medium carrots, peeled
3½ tablespoons sweet butter
3¾ quarts water
 1 medium turnip, peeled
 1 stalk celery
 1 small parsnip, peeled
 1 sprig fresh thyme or ⅛ teaspoon dried
10 whole parsley sprigs with stems

 1 small garlic clove, peeled
 2 whole cloves
1½ tablespoons salt
 5 or 6 small leeks, well washed, white part only, roots trimmed off
 6 1-inch-thick slices of French bread, toasted lightly

In a 3-quart saucepan, put the beans and enough water to cover by 2 to 3 inches. Bring to a boil over moderate heat and let simmer 1 minute. Remove from heat and let stand while preparing the remaining vegetables.

Process the onion and half of the carrots in a food processor with the slicing disc. Reserve the remaining carrots for the second half of the cooking period.

In a 5-quart stockpot or casserole, melt the butter over moderate heat. Add the sliced carrots and the onions and cook slowly, stirring constantly. It is important that the vegetables take on color slowly, and that they form a delicate caramel-like base. After about 20 minutes, add the water to the vegetables.

Remove any of the beans that float to the

top of the saucepan. Drain the beans in a colander and add to the liquid in the large stockpot.

Process the turnip, the celery, and the parsnip in the food processor with the slicing disc, and add to stockpot. Tie the thyme, the parsley sprigs, the garlic, and the cloves in cheesecloth and add to the soup. Add the salt. Bring to a slow simmer, cover and let cook very slowly for 3 hours (the liquid should just barely bubble). Check frequently to make sure the soup is not boiling.

At the end of 3 hours, add the leeks. Cut the remaining whole carrot in half and cut carrots into lengthwise slices about ¼-inch thick. Add to soup. Cover pot and continue to simmer very slowly for 3 hours.

To serve, remove the leeks and the large carrot slices with a slotted spoon and place in a serving dish. Carefully strain the bouillon into another pot, reserving the beans for another use (see note below). Reheat the bouillon slowly and pour over the toast in serving dishes. Pass the whole leeks and carrots separately to garnish each serving.

Serves 6

NOTE: The cooked beans and vegetables, strained from the *Pot-au-Feu*, can easily be transformed into a hearty bean soup. Purée in two batches in the processor, transfer to a saucepan, and thin to the desired consistency with milk, cream, or broth. Season as necessary.

Beets

Jewellike and slightly sweet, the garnet beet used to be the only variety sold at the market. Now, however, there are yellow, white, and even striped beets. Most abundant from June to September, these root vegetables are usually sold with their thick fibrous greens, which can be delicious when cooked, still attached.

When buying, choose small beets that have firm, fine-textured flesh. The greens should be a brilliant green, without wilting or yellowing. For tender-cooking greens, select small bunches with small, bright green leaves and narrow ribs. Keep them wrapped loosely in the refrigerator. The roots will keep longer than the greens, so cut off the greens just above the root and cook them within a day or two. The beets themselves will last for up to 3 weeks in a cool, dark, airy place. Wash the beets just before cooking and peel them after they've been cooked to help prevent them from losing color.

Beet Greens with Cashews

1 to 1¼ pounds fresh beet greens (greens from 2 bunches, about 1¼ pounds each, fresh beets)
3 tablespoons vegetable oil
¼ cup roasted, salted cashews, coarsely chopped
Salt and freshly ground black pepper

Cut off the beet greens, leaving 1 or 2 inches attached to the beets. Remove and discard the large stems and wash the greens thoroughly. Drain and dry well. Cut the greens crosswise at 2-inch intervals.

Heat the oil in a wok or large skillet over moderately high heat. Add about half of the greens and stir constantly until they begin to wilt, about 1 minute. Add the rest of the greens and stir constantly for about 1 minute more or until all the greens are wilted. Stir in the cashews and salt and pepper to taste. Cook for 30 seconds more, stirring constantly.

Serves 4

[MARLENE SOROSKY]

Pickled Beets

2 cups distilled white vinegar
½ cup sugar
10 to 16 whole cloves, or to taste
1 teaspoon salt
1 bay leaf
3 bunches beets (about 2 pounds total), peeled and cut horizontally to fit feed tube of a food processor

To make a syrup, boil the vinegar, sugar, and seasonings in a nonreactive saucepan for 10 minutes. Keep hot.

Slice the beets with the French-fry disc of a food processor and cook in boiling water until just tender, 10 to 15 minutes. Drain. Add to the syrup and return to a boil. Remove from the heat, transfer to a glass bowl or jar, and cool. Refrigerate, covered, overnight or up to 2 weeks.

Makes about 4 cups

[JEHANE BENOIT]

Cook the pasta in boiling salted water until *al dente*, about 9 minutes, adding the broccoli in the last minute. Drain, reserving 3 tablespoons water.

Return the pasta, broccoli, and reserved water to the pan, add the butter and seasonings, and stir over low heat until well coated. Add the Gruyère, Crème Fraîche, and pine nuts and stir until the cheese is melted, about 3 minutes. Top with the Parmesan shavings.

Serves 6

Crème Fraîche

- 1 cup sour cream
- 2 cups heavy cream
- 2 teaspoons fresh lemon juice

Put the sour cream in a large bowl. Gradually whisk in the heavy cream until thoroughly blended. Cover with plastic wrap and put in a warm place for 8 to 24 hours or longer, until the mixture has thickened.

Place a plastic coffee filter holder or strainer over a bowl and insert a filter paper. Pour the thickened cream into the filter. Cover with plastic wrap, refrigerate, and leave to drain for 24 to 36 hours. Tear away the filter paper along its seam, transfer the mixture to a bowl, and stir in the lemon juice. Cover and refrigerate for up to 1 week.

Makes about 2½ cups

Broccoli and Pork Strings in Garlic Sauce

- 1 pound fresh dark green broccoli
- 8 ounces pork loin, cut into 3 × ⅛-inch pieces (use meat frozen three-fourths of the way for easier slicing)
- 3 cups vegetable oil

Pork Marinade

- 1 tablespoon thin soy sauce
- 1 teaspoon sugar
- 2 tablespoons water
- 1 teaspoon cornstarch

Sauce

- 1 tablespoon plus 1 teaspoon minced fresh ginger
- 1 to 1½ teaspoons hot bean paste (available in Asian food markets)
- 1 tablespoon thin soy sauce
- 1 tablespoon Chinese rice wine or pale dry sherry
- 1 tablespoon sugar
- 2 teaspoons black Chinese vinegar
- 1 teaspoon cornstarch dissolved in 2 tablespoons cold water
- ½ teaspoon sesame oil

Using a sharp paring knife, cut the broccoli florets from the main stalk where they first branch off. Carefully strip away the outer layer of fibrous bark from the stems of the florets. Cut off and discard the woody bottom inch of the main stalk, and strip the stalk of its outer peel, peeling away the fiber until the lighter green inner core of stalk is laid bare. Cut the main stalk (or stalks) into spears about 3 inches long and the diameter of a chopstick.

Bring to a full boil in a large pot with enough water to cover the broccoli. Have a metal colander ready in the sink. With the water at a furious boil and the heat on high, add the broccoli to the water. After 2 minutes, drain the broccoli in the colander under cold running water. When the broccoli is cool, shut off the water. Put the broccoli aside to drain.

Mix the soy sauce, 1 teaspoon sugar, the water, and cornstarch in a medium-size bowl. Add the pork sticks to the mixture and mix well with your hands. Put the pork aside to marinate while you prepare the rest of the dish.

Put a deep-frying vessel over high heat for 20 seconds, and fill it with at least 3 inches of oil.

While the oil is heating, combine the minced garlic, hot bean paste, and 1 tablespoon of the minced ginger in a small bowl. Combine the soy sauce, wine, 1 tablespoon sugar, and the vinegar in another bowl and stir well to mix.

When the oil is surmounted by a heavy haze, or registers 350°F on a deep-fry ther-mometer, stir the pork and then drop it at arm's length into the oil. Expect a layer of white bubbles to rise at once a good inch or two above the level of the oil. Immediately stir the pork sticks with a long cooking chop-stick or long-handled wooden spoon to keep them separate. After 30 seconds, remove the pork sticks from the oil with a Chinese mesh spoon, a shallow mesh strainer, or a slotted spoon. Set them aside on a small plate.

Set a wok or 12-inch skillet over high heat for 20 seconds. Add 2 tablespoons of the oil used for deep-frying to the pan, and swirl to coat the cooking surface evenly with the oil. Reduce the heat to moderate and add the gar-lic, bean paste, and the remaining 1 teaspoon of the minced ginger to the pan. Gently stir until fragrant, about 30 seconds. Add the broccoli and the pork to the pan, and stir-fry for 1 minute. Add the combined soy sauce, wine, sugar, and vinegar to the pan next, and stir-fry for 2 minutes until the vegetables and liquids are heated through. Stir the corn-starch mixture to recombine it, and add it to the pan. Stir for 1 minute, until the sauce thickens and clears somewhat.

Turn off the heat. Sprinkle in the sesame oil and stir to mix. Arrange the pork sticks and broccoli attractively on a platter and serve im-mediately.

Serves 6 to 8 as part of a Chinese meal, 3 as a main dish served Western-style

[BARBARA TROPP]

Cabbage

Cabbage belongs to the brassica family, which also includes broccoli, cauliflower, kohlrabi, and Brussels sprouts. During winter when other vegetables are in short supply, cabbage becomes an important ingredient. And although it may have developed a reputation of being commonplace and ordinary, with the right preparation it can become a sophisticated vegetable. There are a number of varieties with different growing seasons, so there is usually some kind of cabbage at the market year-round. When purchasing most types of cabbage, look for heavy ones that are thick and firm, with shiny, crisp outer leaves. The leaves should show no sign of yellowing or other discoloration. Keep cabbage tightly wrapped in the refrigerator for up to one week. Cabbage can be eaten raw or cooked—pickling is a popular preparation in many different cuisines.

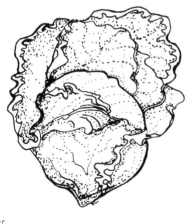

Shrimp with Cabbage and Caviar

5 shrimp (10 to 15 to the pound), peeled
  and deveined
  Salt and freshly ground white pepper
2 tablespoons unsalted butter
1½ cups shredded white cabbage
¾ cup heavy cream
1 teaspoon caviar (optional)

Sprinkle the shrimp with salt and pepper. Melt 1 tablespoon of the butter in a skillet. When hot, add the shrimp. Sauté over high heat for about 50 to 60 seconds. With a slotted spoon, transfer to a plate.

Add the cabbage to the juices in the pan and sauté for about 10 seconds. Add the cream and bring to a boil. Reduce the cabbage-cream mixture over high heat for a few minutes, until the cream coats the spoon. Add salt and pepper to taste.

With a slotted spoon, remove the cabbage to a serving dish. Mix some of the sauce with the cabbage. Add the remaining 1 tablespoon butter, in small pieces, to the sauce remaining in the skillet. Stir the sauce after adding each piece.

Arrange the shrimp on top of the cabbage. Pour the rest of the sauce over and sprinkle with caviar. Serve immediately.

Serves 2

[JACQUES PÉPIN]

Savoy Cabbage Soup, Aosta Style

The Alpine valley of Aosta is just this side of the Alps of the French region of Savoie; and the cultural kinship of the two is apparent, not only in the language and in the many place names, but in the most vital of all manifestations of culture—cooking. As, for example, in this superb soup that seems so much a dainty version of *soupe à l'oignon.*

The only time-consuming procedure in this recipe—the long, slow cooking of the cabbage until it is reduced to creamy softness—can be done in advance, either several hours or the night before. Once that is accomplished, the finishing steps, of which the most important is the "savoring"—*in-saporire*—of the cooked cabbage in a *battuto* of onion and garlic, go very quickly, and the whole soup can be assembled in 20 to 25 minutes.

If you like, you can place the soup in ovenproof bowls and give it a gratin treatment in a very hot oven before serving it. It's a bit of fancy business that is not necessary, but that is up to you. As Matisse said, there are no rules outside of individuals. Let us use the word choices instead of rules and the statement becomes as true of cooking as of painting.

1½ pounds savoy cabbage
¼ cup olive oil

3 tablespoons unsalted butter

1 tablespoon very finely chopped onion

½ teaspoon very finely chopped garlic
  Salt and freshly ground black pepper

2 tablespoons vegetable oil

4 slices good-quality white bread

4 ounces Fontina cheese, sliced very thin
  (see note below)

6 tablespoons freshly grated Parmesan
  cheese

Remove any of the blemished outer leaves of the cabbage. Rinse the remainder in cold water and cut it up into pieces about 1 inch square. You should have about 5 cups. Put the pieces in a soup pot, and add sufficient water to cover by an inch or so; cover the pot and bring the water to a boil. Turn down the heat so that the water bubbles slowly, and cook for at least 3 hours.

When the cabbage has become very soft, drain it, but reserve the cooking liquid.

Put all the olive oil, 2 tablespoons of the butter, and the onion in a medium sauté pan and turn on the heat to moderate. When the onion has become translucent, add the garlic, cooking it until it becomes just slightly colored.

Add the drained, cooked cabbage and a liberal amount of salt and pepper, and turn the heat up to high. Cook the cabbage for about 15 minutes, stirring frequently and mashing it with a fork so that it becomes a creamy pulp.

Transfer the cabbage and all the contents of the pan to a soup pot. Add enough of the cabbage's reserved cooking liquid to cover by 2 to 3 inches and bring it to a moderate boil.

While the soup pot is bubbling, put the remaining 1 tablespoon butter and the vegetable oil in a medium sauté pan or skillet and turn on the heat to moderate. When the butter foam begins to subside, put in the bread slices and brown them on both sides. When browned, transfer to paper towels to drain.

Put a slice of browned bread at the bottom of each of four individual soup plates; cover each with a slice of Fontina and over each put the cabbage with just enough liquid to rise to the top of the cabbage. Sprinkle 1½ tablespoons grated Parmesan over each dish and serve immediately.

Serves 4

NOTE: Genuine Fontina from Val d'Aosta is a tender cheese that mingles savoriness with mildness in an inimitable manner and, in cooking, melts beautifully. The least acceptable substitutes for Fontina are its American and Scandinavian imitations, which are totally lacking in character. If you cannot find authentic Fontina, look for other semisoft cheeses that are creamy in texture and have a little spice to their aroma, such as Münster or Taleggio.

[MARCELLA HAZAN]

Cabbage and Snow Pea Salad

½ medium cabbage (about 11 ounces), cored and cut to fit the feed tube of a food processor

4 ounces snow peas, strings removed

1 small onion (about 2 ounces), peeled and ends cut flat

2 tablespoons vegetable oil

3 tablespoons fresh lemon juice

1 tablespoon fish sauce (preferably *nam pya ye* from Thailand, available at Asian food stores)

½ teaspoon sugar

Process the cabbage in a food processor with the thin slicing disc. Transfer to a large bowl. Pack the snow peas horizontally on edge in the feed tube in a single layer and slice. Add to the bowl, cover the vegetables with cold water, and refrigerate for 30 minutes to crisp. Drain well and pat dry.

Slice the onion with the thin slicing disc. Heat the oil in a skillet over moderate heat and cook the onion, stirring, until crisp and brown, about 5 minutes. Remove with a slotted spoon to paper towels to drain. Reserve the oil.

In a serving bowl, toss together the cabbage, snow peas, onion, reserved oil, lemon juice, fish sauce, and sugar. Serve cold or at room temperature.

Serves 6

[C O P E L A N D   M A R K S]

Danish Cabbage Rolls Stuffed with Veal

1 teaspoon salt

12 large green cabbage leaves (about 2¼ pounds) (see note below)

1 tablespoon fresh parsley leaves

1 small onion (2 ounces), peeled and halved

1 large egg

¼ teaspoon ground allspice

½ teaspoon tomato paste

1½ pounds lean veal, cut into 1-inch pieces

¼ cup seedless dark raisins

½ cup cooked white rice

1½ cups chicken stock, preferably homemade, or more if needed

2 bay leaves

8 fresh medium mushrooms (about 3½ ounces), sliced

¼ cup milk

1 tablespoon unbleached all-purpose flour

3 tablespoons unsalted butter, at room temperature

4 teaspoons finely chopped fresh dill

1 teaspoon finely chopped fresh chives

¼ cup sour cream

Salt and freshly ground white pepper

Bring 3 quarts of water to a boil in a large saucepot. Add the salt and the cabbage leaves, bring the water back to a boil, and cook for 2 minutes, or until the leaves are pliable enough to roll. Drain on paper towels and reserve.

Drop the parsley and onion through the feed tube of a food processor with the metal blade in place and the motor running. Process for 5 seconds or until coarsely chopped. Add the egg, allspice, and tomato paste and pulse 4 to 6 times to combine. Transfer the mixture to a large bowl.

Process the veal in 2 batches with the metal blade, pulsing each batch 10 to 12 times or until finely chopped. Add the veal to the bowl along with the raisins and rice. Using your hands or a wooden spoon, combine all the ingredients thoroughly.

To make the cabbage rolls, place about ⅓ cup of the veal mixture in the center of each cabbage leaf with the core end facing you. Fold the sides over the filling and roll up from the core end to form compact bundles. Place the rolls in one layer, seam side down, in a large skillet. Pour 1 cup of the chicken stock over the rolls and add the bay leaves. Bring to a boil, cover, reduce the heat, and simmer gently for 1 hour, checking occasionally to make sure that the liquid has not evaporated. Add additional stock if necessary.

When the rolls are cooked, remove them to a warm serving platter and cover loosely with aluminum foil.

Leave the remaining cooking liquid in the skillet. It will be used for making the sauce.

Add the mushrooms to the skillet with the remaining ½ cup chicken stock. Simmer the mushrooms, uncovered, over moderately low heat until tender, about 2 minutes. Whisk in the milk.

Blend the flour and butter together in a small bowl until well combined and add bit by bit to the skillet, whisking constantly. Stir in half the dill and all the chives and cook 2 minutes longer. Stir in the sour cream and just heat through. Season to taste with salt and white pepper.

To serve, spoon the warm sauce over the cabbage rolls and garnish with the remaining dill.

Serves 6

NOTE: You may need to use 2 heads of cabbage in order to get the 12 large leaves needed for the rolls.

[E L E N E   M A R G O T   K O L B]

Carrots

Carrots contribute a sweet, rich character to everything they are cooked or eaten with. And when served alone, their charm really comes through. They are available year-round. When shopping, look for crisp, firm carrots with smooth unblemished skin. If the tops are attached, they should be bright green. Remove the tops and refrigerate the carrots in a plastic bag in the coldest section of the refrigerator. They should keep for up to 2 weeks.

Curried Carrot and Zucchini Fritters

3 medium carrots, peeled and cut to fit the
    feed tube of a food processor horizon-
    tally
2 medium zucchini, trimmed and cut to
    fit the feed tube of a food processor
    horizontally
1 cup all-purpose flour
1 teaspoon salt
¼ teaspoon freshly ground black pepper
¼ teaspoon curry powder
2 large eggs, lightly beaten
1 cup flat beer
    Vegetable oil, for frying

Process the carrots and zucchini in a food
processor with the medium shredding disc.

Remove to a bowl.

To make the batter, fit the processor with
the metal blade and process the dry ingredients about 3 seconds. Add the eggs and beer
and pulse just to combine, about 5 times. Stir
into the carrots and zucchini.

Heat 2 inches oil in a large skillet to 365°F.
Drop the batter by the teaspoon into the oil in
batches and cook, turning, until golden,
about 2½ minutes. Remove with a slotted
spoon to paper towels to drain. Reheat the oil
between batches, if necessary.

Serve hot, as an hors d'oeuvre.

Makes about 40 fritters

Carrot Salad with Cilantro Dressing

1 pound carrots, peeled and cut into
    2-inch pieces
½ cup tightly packed fresh cilantro,
    coarsely chopped
⅓ cup light soy sauce
¼ teaspoon salt
1 tablespoon sugar
3 tablespoons clear rice vinegar
1 tablespoon rice wine, such as sake
2 tablespoons sesame oil

Process the carrots in a food processor with
the medium shredding disc. Transfer to a
large bowl and add the cilantro.

To make the dressing, process the remaining ingredients with the metal blade for
about 20 seconds or until the sugar has dissolved. Pour over the carrots and cilantro and
toss to coat. Cover and refrigerate for 1 hour.
Transfer to a serving bowl with a slotted
spoon.

Serves 6

[N I N A   S I M O N D S]

Braised Carrots in Dilled Cream

These go excellently with grilled salmon or swordfish steaks and are equally good with a veal or chicken piccata. They can be prepared in advance and reheated, but do not add the dill until the last moment. If you want more sauce, do not reduce the Crème Fraîche to a glaze; simply bring it to a boil, reduce it slightly, and add a bit of beurre manié (2 teaspoons of butter mixed into a paste with 2 teaspoons of flour).

8 to 10 medium carrots (1 pound total), peeled
3 tablespoons unsalted butter
½ teaspoon sugar
Pinch of salt
Freshly ground white pepper
2 to 3 tablespoons chicken broth
Sprig of fresh thyme or pinch of dried thyme
¾ cup Crème Fraîche (page 30)
3 tablespoons minced fresh dill

Cut the carrots so they are matchstick size and 1½ inches long. (Use the julienne disc of your processor, if you have one.) Melt the butter in a 10-inch skillet over moderate heat. Add the carrots, sugar, salt, and a good grinding of white pepper. Sauté the carrots, stirring, for 1 to 2 minutes, or until they begin to brown. Add the broth, lower the heat, and bury the thyme in the carrots. Cover the skillet and simmer the carrots until they are just tender, about 5 minutes.

Uncover the skillet, raise the heat to moderate, and cook until the liquid is reduced and glazes the bottom of the pan. Stir in the Crème Fraîche and boil down the liquid, stirring occasionally, until it thickens and coats the carrots. Correct the seasoning and stir in the minced dill.

Serves 6

[PERLA MEYERS]

Fifteen-Second Carrot Cake

If your food processor has a workbowl with an inside width greater than 6½ inches you can double the recipe to make two cakes: one to serve and one to freeze.

2 medium carrots (8 ounces total), peeled
2 large eggs
1 cup sugar
¾ cup vegetable oil
1 teaspoon pure vanilla extract
1 cup stirred unbleached all-purpose flour
1 teaspoon baking powder
1 teaspoon baking soda
½ teaspoon salt
1 teaspoon ground cinnamon
½ cup pecan halves
Cream Cheese Frosting (recipe follows) and extra pecan halves, for garnish; or Rum Sauce (recipe follows) and whipped cream, if desired, for serving

Preheat the oven to 325°F. Grease and flour an 8½ × 4½ × 2½-inch loaf pan.

Shred the carrots in a food processor with the fine shredding disc. Remove the carrots (there should be 1½ tightly packed cups). Insert the metal blade and process the eggs, sugar, oil, and vanilla just until blended, about 2 seconds. Do not overprocess.

Evenly sprinkle the flour, baking powder, baking soda, salt, and cinnamon over the mixture; process until smooth, about 5 seconds.

Sprinkle with the ½ cup pecan halves; add the carrots and process until the pecans and carrots are evenly distributed, 4 seconds.

Turn the batter into the prepared pan and bake in the preheated oven until a cake tester inserted in the center comes out clean, 1 hour. Loosen the edges and turn out onto a wire rack. Cool completely.

If using the Cream Cheese Frosting, cover the top and sides of the cake with it. Garnish with extra pecan halves, making crosswise rows fairly close together. (Each slice should have its own row of pecans.) Press a row of pecan halves around the sides and ends of the cake, at the bottom, so they are in a standing position, spacing them to match the rows on top.

If using the Rum Sauce, leave the cake unfrosted and pass the sauce with it, and, if you like, a bowl of whipped cream.

Makes 1 carrot cake, serving 8

Cream Cheese Frosting

4 tablespoons unsalted butter, cut into 4 equal pieces

4 ounces cream cheese

1 teaspoon pure vanilla extract

1¾ cups stirred confectioners' sugar

Process together all the ingredients in a food processor with the metal blade until smooth.

Rum Sauce

1 cup firmly packed dark brown sugar

½ cup dark corn syrup

½ cup heavy cream

4 tablespoons unsalted butter

¼ cup light rum

1 teaspoon pure vanilla extract

Combine the sugar, corn syrup, cream, and butter in a medium saucepan and stir constantly over low heat until boiling, about 9 minutes. Remove from the heat and stir in the rum and vanilla. The sauce may be made ahead and stored in the refrigerator. Serve the sauce hot or cold.

Makes about 2 cups

[CECILY BROWNSTONE]

Cauliflower

A member of the cabbage family, cauliflower matures during the cool part of the year. In most parts of the country, it is plentiful during fall and early winter. Cauliflower is mild in flavor and benefits when combined with more assertive flavors. In supermarkets it is sometimes difficult to check the freshness of cauliflower, as it is often stripped of its protective green leaves and wrapped in plastic. Nonetheless, look for the cauliflower to have tight, firm, compact curds without brown spots. Sometimes these discolorations are shaved off at the market, so be sure to check closely. Cauliflower will keep in the refrigerator, wrapped, for up to 1 week. If any discoloration has occurred during storage, simply trim it before cooking.

Cauliflower Cooked with Cumin and Mustard Seeds

1 medium cauliflower (1¾ pounds)

1-inch cube fresh ginger, peeled and quartered

1 medium onion, peeled and quartered

5 tablespoons vegetable oil

½ teaspoon whole cumin seeds

½ teaspoon kalonji (black onion seeds)

½ teaspoon black mustard seeds

½ teaspoon ground turmeric

¾ teaspoon salt

Freshly ground black pepper

1 teaspoon ground coriander

1 teaspoon amchoor (available at Indian food markets)

⅛ teaspoon cayenne pepper

Water, as needed

Trim any leaves off the cauliflower. Break the cauliflower into small florets about 1½ inches long and ¾ inch wide at the head. Set aside.

Fit the workbowl of a food processor with the steel blade. Turn on the machine and add the ginger through the feed tube. When the ginger is shredded, add the onion quarters. When the mixture is pastelike but still grainy, turn off the machine. Leave the mixture in the workbowl.

Heat the oil in a heavy 12- to 14-inch skillet over moderately high heat. When the oil is smoking hot, put in the cumin seeds, kalonji, and black mustard seeds. As soon as they sizzle, crackle, and pop (this takes just a few seconds), put in the paste from the workbowl, keeping your face averted from the skillet. Turn the heat down to moderate. Stir and fry the paste until it turns a golden brown.

Add the turmeric and mix well. Add the cauliflower, salt, pepper (a few turns of the grinder), ground coriander, amchoor, and cayenne. Stir and fry for 1 minute. Add 3 tablespoons water and stir and fry. Keep stirring and frying, adding 3 tablespoons water whenever all the liquid in the skillet dries up, until the cauliflower is cooked through but still crunchy, about 10 to 15 minutes.

Serves 6

[MADHUR JAFFREY]

Cauliflower, Eggplant, and Potatoes in Herb Sauce

Whole wheat bread works well with this dish. A salad of chickpeas, cranberries, and kidney beans, flavored with cumin and lemon juice, is also a nice accompaniment.

¼ cup whole blanched almonds
2 large garlic cloves, minced
1 piece (2 × ¾ inch) fresh ginger, peeled and minced
½ cup loosely packed fresh cilantro leaves, minced
6 tablespoons vegetable oil
2 medium onions, finely chopped
1 tablespoon ground coriander
½ teaspoon ground fennel seeds
½ teaspoon crushed red pepper
¼ teaspoon ground turmeric
½ cup canned tomato purée
1 teaspoon paprika
1½ cups water
1 medium cauliflower (about 2 pounds), cored and cut into 1½-inch florets
1 small eggplant (about 8 ounces), stem removed, cut into 1-inch cubes
2 medium potatoes (about 8 ounces), peeled and cut into 1½-inch cubes
1½ tablespoons cumin seed
  Salt

Process the almonds in a food processor with the metal blade, pulsing twice, then processing for 30 seconds or until the almonds are finely ground; remove from the processor and set aside.

In a bowl combine the garlic, ginger, and cilantro leaves. Set aside.

Heat the oil in a large skillet over moderately high heat. Add the onions and cook, stirring, until they are browned, about 10 minutes. Stir in the reserved garlic mixture and cook 20 seconds more. Stir in the ground coriander, fennel, crushed red pepper, and turmeric until well blended; reduce the heat to low and add the tomato purée, paprika, and reserved almonds. Cook, stirring constantly, for 2 minutes, taking care that the sauce does not stick to the bottom of the skillet.

Add the water and the cauliflower, eggplant, and potatoes; raise the heat to high and bring to boil. Reduce the heat and simmer, covered, for 30 minutes, stirring occasionally, until the cauliflower is almost tender. Remove the saucepan from the heat and let stand 30 minutes, allowing the flavors to blend.

Meanwhile, roast the cumin seed in a

small skillet over moderately high heat, shaking the pan constantly, until well browned, about 2 minutes. Transfer to a plate and let cool; then crush the seeds with a mortar and pestle or on a flat surface with a rolling pin.

Stir the crushed cumin and salt to taste into the vegetables and reheat over moderate heat.

Serves 4 to 6

[J U L I E   S A H N I]

Gobhi Paratha
Cauliflower-Stuffed Breads

- 2 pieces (½ inch each) fresh ginger, peeled
- ½ cup loosely packed fresh cilantro leaves
- 2 fresh mild green chili peppers (Anaheim or poblano), stemmed, cored, and seeded
- 1 small cauliflower (about 1¼ pounds), cored and divided into florets
- 1 cup vegetable oil
- 3 cups whole-wheat flour
- ¾ to 1 cup lukewarm water
- 1 tablespoon fresh lemon juice
  Pinch of salt (optional)

Using a food processor fitted with the metal blade, with the machine running, drop the ginger through the feed tube and process for 12 to 15 seconds, or until minced. Add the cilantro and chili peppers and pulse 10 to 12 times or until finely chopped. Add half of the cauliflower and pulse 6 to 8 times, or until the cauliflower is finely chopped. Transfer to a 2-quart bowl. Process the remaining cauliflower, pulsing 6 to 8 times or until finely chopped. Add to the bowl.

Heat 5 tablespoons of the oil in a large skillet over moderate heat. Add the cauliflower mixture and cook, stirring often, until it is soft but not browned, about 10 minutes. Return the mixture to the bowl and refrigerate, uncovered, for at least 2 hours.

With the metal blade in place, put the flour in the processor bowl. Then, with the machine running, gradually add the water through the feed tube just until the mixture forms a ball. With the machine still running add 1 tablespoon of the oil and process for 45 seconds more. Carefully remove the dough to a lightly floured surface. Spread 1 teaspoon of oil over the top and knead the dough for about 30 seconds.

Shape the dough into an 8-inch cylinder and cut it into 8 equal pieces. Cover them with a kitchen towel.

Stir the lemon juice and salt, if used, into the reserved cauliflower mixture and divide the mixture into 8 equal portions. Shape each portion into a rough ball and set aside.

Shape a piece of dough into a ball, dust with flour and roll it into a 5-inch round. Place a portion of the cauliflower mixture in the center. To enclose the stuffing, gather the edge of the circle and pinch it tightly together at the center to seal. Place the filled bread sealed end down. Dust with flour and roll the bread gently with the rolling pin to flatten it slightly. Carefully roll the bread into a 6-inch round, about ¼ inch thick. Cover with a kitchen towel. Repeat for the remaining dough. Do not stack the breads.

Heat a cast-iron skillet or griddle for about 2 minutes over moderately high heat; or heat an electric skillet to 375°F. Cook the breads, one or more at a time without crowding, for 2 to 3 minutes or until the bottom is flecked with brown. With a metal spatula, flip the bread and cook for 1 minute more. Pour about 1 tablespoon of the oil around the edge of each bread and cook for 1 minute more on each side or until the bread is golden brown; keep covered in a warm oven. Wipe the skillet with a paper towel and repeat for the remaining breads.

The breads may be prepared ahead and set aside until needed or refrigerated up to 4 days. To reheat, brush a skillet with oil and cook one or more at a time over moderate heat for about 1 minute on each side.

Makes 8 breads, serving 4

[J U L I E   S A H N I]

Celery and Celery Root

Celery and celery root have similar flavors, but their textures differ greatly. Celery is prized for its stalks, or ribs, and herbaceous leaves, which grow above ground, whereas celery root is loved for its root, which matures underground. Celery root, also called celeriac, produces a few dark green stalks that are too tough to eat.

Celery should be firm with pale, not dark, green stalks and fresh-looking leaves. It will keep well refrigerated in a plastic bag for up to 5 days. The outer leaves and stalks can be cooked, while the crisp pale inner stalks are best saved for raw preparations.

Celery root is brown, and the best are about the size of grapefruits (not any larger). They should have few stems and roots. Look for ones that are heavy for their size, dense, and tender. Store celery root in the coldest part of the refrigerator, wrapped loosely, for up to 2 weeks. Whether raw or cooked, celery root must be peeled. It will discolor, though, so submerge it in a mixture of water and lemon juice until ready to use. Celery root is delicious raw in salads, roasted, and cooked with other root vegetables.

Triple Celery Bisque

Gunnar Forsell of the Grappe d'Or restaurant in Stockholm created this soup, which is adapted here. You may serve the pale green bisque either hot or chilled.

1   small celery root (about 8 ounces), peeled and cut into pieces to fit the feed tube of a food processor
3   medium celery ribs with leaves (about 8 ounces total), cut into lengths to fit the feed tube vertically
1   medium carrot (about 3 ounces), peeled and cut into lengths to fit the feed tube vertically
1   medium leek (about 5 ounces), carefully washed and cut into lengths to fit the feed tube vertically
2   medium onions (about 10 ounces total), peeled and quartered
4   tablespoons unsalted butter
2   tablespoons fresh parsley leaves, finely chopped
¼   cup stemmed and loosely packed fresh dill, finely chopped
¼   teaspoon celery seed, lightly crushed (see note on page 48)
¼   teaspoon dried tarragon, crushed
½   teaspoon salt
    Freshly ground black pepper
4   cups chicken stock, preferably home-made
2   medium potatoes (about 12 ounces total), peeled and quartered
1   cup milk
    Pinch freshly grated nutmeg
½   cup heavy cream

12 small shrimp (6 ounces), cooked, peeled, and deveined, for garnish
1   small celery rib (about 1½ ounces), trimmed and cut into 1-inch pieces, finely chopped

In a food processor fitted with the medium slicing disc, process the celery root, medium pieces of celery, carrot, leek, and onions, emptying the workbowl as necessary.

Melt the butter in a medium saucepan over moderate heat. Add the sliced vegetables and cook, stirring constantly, until just tender, about 10 minutes. Add the parsley, dill, celery seed, tarragon, salt, pepper, and chicken stock and simmer, covered, for 25 minutes.

Process the potatoes with the medium slicing disc and add to the stock. Stir in the milk and nutmeg. Simmer, covered, for 20 minutes longer or until the potatoes are tender.

Strain the liquid into a large bowl, then return it to the stockpot. Process the cooked vegetables in 2 batches with the metal blade until smooth, about 1 minute for each batch, scraping down the bowl as necessary. Whisk the puréed vegetables into the cooking liquid and stir in the heavy cream. Adjust the seasonings to taste.

Just before serving, slowly reheat the soup, stirring occasionally. Do not boil.

To serve, divide the soup among 6 individual bowls and garnish each with 2 shrimp and a sprinkling of the chopped celery.

Serves 6

NOTE: For lightly crushed celery seed, place in the bowl of a teaspoon. Place another teaspoon of the same size, with the handle pointing in the opposite direction, over the seed. Press down on the seed to release the flavor.

[ELENE MARGOT KOLB]

Mushroom, Celery, and Parmesan Cheese Salad

1½ ounces Parmesan cheese, in one piece, at room temperature
4 medium celery ribs, trimmed and cut into lengths to fit the feed tube of a food processor vertically
8 ounces fresh mushrooms, stems trimmed, opposite sides cut flat
3 tablespoons fruity Italian olive oil
2 teaspoons fresh lemon juice
Salt and freshly ground black pepper

Shave the Parmesan cheese into thin slices with a swivel-bladed vegetable peeler. Reserve.

Stack the celery in the feed tube of a food processor and process with the thin slicing disc. Repeat with the mushrooms, placing them cut side down in the feed tube.

Transfer the vegetables to a bowl. With a fork, blend together the olive oil, lemon juice, salt, and pepper. Pour over the vegetables and toss well.

Divide the mixture among 4 salad plates and top with the sliced Parmesan cheese.

Serves 4

[MICHELE SCICOLONE]

Celery, Pecan, and Spinach Stuffing

3 cups pecan pieces
1½ cups olive oil
3 medium garlic cloves, peeled and minced
3 medium onions (about 15 ounces total), peeled and finely chopped
5 medium celery ribs, chopped
3 cups tightly packed stemmed spinach leaves (8 ounces), washed, dried, and chopped
3 cups unsalted matzo meal

¾ cup chicken stock, homemade
2 teaspoons dried thyme
1 teaspoon dried oregano
Salt and freshly ground black pepper

In a food processor fitted with the metal blade coarsely chop the pecans in 2 batches, about 5 pulses for each batch. Remove and set aside.

In a medium skillet heat ¾ cup of the olive oil over moderate heat. Add the garlic, onions, and celery and cook for about 12 minutes, or until just tender. Transfer the mixture to a large bowl and add the spinach.

Add the remaining ¾ cup olive oil and the remaining ingredients to the bowl and toss to combine. Season to taste with salt and pepper.

Use to stuff a turkey; fill the bird loosely.

Makes about 10½ cups, enough for a 14-pound turkey

[C A R L   J E R O M E]

Braised Root Vegetables

2 large carrots (about ½ pound), peeled
2 large parsnips (about ½ pound), peeled
2 medium white turnips (about ½ pound), peeled
8 ounces celery root, peeled
   Juice of half a lemon
   Salt
2 medium onions (about ½ pound), peeled
2 tablespoons unsalted butter
2 tablespoons unbleached all-purpose flour
2 teaspoons Dijon mustard
1½ teaspoons white wine vinegar
¼ teaspoon freshly ground black pepper

Cut the carrots, parsnips, turnips and celery root into the largest possible pieces to fit in the feed tube of a food processor. Into a 1-quart bowl put 2 cups of cold water and the lemon juice. Add the prepared celery root and set aside.

Bring to a boil 3 cups of water and a pinch of salt in a 3-quart saucepan. Add the large pieces of carrot, cover, and cook for 8 minutes. Add the parsnips, turnips, celery root,

and any small carrot ends and cook, covered, for 5 minutes more.

With a slotted spoon remove the small parsnip and carrot ends and set aside to drain. Cook the remaining vegetables 3 or 4 minutes more, until barely tender. Strain the cooking liquid into a 2-quart saucepan. Set aside the vegetables to drain and cool. Reduce the cooking liquid to 1¼ cups and set aside.

Cut the onions in half vertically. Stand them in the feed tube of a food processor and use the medium slicing disc to process them.

In a medium skillet melt the butter over moderate heat. Add the onions and sauté, stirring constantly, for 1 minute. Lower the heat, cover, and cook for 2 minutes more. Stir in the flour and cook, stirring constantly, for 1 minute. Gradually add the reduced cooking liquid, stirring constantly. Stir in the mustard, vinegar, and pepper. Continue to stir over moderately low heat until thickened, about 30 seconds. Remove the skillet from the heat.

Use the French fry disc of the food processor to process all of the reserved vegetables. Add to the onion mixture, stir gently to mix well, cover, and cook over moderately low heat for 4 minutes, stirring twice. Serve hot.

This may be made ahead and reheated over low heat. Or it can be puréed, using the metal blade of the food processor, and reheated, if necessary, in a double boiler.

Serves 4 to 6

Celery Root Ragout with Essence of Cèpes

- 1 ounce dried cèpes or morels
- 1 cup hot water
- 4 tablespoons unsalted butter
- 2 tablespoons fresh lemon juice
- 2 medium celery roots (about 1 pound each), peeled and diced
  Salt and freshly ground white pepper

Soak the cèpes in the hot water in a small saucepan for 30 minutes. Bring to a boil over moderate heat and simmer, uncovered, for about 10 minutes. Strain the mixture through a sieve lined with dampened cheesecloth into a 1-cup liquid measure. Press the cèpes to extract as much liquid as possible. You should have about ½ cup liquid. Reserve the liquid and cèpes separately (see note below).

Melt 2 tablespoons of the butter with 1 tablespoon of the lemon juice in a skillet over moderate heat. Add the celery root and cook, stirring constantly, until coated with the butter mixture, about 3 minutes. Pour in the cèpe liquid, cover the skillet, and simmer, stirring often, until the celery root is tender, about 10 minutes.

Stir in the remaining 2 tablespoons butter and season to taste with the remaining 1 tablespoon lemon juice and salt and pepper.

NOTE: The cèpes can be rinsed to remove any grit and processed in a food processor with the metal blade until coarsely chopped, about 4 pulses. Fold into the cooked celery root for added flavor and garnish. Or keep the cèpes, refrigerated, for another use.

Serves 4 as a side dish

[BERNARD LOISEAU/
JACQUES MENDA]

Celery Root and Tomato Salad

Claude Deligne, chef of the 3-star Taillevent restaurant in Paris, created this salad at the request of a client on a "régime" or special diet.

- 9 ounces curly endive or chicory, trimmed of white stems
- 7 small firm ripe tomatoes, halved and thinly sliced

1 pound celery root, peeled, cut into uniform pieces to fit the feed tube of a food processor
2 tablespoons fresh lemon juice
½ cup parsley leaves, finely minced with 1 tablespoon fresh basil leaves
    Basil Vinaigrette or Onion Dressing (recipes follow)

Cut the endive into ½-inch lengths. Arrange in a round shallow glass salad bowl, 10 to 12 inches in diameter.

Insert medium slicing disc in a food processor. Place tomatoes in feed tube and slice, using light pressure on pusher. Arrange overlapping slices in a circle on endive or chicory, leaving a 1-inch border of greens.

Insert the julienne disc in bowl of food processor. Place celery root in feed tube. Process, using medium pressure on pusher. If you don't have a julienne disc, you can cut the celery root into julienne (2 × ¼ inch) by hand. With either method, add the lemon juice to the celery root in a bowl and toss gently immediately to prevent discoloring.

Arrange the julienned celery in a circle around tomatoes and greens. Sprinkle with the minced parsley and basil and serve with the Basil Vinaigrette or Onion Dressing.

Serves 8

[ABBY MANDEL]

Basil Vinaigrette

1 shallot, peeled
1 tablespoon fresh basil leaves or 1½ teaspoons dried basil
¾ cup olive oil
¼ cup red wine vinegar
½ teaspoon sugar
½ teaspoon salt
    Freshly ground black pepper

With the metal blade in place, drop the shallot through the feed tube of a food processor with the motor running. Remove the cover and scrape the sides of the workbowl. Add the basil, oil, vinegar, sugar, salt, and pepper to taste. Process, turning the machine on and off several times, until well mixed.

Makes about 1 cup

Onion Dressing

1 small piece of fresh ginger, peeled (for
   1 teaspoon minced)
1 small onion, peeled and cut in half
½ cup parsley leaves
6 tablespoons cider vinegar
1 tablespoon sugar
2 teaspoons dry mustard
2 teaspoons Hungarian paprika
2 teaspoons Worcestershire sauce
1 teaspoon salt
¾ cup olive oil

With the metal blade in place, drop the ginger and onion through feed tube of food processor with machine running. Remove the cover and scrape the sides of the workbowl. Add the parsley, vinegar, sugar, mustard, paprika, Worcestershire sauce, and salt and process for 10 seconds. Add the oil and turn machine on and off 2 times.

Makes about 1¼ cups

Chicory

Chicories belong to the daisy family. Some of the many types available at the market include escarole, Belgian endive, curly endive (frisée), and radicchio. Escarole has broad leaves that are bright green on the outside and pale yellow on the inside. They are the least bitter member of the chicory family. Endive is a small, spear-shaped head of pale, tight, mildly bitter leaves. Curly endive (also called frisée and, erroneously, chicory) has a large, loose head with frizzy green-tinged leaves. Radicchio is the Italian name for red chicory and is small and cabbage shaped. Radicchio, escarole, and endive are crisp and tender enough to be eaten raw as well as hefty enough to be cooked. Select firm chicories that look fresh and crisp. Store them in the refrigerator, wrapped in paper towels and placed in plastic bags, for up to 3 days.

Sautéed Belgian Endives

8 large Belgian endives (about 2 pounds total)
2 tablespoons fresh lemon juice
1 tablespoon plus 1 teaspoon sugar
1½ teaspoons salt
4 tablespoons unsalted butter
Freshly ground black pepper

Core the endives and cut crosswise into ½-inch slices. In a 10-inch sauté pan or skillet, put the endives, lemon juice, the 1 tablespoon of sugar, and 1 teaspoon of the salt. Toss to combine all the ingredients.

Cover the pan and cook over moderately high heat for 12 to 15 minutes, stirring occasionally. The endives should be cooked through but still retain some texture; there will be some liquid in the pan.

Lift the endives out with a slotted spoon and set aside. Reduce the endive juices until the pan is almost dry. Add the cooked endives, the 1 teaspoon sugar and ½ teaspoon salt and the butter; stir over high heat until the butter is melted. Adjust the seasoning, adding the pepper, and serve immediately.

Serves 6 to 8

[F R É D Y G I R A R D E T /
A B B Y M A N D E L]

Braised Escarole with Two Cheeses

2 large heads escarole (about 1½ pounds), washed
2 tablespoons unsalted butter
Salt and freshly ground black pepper
Pinch freshly grated nutmeg
¾ cup chicken stock, preferably homemade
2 medium garlic cloves, peeled
1 ounce imported Parmesan cheese
4 ounces mozzarella cheese, chilled

Preheat the oven to 325°F.

Blanch the escarole in a large saucepan of lightly salted boiling water for 2 minutes. Drain well and squeeze dry with paper towels to remove as much liquid as possible. Cut each head into 4 wedges, leaving the core to hold the leaves together. Bend the leaves and wrap them around the core to make little bundles.

Butter a baking dish large enough to hold all the bundles in a single layer. Arrange the escarole in the dish and season lightly with salt, pepper, and nutmeg. Add the stock and garlic cloves. Cover with parchment paper and bake in the center of the preheated oven until the escarole is soft, about 1 hour.

Meanwhile, drop the Parmesan through the feed tube of a food processor with the metal blade in place and the motor running. Process until finely chopped, about 30 seconds. Remove the metal blade, insert the medium shredding disc, and process the mozzarella. Set aside.

When the escarole is soft, remove the

parchment paper. Drain the juices into a small saucepan and add the garlic cloves. Bring to a boil and cook until the liquid is reduced to about 3 tablespoons. Process the reduced juices and garlic cloves in the processor with the metal blade until smooth, about 30 seconds. Season to taste.

Preheat the broiler to its highest setting.

Drizzle the escarole with the garlic mixture and sprinkle with the cheeses. Broil about 6 inches from the heat source until golden, about 2 minutes.

Serves 6

[DEIDRE DAVIS]

Chicory and Radicchio Salad with Goat Cheese

1 large egg
1 teaspoon water
⅓ cup dry bread crumbs
10 ounces goat cheese, chilled and cut into 16 slices (¼ to ½ inch thick)
1 medium head chicory (½-pound) or curly endive (about 8 ounces), washed, dried, and torn into bite-size pieces
2 heads radicchio or 1 head red leaf lettuce (about 8 ounces total), washed, dried and torn into bite-size pieces
¼ cup olive oil
2 tablespoons fresh lemon juice
¼ teaspoon salt
Freshly ground black pepper
Vegetable oil, for frying

In a small bowl beat together the egg with the water. Spread the bread crumbs on a plate. Dip the cheese slices into the egg and then into the bread crumbs. Place the coated slices on a baking sheet and refrigerate. Thirty min-

utes before serving the salad, move the coated cheese to the freezer.

Shortly before serving the salad, put the greens in a large salad bowl. In a small bowl whisk together the olive oil, lemon juice, salt, and a good grinding of black pepper. Pour over the greens and toss. Set aside.

Heat about ¼ inch of vegetable oil in a medium skillet over moderate heat. (The oil is the correct temperature when a cube of bread dropped into it takes 40 seconds to brown lightly.) Fry the chilled cheese slices in the hot oil for about 1½ to 2 minutes, until crisp and browned on both sides, turning them with a spatula. Drain on paper towels.

Divide the salad among 8 salad plates and top each with 2 slices of fried cheese.

Serves 8

[MARLENE SOROSKY]

Endive Salad with Roquefort and Walnut Oil Vinaigrette

¼ cup walnut oil

3 tablespoons Crème Fraîche (page 30) or heavy cream

1 tablespoon sherry wine vinegar

2 teaspoons Dijon mustard

¼ teaspoon dry mustard

Salt and freshly ground black pepper

6 medium endives (about 1¼ pounds)

1 tablespoon fresh lemon juice

3 tablespoons crumbled Roquefort cheese (about 1½ ounces)

¼ cup walnuts, finely chopped

2 teaspoons minced parsley, for garnish

In a food processor fitted with the metal blade, process the oil, Crème Fraîche, vinegar, Dijon mustard, and dry mustard for about 15 seconds, stopping once or twice to scrape the bowl. Season to taste with salt and pepper. Transfer to a serving bowl and set aside at room temperature for 30 minutes.

Meanwhile, core the endives and cut crosswise into 1-inch slices.

Add the endives to the serving bowl. Sprinkle with the lemon juice and add the Roquefort and the walnuts. Toss gently and refrigerate for about 30 minutes before serving. Garnish with the minced parsley.

Serves 6

[P E R L A   M E Y E R S]

Penne with Endive and Walnuts

2 ounces stale Italian bread, torn into pieces

1 tablespoon unsalted butter

2 tablespoons walnut or olive oil

8 slices bacon (about 6 ounces), cut into ½-inch pieces

2 large garlic cloves, peeled and finely chopped

1 pound penne or other tubular pasta

1 large head curly endive (about 12 ounces), trimmed and cut crosswise into 1-inch slices

1 large head Belgian endive (about 6 ounces), cored, halved lengthwise, and cut crosswise into ½-inch slices

¾ cup walnut pieces, toasted and coarsely chopped

Salt and freshly ground black pepper

2 ounces goat cheese, crumbled

Process the bread to coarse crumbs in a food processor with the metal blade, about 45 seconds.

Heat the butter and 1 tablespoon oil in a

skillet over moderate heat. Add the crumbs and cook, stirring constantly, until golden brown, about 5 minutes. Remove from the skillet and reserve.

Brown the bacon in the skillet over moderate heat, 7 minutes. Drain on paper towels, reserving 2 tablespoons fat in the skillet.

Cook the garlic in the reserved fat and remaining 1 tablespoon oil in the skillet over low heat until soft but not brown, about 2 minutes. Set aside.

Cook the penne in a large pot of boiling salted water until *al dente*, about 10 minutes, adding both endives in the last 15 seconds. Drain.

Toss the penne and endive in a serving bowl with the walnuts, garlic and oil, bacon, and salt and pepper to taste. Top with the goat cheese and crumbs.

Serves 6

Corn

There's nothing like ears of summer corn, so juicy and tender that they can be eaten raw. Corn can be used in a myriad of dishes: soups, soufflés, pancakes, salads. The fresher the corn, the better tasting it will be, so buy it at a farmers market or a roadside stand. A fresh ear will be plump, moist, and healthy with shiny kernels. The husk will rest snugly over the kernels and the silk will be golden brown. If you're not serving the corn immediately, refrigerate it unshucked and wrapped in a damp towel. Remove the husks and silk at the last possible moment before cooking.

Corn Chowder

4 slices lean bacon, cut into ½-inch pieces
½ small onion (about 1 ounce), chopped
1 small celery rib (¾ ounce), chopped
¼ medium green pepper (about ¾ ounce),
    seeds and ribs removed, chopped
3 cups fresh or thawed frozen corn (about
    15 ounces)
2 medium all-purpose potatoes (about
    12 ounces total), peeled and cut into
    ½-inch dice
3 medium tomatoes (about 1½ pounds
    total), peeled, halved, seeded, and
    coarsely chopped
1 teaspoon salt
¾ teaspoon freshly ground black pepper
3 cups milk
    Chopped parsley, for garnish

Sauté the bacon in a large stockpot until browned, about 4 minutes. Transfer to paper towels to drain. Sauté the onion, celery, and green pepper in the bacon fat for 2 minutes. Add the corn and sauté 3 minutes more. Add the potatoes, tomatoes, bacon, salt, and pepper and simmer, covered, for 30 minutes, stirring often. Stir in the milk and heat just to a boil. Garnish with chopped parsley.

Serves 6

[LYN STALLWORTH/
SUZANNE S. JONES]

Bélon Oysters with Corn Sauce

12 unshucked medium to large bélon or
    American oysters (about 2¼ pounds)
    Rock salt
1 cup fresh or thawed frozen corn kernels
½ cup fish broth, preferably homemade, or
    ¼ cup bottled clam juice combined
    with ¼ cup water
2 large shallots, peeled and finely chopped
1 tablespoon raspberry or sherry wine
    vinegar
3 tablespoons unsalted butter, cut into
    small pieces
1 teaspoon Cognac
⅛ teaspoon cayenne pepper

2 tablespoons fresh chervil leaves
1 tablespoon black caviar (optional)

Preheat the broiler.

Shuck the oysters, reserving ¼ cup liquid and the bottom shells. Line a broiler pan with ½ inch rock salt and lay the oysters, in the bottom shells, on the salt. Strain the reserved oyster liquid through a sieve lined with dampened cheesecloth.

To make the sauce, combine the oyster liquid, corn, fish broth, and shallots in a small saucepan and simmer over moderately high heat until the corn and shallots are just tender and the liquid is reduced by half, 4 to 6 minutes. Stir in the vinegar.

Purée the corn mixture in a food processor with the metal blade, about 30 seconds, scraping down the workbowl as necessary. Force the purée through a fine sieve into the saucepan and bring to a boil. Stir in the butter with a wire whisk until combined. Stir in the Cognac and cayenne pepper.

Spoon 2 teaspoons sauce over each oyster and broil 4 inches from the heat source until the edges just begin to curl, 2 to 3 minutes. Divide the oysters among serving plates and sprinkle with the chervil and caviar, if using.

Serves 4

[SALLY TAGER]

Chowder on a Plate

6 small red potatoes (1 pound total), peeled
1 bunch large leeks (about 18 ounces total), trimmed, split, washed well, and cut to fit the feed tube vertically
2 tablespoons unsalted butter
2 tablespoons vegetable oil
4 ounces bacon, cut into ¼-inch dice
¼ cup fresh or thawed frozen corn kernels
1 piece (about 2 pounds) halibut fillet, skinned and cut into 4 serving pieces
¾ cup fish broth, preferably homemade, or 6 tablespoons bottled clam juice mixed with 6 tablespoons water
½ cup heavy cream
    Pinch cayenne pepper
    Salt and freshly ground black pepper
1 tablespoon minced parsley, for garnish

Preheat the oven to 325°F.

Slice the potatoes in a food processor with the thick slicing disc. Remove from the workbowl. Slice the leeks with the medium slicing disc.

Sauté the potatoes, in 2 batches, in the butter and oil in a medium skillet over moderate heat until crisp and golden, about 8 minutes per batch. Remove from the heat and keep warm.

Sauté the bacon in a large skillet over moderate heat until the fat begins to render, about 3 minutes. Add the leeks and sauté until the bacon is lightly browned, about 6 minutes more. Stir in the corn and set aside.

Arrange the fish fillets in a pie pan, tucking under the ends if necessary for even thickness. Spoon ¼ cup fish broth over the fish. Place a buttered piece of wax paper the size of the pan over the fish, buttered side down, and bake in the preheated oven until the fish just flakes when tested with a fork, 12 to 15 minutes. Strain the broth through a sieve.

Add the strained broth to the bacon mixture with the remaining ½ cup broth and the cream. Boil until the sauce is thickened, 3 to 4 minutes. Add the cayenne pepper and salt and pepper to taste.

Serve the fish with the sauce and potatoes and garnish with the parsley.

Serves 4

[SALLY TAGER]

Kernel Corn Pancakes

¼ cup milk

1 stick (2 inches) cinnamon

2 tablespoons unsalted butter

2 tablespoons sugar

1 can (12 ounces) whole-kernel corn, drained

3 tablespoons unbleached all-purpose flour

1 large egg

Vegetable oil, for frying

1 cup honey, warmed

Put the milk and cinnamon stick in a 1-quart saucepan and bring to a boil over moderate heat. Reduce the heat and simmer for 10 minutes. Add the butter and sugar and stir until the butter has melted. Remove from the heat and let stand for 10 minutes. Remove and discard the cinnamon stick.

Purée the corn in a food processor with the metal blade, about 1½ minutes, stopping once to scrape the workbowl. Add the flour, egg, and reserved milk mixture; process for 10 seconds more. Set aside, covered, for at least 20 minutes.

Preheat the oven to its lowest setting. Line a baking sheet with a double layer of paper towels and set aside.

Stir the batter. Pour a thin film of oil into a medium skillet and heat over moderate heat. Drop the batter by tablespoons into the skillet, without crowding the pancakes. Cook for 1½ to 2 minutes or until the bottoms are brown and the tops have begun to dry. Carefully turn the pancakes and cook for about 2 minutes more, until browned. Remove to the prepared baking sheet and keep warm in the preheated oven. Repeat for the remaining batter, adding oil to the skillet as necessary.

Serve with the warm honey.

Makes about 16 pancakes

[C O P E L A N D   M A R K S]

Cucumbers

Cucumbers belong to the gourd family of vegetables. This summer charmer has a high water content, which makes it especially refreshing on hot days. There is the small Kirby, the traditional slicing variety, and the very long, thin English or hothouse cucumber. The English cucumber is milder in flavor and has few seeds. At their peak from May to August, cucumbers should be very firm and vibrant. Avoid ones that show any signs of yellowing or softness. Older cucumbers tend to have large hard seeds that can be bitter, so choose cucumbers that are the smallest in the bunch. They will keep in the refrigerator for up to 5 days, although they are at their best soon after they are picked. Wash cucumbers just before serving and seed only those that are old.

Cold Curried Cucumber Soup

5 medium cucumbers (about 18 ounces total), preferably Kirby, scrubbed and ends trimmed

10 medium scallions (about 5 ounces total)

1½ tablespoons vegetable oil

1 piece fresh ginger, about 1 × 1 inch, peeled and finely chopped

½ cup rice wine

2½ cups chicken stock, preferably home-made

1 teaspoon curry powder

½ teaspoon salt

¼ teaspoon freshly ground white pepper

1 cup plain yogurt

Cut the cucumbers in half lengthwise. Scoop out the seeds with a spoon and discard, then cut the cucumbers into thick slices. Set aside.

Cut the white part of the scallions into 1-inch pieces. Reserve the greens from 3 of the scallions for garnish.

Heat a wok or a large skillet over high heat. Add the oil and, when hot, add the ginger and scallion pieces. Stir-fry until fragrant, about 15 seconds. Add the cucumbers and toss lightly for about 1 minute. Adjust the heat, if necessary, to prevent burning. Add the rice wine and cook for 2 minutes more. Stir in the chicken stock and curry powder, and when the mixture boils, reduce the heat and simmer for 15 minutes.

Strain the mixture and reserve the liquid. Purée the solids in a food processor with the metal blade, about 1 minute, scraping down the workbowl as necessary. With the motor running, add ¼ cup of the liquid through the feed tube and process 15 seconds more.

Transfer the purée to a large bowl. Whisk in the remaining liquid and season with salt and pepper. Cover and refrigerate until chilled, at least 4 hours.

Just before serving, thinly slice the re-served scallion greens. Whisk the yogurt into the soup and serve in bowls, garnished with the sliced scallion greens.

Serves 4

[NINA SIMONDS]

Japanese Crab and Cucumber Salad

2 pounds pickling cucumbers, such as Kirby (see note below)

2 teaspoons salt

4 tablespoons rice vinegar

3 tablespoons mirin (sweet sake)

1 teaspoon sugar

1 pound fresh or canned lump crabmeat, picked over

2 teaspoons fresh lemon juice

Peel the cucumbers and slice them very fine, using the thin slicing disc of a food processor, if desired. Put the slices in a bowl, mix well with the salt, and leave for 2 hours.

Squeeze all the liquid from the cucumbers and discard it. Pour out any liquid that may have accumulated in the bowl. Dry the bowl and return the cucumbers to it. Add 2 tablespoons of the vinegar, 1 tablespoon of the mirin, and the sugar. Mix well, cover, and refrigerate.

Just before serving, put the crabmeat in a bowl. Add the remaining 2 tablespoons each vinegar and mirin and the lemon juice. Mix well.

In pretty Japanese, Chinese, clear glass, or ceramic bowls (one for each diner), make two mounds each—one of cucumbers (squeeze them out again before you put them in the bowl) and the other of crabmeat. Serve immediately, with chopsticks.

Serves 6 to 8 as an appetizer

NOTE: If Kirbies are unavailable, use English cucumbers or 2½ pounds regular cucumbers, peeled, cut in half lengthwise, and seeded.

[MADHUR JAFFREY]

Poached Salmon Steaks with Cucumber Sauce

6   salmon steaks, ¾ inch thick (about 6 ounces each)
1¼   cups coarsely chopped mushrooms
1   medium leek, well washed, halved lengthwise, and thinly sliced (about ¾ cup)
1   large cucumber, peeled, seeded, and coarsely chopped (about 1½ cups)
1   teaspoon salt
½   teaspoon freshly ground black pepper
1   cup dry white wine
4   tablespoons unsalted butter
3   sweet red peppers, stemmed, cored, seeded, quartered lengthwise, and cut crosswise into ¼-inch slices

Preheat the oven to 400°F.

Butter a 12-inch ovenproof sauté pan or a flameproof casserole large enough to hold the steaks in one layer. Distribute the mushrooms, leek, and cucumber over the bottom of the pan and then the salmon steaks, in one layer, on top of them. Sprinkle with the salt and pepper and add the wine. Put a round of buttered wax paper over the steaks, cover the pan, and bring to a boil over moderate heat. Transfer the pan to the preheated oven and cook the fish for about 10 minutes, until the flesh is just beginning to flake.

With a slotted spatula, transfer the steaks to a warm platter, carefully scraping off bits of vegetables that are clinging to them. Scrape the contents of the pan into a food processor fitted with the metal blade and process for 1 minute. Transfer the purée to a 2-quart saucepan and bring to a boil over moderate heat.

Meanwhile, cut 3 tablespoons of the butter into 12 pieces and whisk the butter into the sauce, one piece at a time.

Melt the remaining 1 tablespoon butter in a medium skillet over moderate heat. Add the pepper slices and sauté them, stirring constantly, for 30 to 40 seconds, until they are slightly wilted.

To serve, pour about ⅓ cup of sauce on each of 6 plates. Put a steak on top and coat it with a little more sauce. Arrange the peppers in a circle around the sauce on the plate. Place a small piece of pepper on top of each steak and serve immediately.

Serves 6

[JACQUES PÉPIN]

Eggplant

Eggplants vary in color, shape, and size, from the common dark purple, bell-shaped variety to the egg-shaped white and the long, thin Japanese types. Eggplants reach their peak in August and September, although they are available year-round. Choose ones that are firm, shiny, and blemish-free. Avoid soft eggplants; these are old and will be bitter with hard seeds. Use eggplants soon after they are picked and don't refrigerate them, as they suffer under cold temperatures. There are many theories concerning the necessity of degorging, or sprinkling eggplant with salt and letting it stand for 30 minutes to leach out some of its bitterness. The bitterness-causing substance, called solanine, is found in the seeds of the eggplant; so if there are many hard seeds—as is the case when the vegetable is old—then salting is useful. Salting before frying eggplant is also a good idea, because this will draw out some of the vegetable's moisture, reducing the amount of oil absorbed during cooking.

Imam Bayildi
Eggplant with Tomatoes and Onion

 1 medium eggplant (about 1 pound), ends trimmed, cut crosswise into four 1-inch slices
2½ teaspoons salt
 ½ cup loosely packed parsley leaves
 1 small onion, peeled
 1 medium green pepper, cored and seeded
 2 medium tomatoes, halved, seeded, and juiced
 1 tablespoon tomato paste
 ½ teaspoon Hungarian sweet paprika
   Freshly ground black pepper
 ⅓ cup olive oil

Sprinkle the eggplant slices on both sides with 2 teaspoons of the salt and set aside in a colander to drain for 30 minutes.

Meanwhile, mince the parsley in a food processor with the metal blade for about 15 seconds. Use the French-fry disc to process the onion and green pepper, standing them in the feed tube. Transfer the mixture to a small saucepan.

Use the French-fry disc to process the tomatoes, With a slotted spoon, transfer the to-mato pulp to the saucepan; discard the juice in the processor bowl. Stir in the tomato paste, paprika, remaining ½ teaspoon salt, and black pepper to taste. Cook over moderate heat for about 1 minute or until just heated through. Set aside.

Remove the drained eggplant slices to paper towels and pat them dry.

Preheat the oven to 375°F.

Heat the oil in a medium skillet over moderately low heat. Add the eggplant slices and cook for about 3 minutes on each side, until soft but not browned.

With a spatula, transfer the eggplant slices to a 9-inch-square baking dish. Spoon the tomato mixture evenly over them. Cover tightly with aluminum foil and bake in the center of the preheated oven for 20 to 25 minutes, or until the vegetable mixture is tender.

Serve hot or at room temperature.

Serves 4

[A B B Y   M A N D E L]

Melanzane in Carrozza
Eggplant and Mozzarella Sandwiches

 2 eggplants (about 1 pound each), ends trimmed, cut into ⅓-inch thick slices
   Coarse (kosher) salt
 6 anchovy fillets, rinsed
1½ tablespoons capers, drained
 10 fresh basil leaves, stems removed, washed and dried
   Olive oil, for frying

8   ounces whole-milk mozzarella cheese,
        well chilled and cut into ⅓-inch-thick
        slices
    Freshly ground black pepper

Sprinkle the eggplant slices on both sides
with coarse salt and drain them in a colander
for 1½ hours. Pat the slices dry with paper
towels and set aside.

Process the anchovies, capers, and whole
basil leaves in a food processor with the metal
blade until smooth, about 20 seconds, scraping down the workbowl as necessary. Reserve.

Sauté a few eggplant slices at a time in 3
tablespoons of olive oil until browned, about
3 minutes on each side. Drain on paper towels. Repeat with the remaining eggplant
slices, adding more oil as necessary (see note
below).

Preheat the oven to 400°F.

Spread the anchovy mixture on half the
eggplant slices and top each with a slice of
mozzarella and then with another eggplant
slice. Place on a baking sheet and sprinkle
with pepper. Bake for about 8 minutes or until the cheese just begins to melt.

Transfer to a serving platter.

Makes about 18 sandwiches

NOTE: The eggplant slices may be baked instead of sautéed. Preheat the oven to 375°F.
Brush both sides with olive oil and place on a
baking sheet. Bake until soft and golden
brown, 15 to 20 minutes, turning once.

[N A O M I   B A R R Y]

Penne with Tomato, Eggplant, and Anchovy Sauce

2   medium eggplants (about 1 pound each)
    Salt
¾   cup olive oil, or as needed
5   anchovy fillets
1   large onion, chopped (about 1¼ cups)
2   large garlic cloves, minced
1   pound ripe Italian plum tomatoes,
        peeled and chopped
½ to 1 cup dry white wine
    Freshly ground black pepper
⅓   cup shredded fresh basil leaves or 1 table-
        spoon dried basil

1   pound penne or other short pasta
¾   cup grated pecorino cheese

Peel the eggplants, leaving a ½-inch strip
on each of four sides. Trim the ends and
cut into ½-inch slices. Layer the slices in
a colander and sprinkle each layer with a
little salt. Cover with wax paper and weigh
down with something heavy, such as a large
can. Set the colander in the sink. Let the
eggplant stand for 30 minutes to an hour
to drain off the bitter juices. Press down with

your hands to extract all possible liquid.

Dry the eggplant. Heat 3 tablespoons of the oil in a skillet over moderately high heat. Fry about one third of the eggplant slices until golden on both sides. Remove with a slotted spoon to paper towels to drain. Add 2 to 3 more tablespoons oil to the skillet and fry another third of the eggplant slices. Remove and drain. Add 2 more tablespoons of oil and fry the remaining eggplant. Drain and reserve.

Place the anchovies in lukewarm water to cover to remove the salt. Soak for 5 minutes; change the water; let stand for 10 more minutes. As the anchovies are soaking, heat the remaining 4 tablespoons oil in a medium saucepan. Add the onion and garlic and cook over moderate heat, stirring constantly, until soft. Add the tomatoes. Bring to a boil. Lower the heat and cook, uncovered, for 10 to 15 minutes, or until the sauce has thickened.

While the sauce is cooking, chop the anchovies fine. Stir the anchovies and fried eggplant slices into the sauce with a fork,

mashing the eggplant into lumps. Depending on the tomatoes, the sauce may be very thick. Thin it with the wine to the consistency of pancake batter. Taste for saltiness and, if necessary, add a little more salt. Add a generous amount of pepper, stir in the basil leaves, and continue to cook. In a kettle of boiling salted water cook the pasta until it is *al dente* and drain.

Pour the sauce into a heated serving dish and add the pasta. Toss and sprinkle with the pecorino. Toss again at the table.

Serves 6

NOTE: If you prefer, combine the sauce and pasta in an 8- to 10-cup lightly oiled baking dish. Stir in half of the pecorino and sprinkle the remaining cheese on top. Bake for 15 minutes in a preheated hot (400°F) oven to amalgamate the pasta and sauce.

[N I K A   H A Z E L T O N]

Eggplant and Chicken Swirls

4 small eggplants (about 10 ounces each)
1½ teaspoons salt
1 ounce fresh ginger, peeled
1 medium scallion, white part only, cut into 1-inch pieces
½ skinless boneless chicken breast (4 ounces), cut into 1-inch pieces
1 teaspoon rice wine, such as sake
   Pinch salt

   Vegetable oil, for deep frying
   Cornstarch, for coating
⅓ cup soy sauce
   Lemon wedges, for garnish

Remove the stems from the eggplants. Slice each eggplant in half lengthwise. Cut 2 or 3 large ⅛-inch-thick slices of a uniform size from each half, setting the unused eggplant

69

Fennel

Fennel looks similar to celery, although the bulb is fatter and paler and the stalks fewer, with delicate feathery fronds. The stalks are generally too tough to eat, and the fragrant fronds are mostly used as a garnish. The fennel bulb has a faint licorice flavor that mellows as it is cooked. Buy firm, round, undamaged fennel without bruising and refrigerate it in a plastic bag for up to 5 days. To prepare fennel, trim away the coarse outer part of the bulb, and if there are any stalks attached, cut them flush with the bulb. Core the bulbs, except those that are very small, and cut them according to the recipe. Fennel can be eaten raw or cooked.

Oven-Braised Fennel

2 medium fennel bulbs (1 pound each)
3 tablespoons unsalted butter
½ cup chicken stock, homemade
  Salt and freshly ground black pepper
1 ounce Parmesan cheese, finely grated

Preheat the oven to 350°F.

Wash and trim the fennel bulbs. Discard any tough or brown outer layers. Cut each bulb in half lengthwise, then cut each half into 4 wedges about 1 inch wide.

Use 1 tablespoon of the butter to grease a 13 × 9 × 2-inch baking dish. Arrange the fennel wedges cut side down in a single layer. Pour the chicken stock over the fennel and season with salt and pepper. Sprinkle with the Parmesan cheese and dot with the remaining 2 tablespoons butter.

Bake, uncovered, in the preheated oven until the fennel is tender, about 45 minutes.

Serves 4

[MICHELE SCICOLONE]

Shrimp, Red Pepper, and Fennel Sauté

1½ pounds unshelled raw shrimp
7 tablespoons unsalted butter
1½ pounds sweet red peppers, stemmed, cored, and seeded
1 large fennel bulb (about 1½ pounds), trimmed
1 large garlic clove, minced
  Salt and freshly ground black pepper
½ cup Pernod
1½ cups heavy cream
  Juice of ½ lemon
1 tablespoon minced chives
1 tablespoon minced fennel leaves

Shell the shrimp, reserving 1 cup of the shells.

Melt 4 tablespoons of the butter in a small skillet. Add the reserved shrimp shells and sauté over moderately high heat for about 1 minute, or until the shells turn pink.

Place the melted butter and shrimp shells in a food processor fitted with the metal blade. Process until the shells are ground to a paste, turning the machine on and off several times to scrape down the side of the workbowl. Pass the shrimp butter through a fine sieve; refrigerate until firm.

Slice the peppers into ¼-inch wide strips. Cut the fennel bulb into strips the same size as the peppers.

Melt the remaining 3 tablespoons butter in a large skillet. Add the peppers, fennel, and garlic. Cover and cook over moderately low heat for 10 to 15 minutes, stirring occasionally, until the vegetables are just tender.

Raise the heat and add the shrimp to the skillet. Stir-fry over moderately high heat for about 3 minutes, or until the shrimp are pink and opaque. Remove the shrimp and vegetables to a bowl with a slotted spoon. Season them with salt and pepper.

Pour the Pernod and cream into the skillet and boil until reduced to a thick sauce.

Reduce the heat to low. Whisk in the lemon juice and the shrimp butter, a tablespoon at a time.

Add the shrimp and vegetables to the sauce and cook over low heat until just heated through. Check the seasoning, then sprinkle with the minced chives and fennel and serve immediately.

Serves 4

[JAN WEIMER]

Fennel Bulbs, Parma Style, with Sausage

This is one of two versions of cooked fennel that is popular in Parma. Like most dishes in the style of that region, it employs Parmesan cheese with its butter.

It should accompany sauceless boiled or roasted main courses or those having a sauce without a cream or cheese base. It may also be served by itself as an in-between course.

- 4 medium fennel bulbs (1 pound each)
  Coarse (kosher) salt
- 2 sweet Italian sausages
- ½ cup butter
- ¾ cup freshly grated Parmesan cheese
  Salt and freshly ground black pepper

Cut the fennel bulbs vertically into quarters. Remove the small knob at the bottom and cut out the hard inner part—a continuation of the knob. Place the fennel in a large bowl of cold water and soak for about 15 minutes. Heat a large quantity of cold water, with coarse salt added, in a flameproof casserole. When the water reaches the boiling point, add the fennel and let it boil for about 10 minutes. Drain the fennel, then place it on paper towels to absorb all excess liquid. Remove the skin from the sausages and slice them into 5 or 6 pieces each. Heat 2 tablespoons butter in a frying pan. When butter is melted, add the sausage pieces and sauté for about 5 minutes. Remove the sautéed sausage pieces from pan to small bowl and let cool.

Preheat oven to 375°F. Butter well the bottom and sides of a 10 × 4 × 1¾-inch baking dish and cut the remaining butter into small pats. Cover the bottom of the prepared dish with three-quarters of the fennel. Sprinkle half of the Parmesan over it, then half of the sausage pieces, one-third of the butter pats, then salt and pepper to taste. Make one more layer of fennel with the remaining sausage, Parmesan, and butter. Season with salt and pepper. Bake in the preheated oven for about 25 minutes. Serve hot.

Serves 6 to 8

[GIULIANO BUGIALLI]

Pork Roast with Fennel

3 tablespoons unsalted butter
1 tablespoon olive oil
1½ teaspoons dried rosemary
1 teaspoon fennel seeds
　Salt and freshly ground black pepper
4 medium garlic cloves, peeled
1 center-cut pork loin roast (about
　　6 pounds), bones split for slicing
2 large fennel bulbs (about 2¼ pounds
　　total), trimmed and cut into eighths
¼ cup water
1 cup dry white wine
　Fresh rosemary, for garnish

Place a rack in the center of the oven and preheat the oven to 400°F.

Put 1 tablespoon butter and the olive oil in a roasting pan and place in the oven to melt the butter.

Put the dried rosemary, fennel seeds, ½ teaspoon salt, and 1 teaspoon pepper in a food processor with the metal blade in place. Drop the garlic through the feed tube with the motor running and process until the garlic is finely chopped, about 10 seconds.

Cut ½-inch-deep slits in the pork loin at random and fill with the herb-garlic mixture. Season the meat with additional salt and pepper.

Put the pork loin in the prepared roasting pan and cook in the preheated oven until the meat registers an internal temperature of 170°F, 1¼ to 1½ hours.

Meanwhile, process the fennel bulb pieces, in 2 batches, in the processor with the metal blade until finely chopped, about 8 pulses for each batch. Simmer the chopped fennel in a saucepan with the water until tender, about 30 minutes.

Drain the fennel thoroughly and purée with the remaining 2 tablespoons butter in the processor, about 1 minute, scraping down the workbowl as necessary. Return the purée to the saucepan, season with salt and pepper, cover, and set aside.

When the pork is done, transfer it to a cutting board and cover loosely with aluminum foil to keep warm. Discard the fat from the roasting pan, leaving only the juices. Place the pan over high heat and deglaze it with the white wine. Boil for 2 minutes, then strain the juices and discard the solids.

Reheat the fennel purée over low heat while you slice the pork through the split bones. Serve with the pan juices and the fennel purée. Garnish with fresh rosemary.

Serves 8

[LORENZA DE MEDICI/
ABBY MANDEL]

Star Anise Beef with Fresh Fennel

3 pounds flank steak or London broil,
  trimmed of excess fat
2 tablespoons vegetable oil
2 cups water
½ cup soy sauce
½ cup rice wine, such as sake
2 tablespoons sugar
2 whole star anise
2 pieces dried orange peel, each about
  2 inches long
1 stick (about 3 inches) cinnamon
3 medium scallions (about 1 ounce),
  trimmed, halved crosswise and
  smashed with the flat side of a cleaver
3 slices fresh ginger, each about the size of
  a quarter, peeled and smashed with the
  flat side of a cleaver
2 medium fennel bulbs
1 teaspoon sesame oil
  Dressing (recipe follows)
  Fresh cilantro (optional), for garnish

Cut the meat lengthwise into long strips
about 3 inches wide. Pat dry with paper towels. Heat the oil in a large heavy skillet over
high heat. Add half the beef strips and cook
briefly, turning them to brown on all sides.
Transfer to paper towels to drain and repeat
with the remaining beef strips.

Bring the water, soy sauce, rice wine,
sugar, star anise, dried orange peel, cinnamon stick, scallions, and ginger to a boil in a
nonreactive large saucepan or wok. Add the
beef strips and simmer, partially covered, until tender, about 1½ hours. Remove from the
heat and cool the beef in the cooking liquid
to room temperature.

Meanwhile, rinse the fennel and trim off
the stalks. Trim the root end, leaving ⅛ inch
of the base. Cut the bulb in half vertically,
leaving the core intact. Place each half cut
side down and cut into ¼-inch vertical slices.

Bring 2 quarts water to a boil in a large
saucepan. Add the fennel and simmer until
just tender, about 5 minutes. Rinse under
cold running water and drain thoroughly.
Toss to coat with the sesame oil and arrange
on a large serving platter.

Remove the cooled beef from the liquid;
discard the liquid. Thinly slice the beef strips
across the grain and arrange over the fennel
on the platter.

Prepare the dressing and pour it over the
beef and fennel. Just before serving, toss to
coat.

Serve at room temperature or slightly
chilled.

Serves 6

[N I N A   S I M O N D S]

Dressing

1 large scallion, trimmed and cut into
    1-inch pieces
2 medium garlic cloves, peeled
1 piece fresh ginger (about 1 × 1 × ½ inch),
    peeled and halved
¼ cup soy sauce
1½ tablespoons rice wine, such as sake
1½ tablespoons black Chinese vinegar
1½ tablespoons sugar
2 tablespoons sesame oil

Drop the scallion, garlic, and ginger through the feed tube of a food processor with the metal blade in place and the motor running. Process until finely chopped, about 10 seconds, scraping down the side of the bowl once. Add the remaining ingredients and process for 10 seconds to combine.

Makes about ¾ cup

[NINA SIMONDS]

Garlic

Garlic is loved the world over. The head of garlic, a cluster of cloves surrounded by a papery membrane, grows underground. The most common varieties sold in the United States are the Gilroy, California, Mexican, and the mild elephant garlic. Mature heads are their freshest from June until the fall. The qualities to look for are tight, hard, firm heads. In winter, a bitter and very pungent green sprout grows in the center of each clove, which should be removed. Also be sure to cut away any brown spots. Garlic will keep in a cool, dark place for several weeks.

Stir-Fried Rainbow Peppers and Snow Peas in Spicy Garlic Dressing

Served cold for a picnic, this is a piquant vegetable pickle. Hot from the pan, it is an excellent side dish for an indoor meal.

  2 medium sweet yellow peppers
  2 medium sweet red peppers
  3 large Anaheim peppers
 12 ounces fresh snow peas, ends trimmed
       and strings removed
1½ tablespoons vegetable oil
  1 tablespoon sesame oil
1½ tablespoons rice wine, such as sake
  1 cup 1-inch pieces scallion greens
       Spicy Garlic Dressing (recipe follows)

Stand the yellow and red peppers stem side up on a cutting board. With a sharp knife cut 3 or 4 vertical slices, leaving only the core and stem. Remove any seeds and ribs from the slices.

Cut the Anaheim peppers in half lengthwise and remove cores, seeds, and ribs. Cut in half crosswise.

Stack all the peppers upright in the feed tube of a food processor and process with the thin slicing disc. Remove to a colander to drain.

Rinse the snow peas and pat them dry with paper towels.

Heat the oils in a wok or large skillet. When hot, add the peppers and snow peas and stir-fry for 1 minute. Add the rice wine and cook 1 minute more. Add the scallion greens and stir-fry for 15 seconds. Add the dressing, toss, and cook about 30 seconds more. Serve immediately or cool to room temperature and refrigerate until cold.

Serves 6

[N I N A   S I M O N D S]

Spicy Garlic Dressing

  2 large garlic cloves, peeled
  3 tablespoons soy sauce
1½ teaspoons sugar
  2 teaspoons sesame oil
  ½ teaspoon hot chili paste

Drop the garlic through the feed tube of a food processor with the metal blade in place and the motor running. Process until finely chopped, about 5 seconds. Add the remaining ingredients and pulse to mix, about 4 times.

Makes about ¼ cup

[N I N A   S I M O N D S]

Chicken with Forty Cloves of Garlic

This needs rolls with crispness and a good crumb to sop up the sauce. With it, serve pickled beets. Believe it or not, the garlic is disarmed! The flavor is earthy but not overwhelming.

      2 tablespoons olive oil
      2 medium onions, peeled and chopped
      2 medium carrots, peeled and chopped
      4 celery ribs, chopped
     40 garlic cloves, unpeeled (about 3 heads)
      2 sprigs parsley
      1 bay leaf
      1 teaspoon dried thyme
      8 chicken legs
      8 chicken thighs
     ⅔ cup dry white wine
    2½ teaspoons salt
     ½ teaspoon freshly ground black pepper
     ¼ teaspoon freshly grated nutmeg

Preheat the oven to 325°F.

Heat the oil in a large ovenproof sauté pan over moderate heat and add the onions, carrots, celery, and garlic. Cook, stirring occasionally, until the onions are soft and lightly browned, about 10 minutes.

Tie the parsley, bay leaf, and thyme in a piece of cheesecloth and add to the pan. Add the chicken, wine, salt, pepper, and nutmeg. Bring to a simmer, cover tightly, and bake in the preheated oven for 2 hours.

Transfer the chicken pieces to a heated platter. Drain the vegetables in a sieve, reserving the liquid in a 2-quart saucepan. Remove the garlic cloves from the vegetable mixture, reserving the vegetables, and squeeze the cloves from the root end into the workbowl of a food processor fitted with the metal blade. Process them until smooth, about 20 seconds, stopping once to scrape down the workbowl. Whisk the garlic purée into the reserved liquid and bring to a simmer over moderate heat.

Spoon the drained vegetables around the chicken and pour a little of the garlic sauce over the chicken and vegetables. Pass the remaining sauce separately.

Serves 8

[J A M E S   B E A R D]

Roast Lamb with Garlic Sauce and Stuffed Onion Cups

When this recipe is done, you won't even know that three large garlic cloves were used: all their pungency disappears during cooking. The port gives the sauce a slightly sweet accent.

3 large garlic cloves, peeled and thinly sliced crosswise
½ cup unsalted butter, chilled
½ cup ruby port
½ cup beef stock
1 leg of lamb (8 to 9 pounds), boned
2 tablespoons vegetable oil
Salt and freshly ground black pepper
Watercress, for garnish
Stuffed Onion Cups (recipe follows)

Melt 2 tablespoons of the butter in an 8-inch skillet over low heat and cook the garlic until soft but not brown.

Add the port and the stock. Raise the heat to high and cook until the liquid is reduced by one third. Remove from the heat and set aside while you prepare the meat.

Preheat the oven to 500°F.

Cut the leg of lamb so that you end up with the two large muscles from the upper leg—the top round and bottom round—in a whole piece. Trim off the small shank portion, the knuckle flap, and the thin, fatty flap near the top of the butt and set these aside or freeze them for use in other recipes, such as shish kebab, lamb stew, or lamb patties. The remaining large segment of meat will weigh about 3½ to 4 pounds. Find the area where the membrane connects the two muscles in the middle and cut the meat in half along this juncture. One piece will be slightly larger than the other.

Oil these pieces of lamb all over and season well with salt and pepper. Place the meat in a heavy, ovenproof skillet or roasting pan and roast in the preheated oven for 25 minutes, or until the internal temperature of the meat registers 115°F for rare or 120°F for medium rare. Set aside in a warm place.

Skim the fat from the juices in the roasting pan and discard. Pour the remaining juices into the skillet with the sauce base. Cook over high heat until the liquid measures ⅔ cup. Whisk in the remaining butter, 1 tablespoon at a time, adding each piece just as the previous one is melted. Taste and adjust the seasoning if necessary.

To serve, cut the lamb against the grain on an angle into ⅜-inch-thick slices. Arrange the slices on a warm platter. Spoon about 3 tablespoons of the hot sauce over the meat, including some of the garlic slices, and pass the rest separately. Garnish with watercress and serve with Stuffed Onion Cups.

Serves 8

[F R É D Y   G I R A R D E T]

Stuffed Onion Cups

8 small onions (about 4 ounces each)
1 tablespoon salt
2 medium carrots, peeled and cut into
  2-inch pieces
4 ounces fresh or frozen lima beans
3 tablespoons unsalted butter
4 ounces fresh mushrooms, cut into
  ½-inch dice
  Salt, freshly ground black pepper, and
  freshly grated nutmeg

Cut off the tops of the onions and remove the brown skins. With a small melon baller, scoop out the insides of the onions, leaving a ⅜-inch shell all around. Bring 2 quarts water and the salt to a boil in a large saucepan and blanch the onions for 4 minutes. Remove them with a slotted spoon and rinse in cold water. Invert the onions to drain.

Add the carrots to the boiling water and cook for 10 to 12 minutes, until they are easily pierced with a fork. Remove the carrots with a slotted spoon and rinse them in cold water.

Add the lima beans to the boiling water and cook for 12 minutes. While they are cooking, melt 2 tablespoons of the butter in an 8-inch skillet. Add the mushrooms and sauté over moderate heat, stirring, until they are soft, about 5 minutes. Remove from the heat.

Cut the carrot pieces into ¼-inch dice. Add them to the mushrooms. Add the remaining 1 tablespoon butter and toss to mix well.

When the lima beans are done, drain them into a colander and rinse under cold running water. Remove the skin from each bean by gently squeezing the outer edge with the thumb and forefinger until the skin slips off and the tender bean pops out. Add the lima beans to the mushrooms and carrots and toss to coat them with butter. Season with salt, pepper, and nutmeg. The onion cups and vegetable filling can be prepared in advance up to this point.

To finish the dish, season the insides of the onions with salt and pepper. Fill each cup generously with the buttered vegetable mixture.

Arrange the stuffed onions in an 8-inch skillet with a lid. Add ½ inch of water to the pan. Bring to a boil, cover, and cook over moderate heat until the onions are tender and the vegetables are heated through, about 6 to 8 minutes.

Serves 8

Kale

A member of the mustard family and related to cabbage and broccoli, kale is a winter standby, as it comes to market at about the time that the availability of other vegetables is waning. Curly leaf kale is most widely available, although there are a number of other kinds that vary in shape and color. The best kale is also the most attractive; it ought to be brightly colored without wilting or bruising. Keep kale in a plastic bag in the refrigerator for no more than a few days. It has a rather assertive flavor and is best paired with other strong flavors like garlic. Young tender kale should be cooked briefly, and thick leaves ought to be used in long-cooking preparations such as soups and stews.

Kale and Lettuce Soup

3 medium carrots, peeled and cut into
    1-inch pieces
3 medium scallions, trimmed and cut into
    1-inch pieces
4 tablespoons unsalted butter
8 ounces kale, stems removed, washed,
    drained, and cut crosswise into thirds
12 ounces all-purpose potatoes, peeled and
    cut into 1-inch pieces
5 cups chicken broth
2 medium heads Boston or butter lettuce
    (about 1 pound total), washed and
    drained
1 cup sour cream, at room temperature
1 teaspoon salt
¼ teaspoon freshly ground white pepper
¼ teaspoon Chinese five-spice powder
    (optional)
2 tablespoons minced parsley

Chop the carrots coarsely in a food processor with the metal blade, pulsing about 5 times. Add the scallions and pulse 3 times, or until the carrots and scallions are chopped to a medium coarseness.

Melt the butter in a 5-quart saucepot over moderately low heat. Add the carrots and scallions. Cover and cook, stirring occasionally, until the vegetables are soft, about 20 minutes.

Meanwhile, use the processor with the metal blade to chop the kale, in 2 batches, pulsing 10 to 12 times or until coarsely chopped. Set aside. Use the metal blade to chop the potatoes, pulsing about 8 times.

When the carrots are soft, add the potatoes, chicken broth, and reserved chopped kale to the saucepot. Bring to a boil over high heat, then reduce the heat, cover, and simmer for 20 minutes, or until the vegetables are tender.

Meanwhile, use the metal blade to chop the lettuce, in 2 batches, pulsing 10 to 12 times.

When the potatoes and kale are tender, add the lettuce to the saucepot, stir, and simmer, uncovered, for 10 minutes more. Strain the broth into a 4-quart saucepan. Use the metal blade to purée the vegetables, in 2 batches, in the processor, processing about 30 seconds or until smooth. Add the purée to the broth and stir well.

Whisk in the sour cream, salt, pepper, and five-spice powder, if used. Stir over moderately low heat just until the soup is heated through, taking care that it doesn't reach a simmer. Sprinkle with the minced parsley and serve.

Serves 10

[M A R L E N E S O R O S K Y]

Caldo Gallego
Galician Kale, Potato, and White Bean Chowder

1   medium carrot (about 3 ounces), peeled and cut into lengths to fit the feed tube of a food processor vertically
2   medium celery ribs (about 6 ounces total), trimmed and cut into lengths to fit the feed tube vertically
2   medium turnips (about 10 ounces total), peeled and cut to fit the feed tube
2   medium onions (about 10 ounces total), peeled and quartered
8   ounces dried navy beans, rinsed
4   cups water
4   cups beef broth
4   cups chicken broth
2   medium bay leaves
4   whole black peppercorns
1   meaty ham bone (about 1 pound)
4   ounces salt pork, cut into ¼-inch dice and blanched for 1 minute
8   ounces smoked ham, cut into ½-inch dice
4   ounces mild chorizo sausage, cut into ½-inch dice
2   large all-purpose potatoes (1 pound total), peeled and cut into eighths
¼   cup finely chopped parsley leaves
1   pound fresh kale, stems removed, washed, drained, and dried

Process the carrot, celery, and turnips in a food processor with the medium slicing disc. Remove.

Process the onions with the metal blade until coarsely chopped, pulsing about 8 times.

Put the sliced vegetables, chopped onions, beans, water, beef and chicken broth, bay leaves, peppercorns, ham bone, salt pork, ham, and chorizo in a large stockpot. Bring slowly to a boil, skimming often. Reduce the heat, cover, and simmer for 2½ hours. Add the potatoes and chopped parsley and continue cooking until the potatoes are almost tender, about 15 minutes.

Remove the soup from the heat, cool to room temperature, and refrigerate overnight.

To finish the soup, roll 4 kale leaves together lengthwise. Cut crosswise in half and place cut side down in the feed tube of the food processor with the medium slicing disc in place, packing the feed tube tightly. Process with light pressure. Repeat with the remaining kale.

When all the kale has been sliced, remove and discard the fat from the top of the refrigerated soup. Bring it slowly to a boil and add the kale. Reduce the heat and cook, uncovered, until the kale is just cooked through, about 5 minutes.

Serve hot.

Serves 8 to 10

[E L E N E   M A R G O T   K O L B]

Leeks

Leeks belong to the garlic and onion family and look like large scallions. They are used in much the same ways as onions, though the results are more subtle and sweet. Generally available from late summer to early spring, they are most abundant in the fall. At the market choose leeks with firm, unblemished white stalks and bright stiff green leaves. Also, keep in mind that the smaller the leek, the more tender it will be. Bundle the leeks with their roots in a dampened towel and refrigerate them in a plastic bag for up to 5 days. Dirt gets trapped between the many leaf layers, so it's important to wash them thoroughly. If the recipe calls for cooking the leeks whole, trim off as much of the tops as you want to discard, then clean each one by making a lengthwise cut, starting at the top and ending 2 inches from the base. Hold the leek under cold running water, fanning out the layers. If the leeks will be chopped, cut them first and then rinse them in a bowl of cold water. Swish the pieces around the bowl for a few minutes until no traces of dirt or sand are left clinging to them. Let the dirt settle to the bottom of the bowl and lift the leeks carefully out of the water with a slotted spoon.

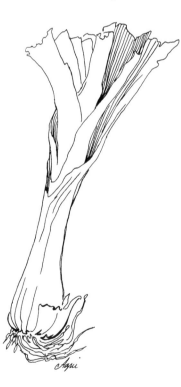

Leek and Potato Soup

As the leek is the national emblem of Wales and St. David, the country's patron saint, this hearty soup is often served on his feast day, March 1.

4   medium all-purpose potatoes (about 1½ pounds total), peeled
3   medium onions (about 12 ounces total), peeled and quartered
2   large leeks (about 14 ounces total), trimmed, split, washed well, and cut to fit the feed tube of a food processor vertically
4   cups chicken broth
½   teaspoon salt
½   cup heavy cream or milk
1   teaspoon dried chervil
½   teaspoon freshly ground black pepper

Slice the potatoes, onions, and leeks in a food processor with the medium slicing disc.

Bring the broth and salt to a boil in a large saucepan, add the vegetables, and reduce the heat. Simmer, covered, until the potatoes are tender, 20 to 25 minutes. Break up the potatoes with a spoon, add the cream, chervil, and pepper, and simmer until heated through, about 2 minutes.

Serves 6

[FAY CARPENTER]

Leek and Oyster Salad

3   large leeks (7 to 8 ounces each), trimmed of all but 1 inch of green
    Pinch salt
1   cup water
2   teaspoons olive oil
12 oysters, shucked, in their liquor
2   tablespoons unsalted butter
1   tablespoon fresh lemon juice
    Pinch cayenne pepper, plus additional for garnish (optional)

Cut the leeks in half lengthwise and remove the thin center piece. Cut the halves lengthwise into quarters, then crosswise into 3-inch lengths. Wash well and drain.

Cook the leeks with the salt and water, stirring, in a large saucepan over high heat for about 3 minutes to remove the acidic taste. Drain and toss in a bowl with the olive oil. Set aside, covered.

Cook the oysters in their liquor, stirring occasionally, in a medium saucepan over moderate heat for 2 minutes. Do not let boil. Remove the oysters to a separate bowl with a slotted spoon and set aside, covered. Whisk the butter, lemon juice, and pinch of cayenne pepper into the liquor in the saucepan over low heat. Keep warm.

Divide the leeks evenly among 4 serving plates. Cut the oysters into thirds and divide them among the 4 plates, placing them on top of the leeks. Drizzle about 2 tablespoons of the warm sauce over each serving. Garnish with cayenne pepper, if desired.

Serves 4

[JEAN-LOUIS GERIN]

Leeks Vinaigrette with Mint

Plan to use 3 medium (½ inch thick) or 6 slender young leeks per serving. Do not use leeks more than ½ inch in diameter.

18   medium or 36 slender leeks
     Salt
½   cup plus 1 tablespoon peanut oil
3   tablespoons white wine vinegar
1   teaspoon Dijon mustard
1½   teaspoons coarse (kosher) salt
¼   teaspoon freshly ground black pepper
1   large bunch fresh mint

Bring a large pot of salted water to a boil. Trim off the root and tough green ends of the leeks. Wash thoroughly.

Place the leeks in the boiling water. When the water returns to a boil, reduce the heat and simmer until the bulb ends of the leeks are tender when pierced with the point of a thin, sharp knife. Depending on the size of the leeks, this will take anywhere from 6 to 60 minutes. Remove each leek as soon as it tests done. When all the leeks are done, return them to the pot and cook for about 30 seconds to reheat.

While the leeks are cooking, combine the oil, vinegar, mustard, salt, and pepper in a small bowl. Mix well and set aside.

Trim the cooked leeks to a length that will fit attractively on small serving plates. Medium-size leeks should be cut in half lengthwise; small slender leeks should not.

Arrange the leeks on 6 serving plates and pour some of the vinaigrette over them.

Remove the large mint leaves from their stems; wash and dry. Make 3 or 4 stacks of 4 or 5 leaves and roll them from the point to the base. With a thin, sharp knife, cut the mint lengthwise into strips. Sprinkle mint over the leeks and serve immediately.

Serves 6

[JEAN-JACQUES JOUTEUX/
NAOMI BARRY]

Sauté of Shrimp in Leek Cream

4 medium leeks (about 1½ pounds total)
8 tablespoons unsalted butter
⅓ cup water
  Salt and freshly ground white pepper
  Pinch sugar
2 cups fish stock or clam juice
1½ cups Crème Fraîche (page 30)
1½ pounds medium raw shrimp, peeled and
    deveined
1 tablespoon minced fresh parsley,
    for garnish

Cut off and discard the root end of the leeks. Trim off all but 2 inches of the leeks' green tops. Slit the leeks lengthwise and wash thoroughly under cold running water. Cut into 2½ × ¼-inch strips.

Melt 2 tablespoons of the butter in a large skillet over moderate heat. Add the leeks, water, salt, pepper, and sugar. Cover and braise over low heat until almost tender, 5 to 8 minutes. Uncover and continue cooking until the leeks are tender and their liquid has evaporated. Reserve off the heat.

In a 2-quart saucepan, reduce the clam juice by half over moderately high heat. Off the heat, whisk in the Crème Fraîche. Return the mixture to a boil over medium heat and reduce to 1¼ cups, stirring constantly. This will take about 20 minutes (see note below). Stir in the reserved leeks and remove from the heat.

Heat 3 tablespoons of the remaining butter in the large skillet over medium heat until it starts to bubble. Add the shrimp, stirring constantly, until they begin to turn opaque, about 3 minutes. Gradually stir in the reserved leek sauce and heat thoroughly. Remove the skillet from the heat and stir in the remaining 3 tablespoons butter, 1 tablespoon at a time, until blended. Garnish with the parsley to serve.

Serves 6

NOTE: The cream should coat a spoon heavily; if not, make a beurre manié by combining 1 tablespoon of unbleached all-purpose flour with 1 tablespoon unsalted butter, blending them together with the back of a spoon. Whisk into the sauce by ½ teaspoons until the desired consistency is reached.

[P E R L A   M E Y E R S]

Lentils

Lentils are a type of pulse—the ripe, dried seeds of the legume family. (Beans are also legumes.) These small round seeds have long been consumed as a substitute for meat, as they are rich in protein as well as carbohydrates. The most common types are the small dark green lentils from Puy, France, and the larger brown lentil. In India, they favor the brilliantly colored orange, yellow, and red lentils that cook down into a smooth purée. Rinse and pick over lentils before cooking to remove any pebbles and sand.

Lentil Soup

1½ cups lentils, picked over
1 garlic clove, peeled
1 small onion, peeled and halved
1 celery rib, cut into 2-inch pieces
1 carrot, peeled and cut into 2-inch pieces
2 medium tomatoes, peeled, seeded, and quartered
3 cups beef broth
3 cups water
1 Polish kielbasa or other smoked sausage (about 1 pound)
1½ tablespoons white wine vinegar
1 teaspoon paprika
1 teaspoon salt
½ teaspoon freshly ground black pepper
Pinch dried thyme

Wash the lentils under cold running water and drain. Put them in a 4-quart saucepan.

Drop the garlic through the feed tube of a food processor with the metal blade in place and the motor running. Process to chop it finely. Stop the machine, scrape down the workbowl, and add the onion, celery, and carrot. Turn the machine on and off 8 to 10 times to chop the vegetables. Add the mixture to the lentils.

Use the metal blade to chop the tomatoes, turning the machine on and off 4 or 5 times. Add the tomatoes and all the other ingredients to the saucepan and cook, covered, over moderately low heat for 1 hour, stirring occasionally, or until the lentils are soft.

Remove the sausage from the soup and set aside. Strain the soup through a colander into a 3-quart saucepan. Use the metal blade of the food processor to purée the solids, about 2 cups at a time, turning the machine on and off 2 or 3 times and then letting it run for 30 to 45 seconds, stopping once to scrape down the bowl. Stir the purée into the liquid in the saucepan. Repeat with the remaining solids.

Cut the reserved sausage into ¼-inch slices and return to the soup. Heat the soup through and serve.

Serves 6

[J U L E S   B O N D]

Lemon Lentil Salad

2 cups lentils, picked over, washed, and drained
4 whole cloves
1 medium onion (about 5 ounces), peeled
2 teaspoons ground cumin
3 tablespoons olive oil
Salt and freshly ground black pepper
1 cup loosely packed parsley leaves
1 medium garlic clove, peeled
2 medium scallions (about 1½ ounces total), about 1 inch of greens trimmed, cut into 1-inch pieces

½ cup fresh lemon juice

1 large hard-cooked egg white, chopped

Put the lentils with enough water to cover in a large saucepan. Stick the cloves into the onion and add the onion, cumin, 2 tablespoons of the oil, salt, and pepper to the pot. Bring to a boil, then reduce the heat and simmer, covered, until the lentils are just tender, about 20 minutes. Drain, removing and discarding the onion. Cool the lentils to room temperature.

Meanwhile, process the parsley in a food processor with the metal blade until finely chopped, about 15 seconds. With the motor running, add the garlic and scallions through the feed tube and process until finely chopped, about 10 seconds. Reserve.

Stir the lemon juice into the cooled lentils. Season with salt and pepper to taste. Transfer the lentils to a serving dish and sprinkle with the parsley mixture, then the chopped egg white. Drizzle the remaining 1 tablespoon olive oil over all and add a generous grinding of black pepper.

Serves 8

[LYN STALLWORTH AND SUZANNE S. JONES]

Rice and Lentils

Toasting the lentils enhances their earthy flavor. This makes a satisfying vegetarian main dish.

    1 cup yellow lentils (see note below), picked over
    1 small onion (about 2 ounces), peeled
    3 tablespoons vegetable oil
    2 cups long-grain rice, washed and drained well
    1 stick (about 2 inches) cinnamon
    4 whole cardamom pods
    4 whole cloves
    3 medium bay leaves
    1 teaspoon salt
 3½ cups water, or more as needed

Lightly toast the lentils in a large, dry skillet over low heat, stirring often, about 10 minutes. Be careful not to scorch the lentils. Transfer to a strainer and rinse under cold running water. Drain well.

Stand the onion in the feed tube of a food processor and process with the fine slicing disc.

Heat the oil in the skillet over moderate heat. Add the onion and cook, stirring, until lightly browned and crisp, about 5 minutes.

Remove half the onion to paper towels with a slotted spoon. Stir the rice and lentils into the onion remaining in the skillet, then add the cinnamon, cardamom, cloves, bay leaves, and salt. Cook, stirring, over moderate heat for 2 minutes.

Add the 3½ cups water and bring to a boil. Cover the pan, reduce the heat to low, and cook until the water is absorbed, about 15 minutes. Stir the mixture. If it appears to be too dry, stir in 1 or 2 tablespoons more water. Remove from the heat and keep covered for 10 minutes before serving.

Remove the bay leaves (and other whole spices, if desired) before serving warm, sprinkled with the reserved onions.

Serves 6 to 8 as a side dish

NOTE: Small yellow lentils *(moong dahl)* are available in Indian or Asian food shops.

[C O P E L A N D   M A R K S]

Ragout of Lentils and Sausage

  2 large onions (about 14 ounces total),
       peeled and quartered
  3 tablespoons olive oil
  2 dried red chili peppers (about 2 × ⅜ inch
       each), cut in half
  2 large garlic cloves
  1 can (35 ounces) Italian plum tomatoes,
       drained
  1 tablespoon tomato paste
1½ teaspoons imported paprika
  1 teaspoon dried thyme
  1 teaspoon dried marjoram
       Salt and freshly ground black pepper
  6 German knockwurst (about 1 pound
       total), cut into ¼-inch slices
3¼ cups Braised Lentils (recipe follows),
       plus ½ cup cooking liquid
  ½ cup finely chopped parsley

Process the onions in a food processor with the medium slicing disc. Heat the oil in a large sauté pan over moderate heat. Add the onions and chili peppers, reduce the heat to moderately low and sauté, stirring often, until the onions are soft and lightly browned, about 12 minutes.

Drop the garlic through the feed tube of the processor with the motor running and process until finely chopped, about 10 seconds. Scrape down the workbowl, add the tomatoes, and pulse 3 times to chop.

Add the tomato paste, paprika, thyme, and marjoram to the pan and stir to coat the onions. Season with salt and pepper to taste. Add the garlic-tomato mixture and cook until the tomato liquid evaporates, about 10 minutes. Reduce the heat to low, add the knockwurst, and simmer, covered, for 20 minutes. Add the lentils and the ½ cup cooking liquid; partially cover the pan and simmer, stirring occasionally, until the liquid is absorbed, about 20 minutes. Remove and discard the chili peppers. Sprinkle with chopped parsley and serve.

Serves 6

Braised Lentils

1 cup lentils, picked over

8 cups water

1 medium carrot (about 3 ounces), peeled and cut in half

2 medium celery ribs with leaves, cut in thirds

1 medium onion (about 6 ounces), peeled and stuck with 1 clove

¼ teaspoon salt

4 whole black peppercorns

Bouquet garni: 1 bay leaf, 2 large sprigs parsley, 1 teaspoon dried thyme, tied in dampened cheesecloth

Soak the lentils in warm water for 1 hour. Drain and place in a large pot with the remaining ingredients. Bring to a boil, cover, and reduce the heat to low. Simmer until tender, about 10 minutes. Drain the lentils and reserve the liquid.

Makes 5½ cups

[P E R L A   M E Y E R S]

Mushrooms

There are thousands of varieties of this edible fungus, appearance and taste varying from mushroom to mushroom. The most common cultivated type, white or button, is being replaced at the supermarket with all manner of exotic mushrooms, including oyster, chanterelle, shiitake, and portobello. Choose white mushrooms that are firm and evenly colored and avoid ones that have soft or dark spots. For exotic mushrooms, look for ones that feel firm and heavy for their size and appear fresh without any shriveling or darkening. As a rule, smaller and less mature mushrooms are better. Mushrooms can be stored in the refrigerator for several days, just as long as they have air circulating around them. Keep them in a paper bag with holes in it. Do not store them in plastic bags or the mushrooms will deteriorate quickly.

Before cooking, trim away any discoloration with a knife and wipe them clean with a soft-bristled brush or paper towel, dampened if necessary. If the dirt still won't come off, rinse quickly and let them dry thoroughly on paper towels.

Creamed Mushrooms on Toast

1 pound mushrooms, halved
6 tablespoons unsalted butter
1 cup heavy cream
2 tablespoons dry sherry
   Salt and freshly ground black pepper
4 slices white bread, toasted and halved
   diagonally

Sauté the mushrooms in the butter in a large skillet over moderate heat until lightly col-ored, about 5 minutes. Add the cream, sherry, and salt and pepper to taste and boil, stirring, over high heat until the sauce coats the back of a spoon, about 10 minutes. Spoon over the toast.

Serves 4

[MARION CUNNINGHAM]

Mushrooms Stuffed with Shrimp

This recipe calls for last-minute cooking, although the mushrooms may be stuffed up to an hour ahead.

1 slice (about ⅛ inch) fresh ginger, peeled
1 medium scallion, trimmed and cut into
   1-inch lengths
4 water chestnuts, drained
8 ounces medium raw shrimp, shelled,
   deveined, and halved crosswise
2 teaspoons dry sherry
2 teaspoons light soy sauce
¼ teaspoon sugar
24 fresh mushrooms (1½ to 2 inches in
   diameter), stems removed, thoroughly
   cleaned
2 tablespoons vegetable oil
½ cup chicken stock, preferably homemade
2 tablespoons oyster sauce

Drop the ginger through the feed tube of a food processor with the metal blade in place and the machine running. Process until minced. Add the scallion and water chestnuts, pulse 3 or 4 times and then process until minced, about 10 seconds. Add the shrimp; pulse 6 to 8 times or until finely chopped. Add the sherry, soy sauce, and sugar and pulse 4 or 5 times to blend well.

Divide the filling among the mushroom caps, mounding it and smoothing the tops.

Heat the oil in a large skillet over moderate heat. Add the mushrooms, filling side up, and cook until sizzling, about 30 seconds. Pour in the chicken broth, cover, and cook until the filling turns white, about 2 minutes.

Uncover the skillet and drizzle the oyster sauce over the mushrooms. Raise the heat to high. Spoon the pan juices over the filling 4 or 5 times, tipping the skillet if necessary. Continue to cook until the sauce has formed a brown glaze on the mushrooms and evaporated from the bottom of the skillet, about 4 minutes. Transfer the mushrooms to a serving plate and serve immediately.

Serves 8 as an appetizer

[HUGH CARPENTER]

Wild Mushroom Pâté

If the fresh wild mushrooms called for here are unavailable, use a combination of fresh cultivated mushrooms and additional dried wild mushrooms, soaking them with the others as directed.

- 3 ounces dried cèpes or porcini mushrooms
- 4 cups boiling water
- 2 tablespoons unsalted butter
  Salt and freshly ground black pepper
- 1½ pounds skinned boneless chicken breasts, quartered
- 2 large egg whites
- 1 tablespoon fresh tarragon or 1 teaspoon dried
- 1¾ cups heavy cream
- 12 ounces assorted fresh wild mushrooms, preferably chanterelle, pleurotte or oyster, and shiitake, stemmed and quartered if large
- 3 tablespoons olive oil
  Tarragon leaves, for garnish

Soak the cèpes in the boiling water for 2 hours. Drain, reserving the mushrooms and liquid separately, first cutting off the stems.

Strain the soaking liquid through dampened cheesecloth into a saucepan and boil until reduced to 1¼ cups, about 20 minutes.

Sauté the cèpes in the butter in a small skillet over moderate heat until tender, about 3 minutes. Season with salt and pepper.

Chop one third of the cèpes coarsely in a food processor with the metal blade, about 5 pulses. Set aside.

Process the chicken, remaining cèpes, egg whites, tarragon, and 2 teaspoons salt until the chicken is finely ground, about 10 seconds. With the motor running, add 1½ cups cream and ½ cup of the reduced soaking liquid through the feed tube in a slow, steady stream. Process until smooth, about 20 seconds. Transfer to a bowl and stir in the chopped cèpes. Chill for 30 minutes.

Preheat the oven to 350°F. Butter a 5-cup terrine or mold.

Pack the mixture in the prepared terrine, cover, and place in a large baking pan. Pour enough boiling water into the pan to come one fourth of the way up the terrine and bake in the center of the preheated oven until springy to the touch or a meat thermometer registers 160°F, about 55 minutes.

To make a sauce, pour the terrine juices into a saucepan. Add the remaining ¾ cup reduced soaking liquid and ¼ cup cream and boil until slightly syrupy, about 10 minutes.

97

Pâte Brisée

¾ cup unsalted butter, chilled and cut into
   12 pieces
1 large egg
2 tablespoons cold water
⅛ teaspoon salt
1¾ cups unbleached all-purpose flour

Put the butter, egg, water, and salt in a food
processor fitted with the metal blade. Turn
the machine on and off 6 times and then
leave the motor running for 5 seconds to mix
the ingredients. Do not be concerned if small
lumps of butter remain.

Add the flour. Process just until the dough
begins to come together. Do not overprocess.

Put the dough, including the little scraps
that remain on the bottom of the workbowl,
in a plastic bag. Press the dough together into
a ball and then flatten it into a disc. Refrigerate at least 2 hours or overnight before use.

Makes enough for a single 11-inch crust

[F R É D Y   G I R A R D E T /
A B B Y   M A N D E L]

Onion Soup

8 medium onions (about 2½ pounds
   total), peeled
½ cup plus 2 tablespoons unsalted butter
½ cup Riesling wine
4 cups chicken broth (see note below)
¼ teaspoon salt
⅛ teaspoon freshly ground white pepper
2 tablespoons sweet sherry
4 ounces Gruyère cheese
12 thin slices French bread
2 tablespoons olive oil
1 medium garlic clove, peeled and split

Process the onions in a food processor with
the thin slicing disc. Melt the ½ cup butter in
a large heavy saucepot. Sauté all but 1 cup of
the onions in the melted butter until they are
soft and golden brown, 35 to 40 minutes. Stir

the onions often to prevent them from sticking to the bottom of the saucepot.

Add the wine to the sautéed onions and
cook 5 minutes more. Transfer the mixture to
the processor fitted with the metal blade. Add
1 cup of the chicken broth and process until
smooth, about 45 seconds, scraping down the
workbowl as necessary. Pour the purée back
into the saucepot, add the remaining broth,
salt, pepper, and sherry.

Sauté the remaining sliced onions in the 2
tablespoons butter until soft and golden,
about 20 minutes, watching carefully to avoid
burning. Add them to the purée and reheat
gently, about 5 minutes.

Meanwhile, prepare the croutons. Preheat
the oven to 300°F. Shred the cheese in the
processor with the medium shredding disc

and set aside. Lightly toast the bread slices in the center of the preheated oven, about 5 minutes. Brush them with the olive oil and rub them with the garlic. Sprinkle the shredded cheese over the slices. Increase the oven temperature to 375°F and bake the croutons until the cheese is melted and lightly browned.

Serve the soup in individual bowls, each garnished with 2 croutons.

Serves 6

NOTE: For a thinner soup, add more broth.

[JOANNA PRUESS]

Baked Cod with Onions and Mint

Roasted Potatoes

  1 medium garlic clove, peeled
16 small red potatoes (about 1 pound total)
  2 tablespoons olive oil
     Salt and freshly ground black pepper
 ½ teaspoon dried thyme

Baked Cod

  1 cup fresh mint leaves
  1 cup fresh parsley leaves
  1 medium garlic clove
  3 medium yellow onions (about 12 ounces total), ends cut flat, peeled and halved
  6 tablespoons unsalted butter
     Salt and freshly ground black pepper
  4 cod fillets (about 7 ounces each)
  1 tablespoon olive oil
  2 tablespoons fresh lemon juice
  2 medium scallions (2 ounces total), trimmed of all but 3 inches of green
  1 tablespoon small capers, drained and rinsed, for garnish
  8 flat anchovy fillets, patted dry and cut lengthwise in half, for garnish
     Scallion slivers, for garnish

Preheat the oven to 400°F.

To prepare the potatoes, drop the garlic through the feed tube of a food processor with the metal blade in place and the motor running. Process until finely chopped, about 5 seconds.

Rub the potatoes with the olive oil. Put them in a baking dish and sprinkle with the chopped garlic, salt, pepper, and thyme. Bake in the center of the preheated oven for 20 minutes. Stir occasionally.

While the potatoes are cooking, prepare the cod. Process the mint and parsley with the metal blade until finely chopped, about 10 seconds. Reserve.

Drop the garlic through the feed tube with the metal blade in place and the motor running. Process until finely chopped, about 5 seconds. Reserve.

Slice the onions cut ends down with the all-purpose slicing disc. Cook the onions in the butter, stirring, until barely soft, 10 to 12 minutes. Add the garlic and cook 2 minutes more. Stir in the chopped herbs, ¼ teaspoon salt, and ⅛ teaspoon pepper.

Spoon the onion mixture into a shallow baking pan. Arrange the cod fillets in a single layer on top, brush with the oil and lemon juice, and sprinkle with pepper.

Increase the oven temperature to 450°F. Bake the fish until it flakes easily, 10 to 12 minutes.

While the fish is cooking, cut the scallions into 1-inch pieces. Process them with the metal blade until finely chopped, 6 to 8 pulses.

Transfer the fish and onions to individual serving plates. Garnish with the chopped scallions, capers, anchovy fillets, and scallion slivers. Serve with the potatoes.

Serves 4

[JOYCE GOLDSTEIN]

Steamed Chicken with Green Onions

- 1 whole chicken (about 3 pounds)
- 2 tablespoons rice wine, such as sake, or pale dry sherry
- 1 tablespoon salt
- 3 scallions, cut into 2-inch sections and shredded
- 2 tablespoon-size pieces fresh ginger, peeled and cut into 2-inch shreds
- ¼ cup vegetable oil
- 2 teaspoons cornstarch
- 1 tablespoon water

Coat the chicken inside and out with the rice wine and salt. Let it stand for 1 hour at room temperature.

Place the chicken in a heatproof bowl large enough to hold it. Rest the bowl on top of a round cake rack, or 2-inch aluminum can opened at both ends, inside a 6- to 8-quart stockpot. Add 1½ inches of boiling water to the pot. Cover tightly and put the pot over moderate heat. Steam the chicken for 35 minutes, adding more boiling water to the pot if necessary.

Lift out the chicken and reserve the juices that have collected in the bowl. Using a heavy knife, a cleaver, or poultry shears, cut the chicken into pieces about 1 inch by 2½ inches. On a serving platter, arrange the pieces in the form of the chicken. Cover with the shredded scallions and ginger.

Heat the oil in a wok or small skillet until a haze forms. Carefully pour the oil over the scallions and ginger.

In a small pan, bring the reserved chicken juices to a boil. Dissolve the cornstarch in the water and stir it into the juices. Pour over the chicken and serve.

Serves 4 to 6

[LUCY WANG/
LYN STALLWORTH]

Scallion Breads

Scallion breads are made in many ways—deep-fried, pan-fried; with baking powder to yield a hearty bread, without to make a thin pancake suitable for a snack. This recipe produces a chewy and flavorsome bread, a perfect accompaniment instead of rice for many Chinese dishes.

The Chinese name for scallion bread is literally "scallion and oil cake," and refers to the tastes of scallion and oil that lace the bread. Traditionally, Chinese cooks use lard. Barbara Tropp dislikes the taste of the readily available processed lard, so instead uses fragrant dark sesame oil.

Hot water doughs are often found in Chinese cooking. They make for a smoother and more elastic dough than those made without hot water. This particular dough can be refrigerated or frozen until you are ready to roll it out.

Roll out and pan-fry the scallion breads just prior to serving them. They get tough if done in advance and left to sit.

2 cups unbleached all-purpose flour, or as needed
1½ teaspoons baking powder
⅓ cup cold water
2½ teaspoons coarse (kosher) salt
⅓ cup boiling water
2½ teaspoons sesame oil
3 heaping tablespoons thin-cut scallion rings, both green and white parts
½ cup vegetable oil, approximate

Combine 1 cup of the unbleached flour and the baking powder in a food processor fitted with the metal blade. With the machine running, slowly add the cold water through the feed tube in a thin stream, until the dough forms a ball around the blade. Let the machine run for an additional 10 seconds to knead the dough. Remove the cold dough from the workbowl and put aside.

Refit the workbowl with the metal blade, add the remaining cup of flour and 1 teaspoon of the salt to the workbowl, and proceed as above, using the boiling water. Leave the hot dough in the workbowl.

Return the cold dough to the workbowl and process the two doughs together for 15 seconds. The dough should be soft and moist. If the dough is too sticky, add a bit more flour to the bowl and process until smooth (see note below).

Oil a glass or stainless-steel bowl with 1 teaspoon of the sesame oil. Place the dough in it, cover with plastic wrap or a damp towel, and let rest for 2 hours.

Knead the dough for 3 to 4 minutes until smooth, flouring the board lightly only if necessary. With a sharp knife or cleaver, divide the dough into 3 even parts and form each part into a smooth ball.

On a lightly floured surface, roll out the first ball into a 7-inch circle. With your fingers, coat the top evenly with ½ teaspoon sesame oil. Next, sprinkle the top with ½ teaspoon salt and 1 heaping tablespoon of the scallion rings, distributing them evenly over the surface with your fingers.

Roll the circle up into a cylinder and pinch the top and end seams shut. Pull the dough a bit to stretch it lengthwise as you hold it up from the board. Put it down on the board again and, using your fingers, roll the cylinder back and forth along the board. Pick the dough up once more to stretch it.

Put the dough back on the board again. Grasp one end of the cylinder with the thumb and forefinger of your right hand, and use your left hand to grasp the other end of the cylinder and wrap the dough around itself in a flat spiral. Tuck the outer end of the dough under the spiral, and gently press the dough flat with your palm.

The dough will roll out more easily if it rests a bit, so wait a few minutes. Flour the board lightly, and gently roll out the flattened spiral into a 6-inch circle. Don't worry if some of the scallions break through. Cover the finished flatbread with a dry cloth. Repeat this process for the remaining 2 balls of dough.

Heat a 9- or 10-inch skillet over high heat for 20 seconds. Add enough oil to evenly glaze the bottom with ¹⁄₁₆ inch of oil. Let the oil heat for 2 minutes, and then reduce the heat to moderate.

Cook one bread on one side until it is lightly browned (lift it up with a spatula to check) and then turn the bread over. Reduce the heat somewhat and brown the other side. Remove the bread to a double layer of paper toweling, and pat dry. Cover the bread with an inverted plate to keep it warm.

Add more oil to the pan and let it heat for the second and third breads as you did for the first bread. (It is not necessary to preheat the empty pan as you did originally.) Fry the remaining breads, and pat them dry also.

With a sharp knife or cleaver, cut each bread into 6 pie-shaped wedges. Serve them immediately on a plate or in a towel-lined wicker basket to keep them warm through the meal.

Makes three 7-inch flatbreads

NOTE: Scallion breads may, of course, be made by hand. Knead the cold and hot doughs separately and then combine them, kneading until smooth.

[B A R B A R A   T R O P P]

Warm Shrimp Salad with Ginger and Scallions

- 1 large garlic clove, peeled
- ⅓ ounce fresh ginger, peeled and cut into 2 pieces
- 8 medium scallions (4 ounces), trimmed
- 12 tablespoons cold pressed peanut oil (see note below)
- 2 pounds raw medium shrimp, peeled, deveined, washed, and patted dry

Sesame Vinaigrette Sauce (recipe
follows)

14 medium mushrooms [8 ounces], preferably white, of equal size, with caps
tightly closed, wiped

2 medium endives (9 ounces), core removed, separated into leaves (18 leaves
required)

6 small lettuce leaves (2 ounces), washed
and dried

18 sprigs watercress (2 ounces)

Drop the garlic and ginger through the feed
tube of a food processor with the metal blade
in place and the motor running. Process until
minced, about 10 seconds. Remove and reserve.

Place the scallions in the food processor
and pulse 12 to 14 times to chop them finely.
Remove and reserve.

Heat 6 tablespoons of the peanut oil in a
large skillet over moderately high heat. Add
half the shrimp and sauté them until they are
just cooked through, 2 to 3 minutes. Add 2
teaspoons of the garlic and ginger, toss with
the shrimp, and cook for about 30 seconds.
Add half of the scallions and cook, stirring,
for about 30 seconds more.

With a slotted spoon, transfer the shrimp
and scallion mixture to a 3-quart mixing bowl
and combine it with ⅔ cup of the Sesame
Vinaigrette Sauce. Repeat the procedure
with the remaining oil, shrimp, ginger, garlic,
and scallions.

Trim the stems of the mushrooms. Cut off
2 opposite sides of the mushroom cap so it is
flat with the stem. Reserve the side slices for
another use. With the fine slicing disc of a
food processor in place, set the mushrooms,
flat side down, in the feed tube. Make only
one layer. Process using moderate pressure.
Repeat with the remaining mushrooms. You
need 54 good slices.

Pour 2 tablespoons of the Sesame Vinaigrette Sauce over the middle of 6 individual
serving plates. Tilt each plate to enlarge the
circle of sauce. Arrange 3 endive leaves on
each plate so they are evenly spaced and radi-
ating from the center. Place 1 lettuce leaf,
torn into small pieces, in the center of each
plate. Arrange 3 mushroom slices, slightly
overlapping, in each of the 3 spaces between
the endive leaves. Place a sprig of watercress
on each endive leaf. Mound equal servings of
the shrimp and scallion mixture on the lettuce and nap it with additional Sesame Vinaigrette Sauce.

Serves 6

NOTE: Cold-pressed peanut oil is generally
sold in natural foods stores. If not available,
substitute vegetable oil.

[S A L L Y   D A R R]

Sesame Vinaigrette Sauce

⅛ teaspoon minced garlic
1 teaspoon Dijon mustard
2 tablespoons sherry wine vinegar
3 tablespoons dark soy sauce
2 cups cold-pressed peanut oil (see note above)
½ cup sesame oil

In a 3-quart mixing bowl, whisk together the garlic, mustard, vinegar, and soy sauce. Continue to mix with an electric hand mixer at medium speed, adding the 2 oils in a slow steady stream.

Makes about 2¾ cups

[SALLY DARR]

Parsnips

This thick, long white root vegetable does not get the attention it deserves. It has a pleasantly sweet, nutty flavor and is suitable for almost any method of cooking, including baking, boiling, sautéing, and steaming. Its peak season is fall through winter. The important qualities to look for are medium, regularly-shaped firm roots with smooth unblemished skin. They will keep in a cool, airy place for several days. To prepare parsnips for cooking, peel them, trim off the top and root end, and cut them according to the recipe. They are inedible raw.

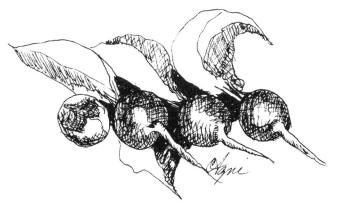

Parsnip Pancakes

Reminiscent of potato pancakes, these tiny griddle cakes are a wonderful side dish when topped with sour cream and chives.

    5 medium parsnips (about 1¼ pounds to-
         tal), peeled and cut into 2-inch pieces
    2 large eggs
    3 tablespoons unbleached all-purpose
         flour
    2 tablespoons milk
    1 teaspoon salt
    ¼ teaspoon freshly ground white pepper
         Melted butter, for brushing the griddle

Cook the parsnips in a saucepan of boiling water until tender, 20 to 25 minutes. Drain and cool. Process in a food processor with the metal blade until almost smooth but still slightly chunky, about 35 seconds. Remove from the processor and reserve.

To make a batter, add the eggs to the processor and process until combined, about 20 seconds. Add the flour, milk, salt, and white pepper and pulse 5 times. Add the parsnips and process until just combined, about 5 seconds.

Heat a griddle or large skillet over moderately high heat and brush with melted butter. Drop the batter by the tablespoon onto the griddle, spreading it evenly. Cook until golden brown, about 3 minutes per side. Wipe off the griddle and brush with more butter between batches.

Makes about 20 pancakes

[WILLIAM WOYS WEAVER]

Parsnip and Spinach Soup

A fresh vegetable soup that is wonderfully flavorful and low in calories.

    5 large parsnips (1 pound total), unpeeled,
         trimmed, and cut into lengths to fit the
         feed tube of a food processor
    1 large Spanish onion (7 ounces), peeled
         and cut into wedges
    1 small celery rib with leaves (1 ounce)
    5 to 6 cups chicken broth
    2 cups fresh spinach, including the stems
    ½ teaspoon freshly grated nutmeg
         Salt and freshly ground black pepper

Slice the parsnips, onion, and celery in a food processor with the medium slicing disc, using firm pressure. Transfer the vegetables to a 4-quart kettle and add 5 cups chicken broth. Cover the kettle and bring the broth to a boil. Reduce the heat and simmer the mixture for 25 minutes.

Fit the processor with the metal blade and transfer the vegetables to the workbowl with a slotted spoon. Add ½ cup of the liquid and purée the mixture for 1 minute, or until smooth. Scrape down the sides of the bowl, add the spinach, and process the mixture for

30 seconds. Stir the mixture into the broth and add the nutmeg and salt and pepper to taste. Heat the soup, stirring in up to another cup of broth if it is too thick. Serve the soup hot or chilled.

Serves 6

[ABBY MANDEL]

Puréed Parsnips

  2 pounds parsnips, trimmed and peeled
1½ teaspoons salt
  4 tablespoons unsalted butter
  2 tablespoons heavy cream
 ¼ teaspoon freshly grated nutmeg
 ⅛ teaspoon fresh white pepper

Cut the parsnips into 1-inch pieces. Cook, covered, with 1 teaspoon salt in a large sauce-pan of boiling water until tender, about 20 to 25 minutes. Drain well.

Add the parsnips to a food processor fitted with the metal blade and process until smooth. Add remaining ingredients and process for 30 seconds longer.

Serves 4

1 teaspoon salt
¼ cup water
5½ ounces fresh snow peas, trimmed and
    strings removed
1 ounce cellophane noodles, softened in
    hot water for 10 minutes, drained, and
    cut into 3-inch lengths

Drop the ginger through the feed tube of a food processor with the metal blade in place and the motor running. Process until finely chopped, about 10 seconds. Remove from the processor and reserve. Process the scallions until finely chopped, about 5 seconds. Remove and reserve.

Pulse the prosciutto until finely chopped, about 15 times. Remove and reserve. Process the chicken until puréed, about 1½ minutes. Add the prosciutto and the pork fat and pulse to combine, about 8 times.

Add the egg white, the 2 tablespoons rice wine, 1 teaspoon of the sesame oil, pepper, reserved ginger, 1½ teaspoons of the chopped scallions, and 2 tablespoons of the cornstarch and pulse 6 to 8 times to combine. Transfer to a large bowl, cover, and refrigerate for 30 minutes.

Shape the chilled chicken mixture into 1-inch balls, using about 1 tablespoon for each.

Bring the chicken broth, ¼ cup rice wine, and salt to a boil in a large saucepot, skimming as necessary. Add the chicken balls and simmer until they float to the surface, about 7 minutes. Stir the water into the remaining 2 tablespoons cornstarch in a small bowl until smooth, then stir into the liquid in the saucepot. Add the snow peas, the cellophane noodles, and the remaining 1 teaspoon sesame oil and cook 15 seconds.

To serve, divide the soup and chicken balls evenly among 6 soup bowls and garnish with the remaining chopped scallions.

Serves 6

[NINA SIMONDS]

Green Pea and Jícama Salad

1 cup toasted pine nuts or roasted Spanish
    peanuts
2 cups shelled fresh or frozen peas
½ medium jícama (about 11 ounces),
    peeled
1 medium garlic clove, peeled
1 large fresh mint leaf
2 tablespoons parsley leaves
    Pinch cayenne pepper
¼ teaspoon salt
½ cup sour cream

¼ cup mayonnaise, preferably homemade
1 medium head Boston lettuce (about 9½
    ounces), washed, drained, and chilled

To toast the pine nuts, preheat the oven to 325°F. Spread the nuts in a 9-inch cake pan and bake them, stirring often, for 8 to 10 minutes, or until lightly browned. Cool completely.

Blanch the fresh peas in a saucepan of boiling water to cover for 4 to 5 minutes or until barely tender. Rinse under cold running water, drain, and set aside in a large bowl. (If you use frozen peas, cook according to package directions until barely tender before rinsing and draining.)

Cut the jícama into ¼-inch dice and add to the peas in the bowl.

To make the dressing, drop the garlic, mint, and parsley through the feed tube of a food processor with the metal blade in place and the motor running. Process until finely chopped, about 10 seconds. Add the pepper, salt, sour cream, and mayonnaise and pulse about 8 times to combine. Scrape down the bowl as necessary. Taste for seasoning.

Toss the dressing with the reserved vegetables. Cover and refrigerate for at least 1 hour or until ready to serve.

Just before serving, add the reserved pine nuts to the vegetables and toss to combine.

Arrange the lettuce leaves on a large serving platter and mound the vegetables in the center.

Serves 6 to 8

[ANNE LINDSAY GREER]

Pastina with Prosciutto and Peas

  4 ounces Parmesan cheese, cut into 1-inch pieces
 ⅓ cup fresh basil leaves
 ⅓ cup parsley leaves
  2 tablespoons fresh sage leaves
  1 large garlic clove, peeled
  3 medium shallots (1½ ounces total), peeled
  2 tablespoons olive oil
  2 tablespoons unsalted butter
  6 ounces prosciutto, cut into ¼-inch dice
 ¾ cup heavy cream
 ½ teaspoon salt
 ¼ teaspoon hot red pepper flakes
 ¼ teaspoon freshly ground black pepper
 12 ounces pastina or other small pasta
  1 package (10 ounces) frozen peas, thawed

Chop the Parmesan fine in a food processor with the metal blade, about 45 seconds. Remove from the processor and reserve. Chop the basil, parsley, and sage fine, about 40 seconds. Remove and reserve.

Drop the garlic and shallots through the feed tube with the motor running and chop fine, about 10 seconds.

Cook the garlic and shallots in the oil and butter in a large skillet over medium-high heat until softened, about 3 minutes. Add the prosciutto and cook for 3 minutes. Add the herbs, cream, salt, hot red pepper, and black pepper and cook until the sauce is thickened, about 5 minutes.

Meanwhile, cook the pastina in a large saucepan of boiling salted water until *al dente*, about 4 minutes, adding the peas in the last 30 seconds. Drain and return to the pan. Stir in the prosciutto mixture and Parmesan.

Serves 8

Peppers

Both hot chili peppers and sweet peppers belong to the Capsicum family. Of the sweet, mild peppers, the best known are the bell—named for their shape. Other varieties include the red, heart-shaped pimiento; the thin, curved green bull's horn; the long tapered yellow Cubanelle; the banana-shaped yellow banana pepper; and the small round cherry pepper. Until a few years ago it was difficult to find anything but green and red bell peppers in the United States, but new strains with vivid colors have been developed, including yellow, orange, purple, and even black. There is also great diversity among hot chilies. The more common of the bunch are jalapeños and serranos. Jalapeños are green and generally measure about 3 inches long and an inch across. The hotter serranos can be green or red and are thinner and shorter.

Most peppers are available year-round and are at their best from summer through fall. Look for shiny, plump, unwrinkled ones and avoid any with soft spots. Placed in a plastic bag, they will keep well in the refrigerator for several days. Before cooking them, remove the seeds and white membrane and cut off the stalk. If you are seeding hot chilies, please use caution and wear rubber gloves.

Red Pepper Caviar

The caviar is a vibrant dip for vegetables, either raw or steamed. Broccoli and cauliflower florets, small new potatoes, baby carrots, green beans, Jerusalem artichokes, and strips of fennel are perfect accompaniments.

You may also wish to try the caviar on toast, sprinkled with grated Gruyère cheese and baked in a 400°F oven until the cheese is lightly browned.

Please note: This recipe calls for raw egg yolks; if eggs are a problem in your area, do not prepare this recipe. Be sure to use salmonella-free eggs.

 2 cups Red Pepper Purée (recipe follows)
 2 large egg yolks
 ½ cup olive oil or vegetable oil
 ½ teaspoon salt
   Freshly ground black pepper or cayenne pepper

Process the Red Pepper Purée and egg yolks in a food processor with the metal blade until combined, about 10 seconds. With the motor running, pour the oil through the feed tube in a slow, steady stream. The mixture should have the consistency of thin mayonnaise. Season with the salt and pepper.

The caviar may be refrigerated, tightly covered, for up to 2 days.

Makes about 2½ cups

[LYDIE MARSHALL]

Red Pepper Purée

The purée freezes beautifully. Make batches in fall, when peppers are most plentiful, so you can keep a number of pints in the freezer.

If the purée has been refrigerated or thawed, drain it in a fine sieve before using. If you prefer a yellow pepper purée, by all means use yellow rather than red peppers.

 8 pounds large sweet red peppers
 ⅔ cup olive oil
 1½ teaspoons salt
 ¼ teaspoon cayenne pepper
 1 teaspoon dried thyme leaves

Place a red pepper stem end up on a cutting board. With a sharp knife cut 3 or 4 vertical slices, leaving only the core and stem. Remove any seeds and ribs from the slices. Repeat for all the peppers.

Insert the medium slicing disc in a food processor. Tightly pack the pepper slices in the feed tube and slice them. Repeat the procedure until all the peppers are sliced.

Heat the oil in an 8-quart stockpot over moderate heat. Stir in the pepper slices and the remaining ingredients. Cover and simmer, stirring occasionally, until very soft, about 1 hour.

Drain the peppers in a colander for 10 minutes, stirring occasionally. With the metal blade in place, purée the peppers in the processor in 3 batches, stopping to scrape down the bowl as necessary. Pass the purée through a fine sieve and discard any bits of skin that remain. Place the sieved purée in a fine strainer and allow to stand for 30 minutes to drain. The purée may be refrigerated, tightly covered, for 2 weeks or frozen, airtight, for up to 6 months.

Makes about 3½ cups

[LYDIE MARSHALL]

Jalapeño Corn Bread

- 1 cup yellow or white stone-ground cornmeal
- 1 cup unbleached all-purpose flour
- 1 tablespoon sugar
- 2 teaspoons baking powder
- ½ teaspoon salt
- 1½ cups buttermilk
- 1 teaspoon baking soda
- 2 large eggs
- ½ cup plus 2 tablespoons unsalted butter, melted
- ¼ cup chopped canned jalapeño peppers
- 1 tablespoon chopped pimiento

Preheat the oven to 425°F. Grease a 13 × 9-inch metal baking pan and heat it in the oven while mixing the batter.

Sift the cornmeal, flour, sugar, baking powder, and salt into a 2-quart bowl. Set aside. Pour buttermilk into a 1-quart measuring cup or a bowl. Add the baking soda and then the eggs and beat lightly with a fork. Stir in the ½ cup melted butter.

Add the liquid mixture, jalapeño peppers, and pimiento to the dry ingredients and stir with a fork just until blended. Pour into the heated pan and bake for 15 to 20 minutes, or until a knife or cake tester inserted in the center comes out clean.

Drizzle the 2 tablespoons melted butter over the top and cut into 3-inch squares. Serve immediately.

Makes 12 squares

[DINAH SHORE]

Red Pota
Crème S

The golden caviar ı
American product,
the Great Lakes. It
than sturgeon cavi
available at good fis
stores.

50 small waxy red
     pounds)
2 quarts vegetab
4 large baking p
     peeled and q
2½ cups Crème F
½ cup loosely pa
2 teaspoons salt
½ teaspoon fresh
4½ ounces golden
     Fresh dill, for

Preheat the oven t
   Put the new po
sheet and bake in
til the potatoes are
with a knife, 25 to
overcook.
   When cool en
tatoes in half and

Prosciutto, Provolone, and Roasted Red Pepper Salad with Basil Vinaigrette

2 large sweet red peppers (about 8 ounces
     each)
1 small head leaf lettuce, cored and cut
     crosswise in half to fit the feed tube of
     a food processor
6 ounces provolone cheese, chilled
1 cup fresh basil leaves
¾ cup extra-virgin olive oil
2½ tablespoons balsamic vinegar
½ teaspoon salt
¼ teaspoon freshly ground black pepper
2 large heads radicchio (about 9 ounces
     each), cored
6 ounces thinly sliced prosciutto, trimmed
     and cut into 1-inch pieces
16 small basil leaves, for garnish

To roast the peppers, preheat the broiler.
Broil the peppers on a rack 4 inches from the
heat source. Turn with tongs until the skin
but not the flesh is completely charred, about
12 minutes. Remove to a paper bag, close, and
set aside to cool for 10 minutes. Peel the peppers, then rinse under cold water to remove
any bits of skin. Pat dry. Remove the cores,
seeds, and membranes and slice each pepper
into 8 thin strips. Reserve.
   Slice the lettuce in a food processor with
the thick slicing disc. Set aside.

Shred the provolone cheese with the fine
shredding disc. Set aside.
   To make a vinaigrette, process the basil,
oil, vinegar, salt, and pepper with the metal
blade until the basil is finely chopped, about
20 seconds, scraping down the sides of the
workbowl as necessary. Transfer the vinaigrette to a small bowl and reserve.
   Separate the radicchio leaves and piece
them together to make sixteen 3-inch cups.
Arrange them in a single layer on a large platter. Place a layer of shredded lettuce in the
bottom of each radicchio cup. Put 2 tablespoons cheese in the center, leaving a border
of lettuce around the cheese. Overlap several
pieces of prosciutto on the cheese in each
cup and top with 2 roasted pepper slices.
(The salad cups may be made ahead, covered
with plastic wrap, and refrigerated overnight.)
   Drizzle each cup with some vinaigrette
and garnish with the basil leaves. Pass the remaining vinaigrette separately.

Serves 8

[ABBY MANDEL]

Potat...

Potatoes are a
nightshade far
color, and coc
own as well as
toes are suited
be considered
and are perfec
named for the
other versatile

New potate
stored. They a
times falsely a

At the mar
tatoes, pick o
any that have
posed to light
off the green
airy place for
tatoes should

Potatoes with Bacon and Clams

2 dozen small clams, shucked and
   drained, ¼ cup liquid reserved
⅓ cup sour cream
2 teaspoons red wine vinegar
   Salt and freshly ground white pepper
8 ounces lean slab bacon, cut into 1½ ×
   ½ × ⅜-inch strips
6 small new potatoes (about 6 ounces
   total), unpeeled, cooked and cut into
   ⅜-inch slices
2 large green spring onions (about 3
   ounces each), root ends and greens
   trimmed, cut into ⅛-inch slices
2 tablespoons water
½ cup coarsely chopped parsley
4 ounces fresh spinach, stems removed,
   washed, dried, and torn into bite-size
   pieces
4 ounces dandelion greens, stems
   removed, washed, dried, and torn into
   bite-size pieces
1 tablespoon olive oil
2 small scallions (about 1 ounce total), cut
   into ½-inch pieces, for garnish

To make a dressing, whisk together the ¼ cup
clam liquid, the sour cream, vinegar, and salt
and pepper to taste. Reserve.

Sauté the bacon in a large skillet over
moderately high heat until lightly browned
on all sides, about 3 minutes. Remove with a
slotted spoon to a warm platter. Drain off all
but 2 tablespoons of the fat.

Cook the potato slices in a single layer in
the bacon fat until heated through, about 1
minute on each side. Transfer to the warm
platter.

Add the clams and pepper to the skillet
and sauté until just cooked through, about 30
seconds. Transfer to the platter. Pour off any
remaining fat.

Cook the onions in a small saucepan with
the water, stirring constantly, until the onions
are limp, about 1 minute. Stir in the parsley
and remove to the platter.

Toss the spinach and dandelion greens
with the oil. Line 4 salad plates with the
greens and divide the ingredients from the
warm platter among them. Spoon 3 or 4 tablespoons of the dressing over each serving
and sprinkle with the scallions.

Serves 4

[JEAN-LOUIS GERIN]

Potato Gratin with Coriander and Tarragon

Each province of France has its own version of scalloped potatoes, baked slowly in the oven, forming a beautiful golden-brown crust. This is Lydie Marshall's adaptation of *gratin dauphinois* that she encountered at L'Ecole des Trois Gourmandes, the Paris cooking classes that were run by Julia Child, Simone Beck, and Louisette Bertholle.

1½ cups milk
¼ teaspoon ground coriander
¼ teaspoon dried tarragon
¼ teaspoon dried thyme
⅛ teaspoon freshly ground black pepper
4 medium russet potatoes (about 1½ pounds)
1 tablespoon unsalted butter
6 to 8 tablespoons heavy cream
½ teaspoon salt
1 bay leaf
3 tablespoons shredded Gruyère cheese

Bring the milk to a boil in a 2-quart saucepan with the coriander, tarragon, thyme, and pepper. Remove from the heat, cover, and let stand for 15 minutes.

Peel the potatoes and cut them into ⅛-inch slices; if using a food processor, use the medium slicing disc. Add to the milk and let stand for another 15 minutes.

Preheat the oven to 375°F.

Drain the potatoes, discarding the milk; do not rinse. Use the butter to grease a shallow 9-inch round or 12-inch oval baking dish. Arrange half of the potatoes over the bottom with the slices overlapping. Dribble 3 tablespoons of cream over the layer of potatoes and sprinkle evenly with ¼ teaspoon salt and pepper to taste. Repeat with the remaining potatoes, adding salt, pepper, and another 3 tablespoons of cream. Put the bay leaf on top.

Cut a piece of parchment or wax paper to fit just inside the dish. Butter it lightly and place it, buttered side down, over the potatoes. Bake in the preheated oven for 30 minutes.

Remove the paper and bay leaf. If the top seems dry, dribble on another 2 tablespoons cream. Sprinkle evenly with the Gruyère. Bake, uncovered, for 30 minutes more, or until the top is golden brown and the potatoes are soft.

Serves 4

[LYDIE MARSHALL]

Potato Gnocchi

2 to 4 ounces Parmesan cheese, cut into
    1-inch pieces
2 medium baking potatoes (about 8
    ounces each), unpeeled
1 cup unbleached all-purpose flour
4 tablespoons unsalted butter, melted
    Salt and freshly ground black pepper

Drop the Parmesan through the feed tube of
a food processor with the metal blade in
place and the motor running. Process until
finely chopped, about 45 seconds. Remove
and reserve.

Cook the potatoes in a medium saucepan
with salted water to cover until tender, 25 to
30 minutes. Drain, peel and quarter them.
Pass them through a food mill or ricer into a
large bowl. Stir in the flour and knead the
mixture on a lightly floured surface for 2 to 3
minutes. If the dough is too sticky, add more
flour by the tablespoon until it is smooth.

To shape the gnocchi, divide the dough
into 6 equal pieces. Roll one piece into a cylinder about 18 inches long and ⅝ inch in diameter. (Keep the remaining pieces covered
until needed.) Cut into ¾-inch pieces; press
each piece with your finger on the back of a
lightly floured fork, rolling it off the end of
the tines to curl slightly. Place on a floured
kitchen towel. Repeat the rolling and shaping
with the remaining dough, flouring the fork
often.

Drop the gnocchi in a large saucepan with
plenty of salted boiling water and cook until
they float to the surface, about 1 minute 15
seconds. Remove with a slotted spoon to a
warmed shallow serving dish.

Toss the gnocchi gently with the melted
butter, season with salt and pepper, and
sprinkle with half the grated Parmesan
cheese. Serve with the remaining grated
Parmesan.

Serves 6

[ADA PARASILITI, MICHI
AMBROSI, ANGELA PARLINGIERI,
AND GIULIANA VICINANZA]

Radishes

A member of the mustard family, radishes are loved for their beautiful color, spiciness, and crispness. New shaped and colored radishes keep cropping up at farmers markets—from white to purple, round to oval or slender, and from thin to fat. The small round red radish we all know is available year-round and can be mild to peppery in taste. Choose radishes that have their leaves still attached; these are good indicators of freshness. The greens ought to be bright green and the radish itself firm and smooth. The large and long white daikon radish, popular in Japan and China, is sold without leaves, so look for one that feels firm and is blemish free.

Keep radishes in a plastic bag in the refrigerator for no more than 5 days.

Chilled Red Radish Rounds

8 ounces firm red radishes
1 scant teaspoon coarse (kosher) salt
1½ teaspoons thin soy sauce
4 teaspoons sugar
1 tablespoon sesame oil

Cut off the root and stem ends of the radishes.

If you want to be quick, slice the radishes in a food processor using the fine slicing disc. To insure that the radishes will be sliced prettily, with a band of red around each slice, stand several radishes on their ends directly on top of the slicing disc and then fit the workbowl cover and pusher over them. Slice them in this manner one layer at a time.

If you wish a fancier cut, slice each radish by hand into a fan by putting the radish on its side and carefully cutting a row of ¹⁄₁₆-inch-thick slices along the radish, starting at the root end and slicing about ¾ of the way through the radish so that the slices remain attached to one another at the stem end, like the ribs of a fan.

Put the sliced radishes into a glass or stainless-steel bowl. Sprinkle with the salt and mix well. Cover the bowl with plastic wrap and leave it to sit 6 hours or overnight, stirring occasionally.

Pour off the salt water and drain the radishes briefly under cold running water. Press them with a kitchen towel to extract their moisture. Return them to the bowl and add the soy sauce, sugar, and sesame oil, stirring gently to mix. Chill slightly before serving.

Serves 4 as an appetizer

[B A R B A R A   T R O P P]

Radish, Cucumber, and Crabmeat Salad

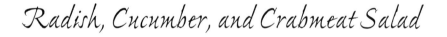

6 small radishes (about 2½ ounces total), ends trimmed
2 small cucumbers (about 8 ounces total), such as Kirby or Japanese (if available), ends trimmed and cut to fit the feed tube of a food processor vertically
8 ounces lump crabmeat, picked over
¼ cup Japanese rice vinegar
2 teaspoons white sesame seeds, for garnish
2 teaspoons black sesame seeds, for garnish

Slice the radishes and cucumbers separately with the ultra-thin slicing disc of a food processor.

Arrange the slices in overlapping circles on 4 serving plates. Arrange the crabmeat on the vegetables. Drizzle each serving with a tablespoon of vinegar and garnish with the white and black sesame seeds.

Serves 4

[R I C H A R D   S E C A R E]

Chicken with Daikon

1¾ cups water
1 piece konbu (giant kelp), about 2 inches square
½ cup dried bonito flakes
1 medium daikon radish (about 1 pound), peeled and cut to fit the feed tube of a food processor vertically
¼ cup mirin (sweet rice wine)
3 cups vegetable oil
1 pound boneless, skinless chicken breasts, trimmed and cut into 1-inch pieces
Unbleached all-purpose flour, for dredging
¼ cup soy sauce

To make the basic broth called *dashi*, bring the water to a boil. Remove from the heat and stir in the konbu and bonito flakes. Let the mixture steep, uncovered, for 30 minutes.

Meanwhile, process the daikon in a food processor with the medium shredding disc. Transfer to a sieve and place over a bowl to drain.

Strain the dashi and combine it with the mirin in a nonreactive saucepan. Bring to a boil, then remove from the heat.

Heat the vegetable oil in a wok or skillet to 375°F.

Dredge the chicken pieces in flour to coat lightly. Add the pieces, without crowding, to the hot oil and fry, stirring occasionally, until they are golden brown, about 3 minutes. As the chicken pieces are cooked, transfer them to paper towels to drain.

Divide the cooked chicken pieces evenly among 4 serving bowls.

Stir the drained daikon into the dashi-mirin mixture and bring to a boil. Remove from the heat and add the soy sauce. Spoon the mixture evenly over the chicken in each bowl and serve immediately.

Serves 4

[RICHARD SECARE]

Shallots

Shallots belong to the onion family and resemble a miniature head of garlic. A reddish-brown papery skin covers a cluster of two bulbs. Their mild yet concentrated flavor is used to enhance, among other things, such classic French sauces as béarnaise and beurre blanc. Available year-round, the shallots to choose are firm and dry, with crackly skin, avoiding any with green sprouts. They can be stored in a cool, dry, airy place for about 3 weeks. Fresh shallots, at the market in spring, will last for only about 1 week; however, if stored in a refrigerator that maintains a temperature below 40°F, they can last up to 2 months.

Shallot Butter

½ cup unsalted butter, cut in 3 or 4 pieces
1 small shallot, peeled
½ teaspoon salt
¼ teaspoon freshly ground black pepper

Process the butter, shallot, salt, and pepper in a food processor with the steel blade until creamy.

Use to top servings of grilled and broiled meats. Refrigerate until firm before using, if desired.

Makes about ½ cup

[CARL JEROME]

Roasted Shallots

24 large shallots (about 1½ ounces each)
2 tablespoons vegetable oil
Salt and freshly ground black pepper

Preheat the oven to 350°F.

Remove the outer peel from the shallots, leaving about ½ inch of the stem. Place the shallots on a baking sheet and drizzle the oil over them. Sprinkle with salt and pepper.

Bake in the lower half of the oven, turning often, for about 1 hour and 15 minutes. The shallots should be almost caramelized on the outside and very soft on the inside.

Makes 4 servings as an appetizer

[LYN STALLWORTH]

Roast Spareribs with Shallot Pepper Sauce

2 pounds meaty pork spareribs
1 cup plus 1 tablespoon dry white wine
½ cup plus 2 tablespoons red wine vinegar
Salt and freshly ground black pepper
½ cup unsalted butter, at room temperature, cut into 8 equal pieces
3 large shallots, peeled and coarsely chopped
2 teaspoons very coarsely ground black pepper (see note below)

To prepare the spareribs, place one jumbo-size plastic bag inside another. Cut the spareribs into 4 serving pieces and put them in the bags. Place the bags in a large bowl and pour the ½ cup white wine and the ½ cup vinegar into the bags, over the spareribs. Seal each bag tightly with a wire twist and turn the bagged spareribs in the bowl to make certain all the ribs are moistened. Marinate for 3 hours at room temperature.

Preheat the oven to 450°F.

Remove the spareribs from the marinade and place them in one layer in a large roasting pan. Discard the marinade. Season the spareribs with salt and freshly ground pepper and dot with 2 pats of the butter. Roast in the center of the preheated oven for 35 minutes, basting 2 or 3 times with the juice and fat that accumulates in the pan.

To make the sauce, bring the remaining 2 tablespoons vinegar, 1 tablespoon white wine, shallots, and coarsely ground pepper to the boil in a small saucepan. Cook over medium heat until the vinegar and wine have evaporated and a moist mixture of shallots and pepper remains, about 2 to 3 minutes. The sauce can be made ahead to this point. Cover and remove from the heat.

Just before serving, reheat the shallot-pepper mixture until it bubbles. Remove the saucepan from the heat and swirl or whisk the remaining butter into the mixture, one piece at a time. Taste for seasoning, adding salt if necessary.

Place the spareribs on a warm serving platter and spoon the sauce over them. Serve immediately.

Serves 4

NOTE: It is important that the pepper be coarsely ground. If your peppermill is not adjustable, crush the peppercorns in a mortar with a pestle or place them between 2 pieces of wax paper and crush them with a heavy rolling pin.

[PHILIP AND MARY HYMAN]

Sorrel

Sorrel is a perennial herb that looks and cooks like spinach, but the similarities end there. Sorrel is distinctively tart and lemony. Its peak season is early spring, although it is available through fall. At the market, look for pale to medium green leaves that appear fresh, without any yellowing. Place the sorrel in a plastic bag and refrigerate for no more than 2 days. Before cooking, strip the leaves from the stems and rinse.

Sorrel Mayonnaise

The mayonnaise will keep, refrigerated, for up to 1 week. (See note on use of raw eggs on page 119).

- 3 cups tightly packed fresh sorrel, stems removed, washed and drained
- 1 bunch fresh watercress, stems removed, washed and drained
- 2 large eggs
- 2 teaspoons Dijon mustard
- 1½ teaspoons white wine vinegar
- ¼ teaspoon sugar
- 1 cup vegetable oil
- 2 tablespoons minced parsley
- 2 tablespoons minced scallion
  Salt and freshly ground white pepper
  Fresh lemon juice

Bring 2 cups of salted water to a boil in a 2-quart saucepan. Add the sorrel and watercress and cook for 2 to 3 minutes. Drain, pressing down on the greens with a spoon to extract the moisture. Set aside.

Process the eggs, mustard, vinegar, and sugar in a food processor with the metal blade until smooth, 15 seconds. Scrape down the bowl. With the machine running, dribble the oil through the feed tube. When all of the oil has been added, the sauce will be thick and smooth.

Add the parsley, scallion, and reserved sorrel and watercress; process until smooth, about 15 seconds. Season with salt, pepper, and lemon juice to taste. Refrigerate until serving.

Makes about 2 cups

[PERLA MEYERS]

Sorrel Timbales

- ½ pound fresh sorrel, stems removed, washed and drained
- 1½ ounces Parmesan or Romano cheese, in ½-inch cubes
- 2 tablespoons unsalted butter
- 1 medium garlic clove, peeled and minced
- 1 medium onion, peeled and finely chopped
- 1 cup heavy cream
- 2 large eggs
- 2 large egg yolks
- ½ teaspoon salt
- ¼ teaspoon freshly ground white pepper

Cut rounds of wax paper to fit the bottoms of six 5-ounce timbale molds. Butter the bottoms of the molds and line them with the paper rounds. Then butter the paper and the sides of the molds. Set aside.

Preheat the oven to 350°F.

Select 12 large sorrel leaves. Put them in a colander and gently pour boiling water over them. Carefully place them on paper towels and pat dry.

Arrange 2 of the blanched leaves in each buttered mold, placing the tips in the center of the bottom and then pressing the leaves against the bottom and sides in a swirl. Set the molds aside.

Bring about 2 quarts of water to a boil in a large saucepan. Blanch the remaining sorrel leaves for 30 seconds. Drain in a colander and refresh under cold running water. Press down on the leaves and then squeeze them to extract as much moisture as possible. Set aside on paper towels.

Drop the cheese through the feed tube of a food processor with the metal blade in place and the motor running. Process until very finely chopped, about 40 seconds. Remove and reserve.

Melt the butter in a medium skillet over moderate heat. Add the garlic, onion, and reserved sorrel and cook, stirring, for 3 to 5 minutes, or until the onion is soft. Process the mixture with the metal blade for about 30 seconds or until puréed, stopping to scrape the bowl as necessary. Add the cream, eggs, egg yolks, salt, pepper, and reserved cheese and process for 10 seconds more or until well blended, stopping once to scrape the bowl.

Divide the mixture among the prepared timbales and put them into an 11 × 7 × 2-inch baking pan. Cover the timbales with a piece of buttered wax paper and pour hot water into the baking pan to come halfway up the sides of the molds. Bake in the center of the pre-heated oven for 25 to 30 minutes, or until a skewer inserted in the center of a timbale comes out clean.

Remove the molds from the water and let stand for 10 minutes. Run a sharp knife around the top edges of the timbales and invert each onto a serving plate.

Serves 6 as a side dish or appetizer

[MARLENE SOROSKY]

Poached Scallops with Sauce Verdoyante

2 cups Fish Stock (recipe follows) or 1⅓
     cups bottled clam broth combined with
     ⅔ cup dry vermouth
1 pound (about 20) fresh sea scallops, cut
     in half crosswise
¾ cup plus 1 tablespoon unsalted butter, at
     room temperature
3 tablespoons water
1 teaspoon sugar
     Salt and freshly ground white pepper

1 pound fresh peas, shelled
3 large egg yolks
1 cup loosely packed fresh sorrel, stems
     removed, washed, drained, and finely
     shredded
2 tablespoons minced fresh chives, for
     garnish

In a 2-quart saucepan over moderate heat bring the Fish Stock to a simmer. Add the scallops, lower the heat slightly, and simmer very gently for 3 minutes, until the scallops turn opaque. With a slotted spoon transfer the scallops to a bowl; add 2 tablespoons of the poaching liquid, place the bowl over warm water, cover, and set aside. Over moderate heat reduce the remaining liquid to ¼ cup.

While the stock is reducing, prepare the peas. Combine the 1 tablespoon butter, the water, sugar, and a pinch of salt in a 1-quart saucepan and bring to a boil over moderate heat. When the butter has melted, add the peas, reduce the heat, cover, and simmer until tender, 3 to 5 minutes. Drain and keep warm.

In the top of a double boiler whisk together the egg yolks and the ¼ cup reduced poaching liquid. Set over barely simmering water and whisk vigorously until the mixture is creamy and has thickened enough so that you can see the bottom of the pan as you whisk. This will take about 5 minutes.

Reduce the heat to very low. Off the heat whisk 1 tablespoon of the butter into the egg yolk mixture. When it is completely incorporated, reset the pan over the water. Whisk in the remaining butter, 1 tablespoon at a time, whisking after each addition until the butter has been fully incorporated into the sauce. The sauce should be smooth and have the consistency of very heavy cream. Stir in the sorrel and season to taste with salt and pepper.

With a slotted spoon, transfer the scallops to heated plates. Spoon the sauce over the scallops and surround with the peas. Garnish with the chives and serve immediately.

Serves 4

[PERLA MEYERS]

Fish Stock

All fish trimmings must be thoroughly cleaned or the stock will be cloudy and bitter. Remove the gills and blood sacs and soak the heads in cold water.

- 2 tablespoons unsalted butter
- 2 ribs celery, with leaves, sliced
- 1 large carrot, peeled and sliced
- 1 large onion, peeled and sliced
- 1 large leek, trimmed, leaving 2 inches of the green tops, well washed and sliced

- 3 garlic cloves, unpeeled, crushed with the flat side of a heavy knife
- 6 black peppercorns
- 3 pounds white fish trimmings (sole, snapper, cod or tile), including bones and heads
- 3 large sprigs parsley
- 1 bay leaf, crumbled
- 1 teaspoon dried thyme
  Pinch salt
- 4 cups water
- 2 cups dry vermouth

Melt the butter in a 4-quart heavy casserole over moderate heat. Add the celery, carrot, onion, leek, garlic, and peppercorns. Stir to coat with butter and cook for 1 to 2 minutes, without letting the vegetables brown.

Place the fish trimmings on top of the vegetables. Add the parsley, bay leaf, thyme, and salt. Lower the heat, cover the casserole, and simmer for 15 minutes.

Add the water and vermouth, raise the heat to moderate, and bring to a boil, uncovered. Partially cover the casserole and simmer for 35 to 40 minutes, skimming the scum from the surface every 10 minutes.

Strain the stock through a double layer of dampened cheesecloth into a 2-quart bowl. Refrigerate, uncovered, until the fat has congealed on the surface. Remove and discard the fat.

Cover tightly and refrigerate for up to 2 days, or freeze for up to 6 weeks.

Makes about 1½ quarts

[P E R L A   M E Y E R S]

Spinach

This popular vegetable grows widely throughout the country and is available throughout the year. The oval or heart-shaped leaves grow in small bunches on short stems. Young tender spinach leaves are excellent raw in salads, while the larger leaves are better for cooking. Choose crisp, fresh, dark green leaves that show no sign of yellowing or wilting and refrigerate them, unwashed, in a plastic bag in the crisper for up to 3 days. Spinach tends to be gritty, so be sure to wash it well. Remove thick central leaves if they are tough or coarse.

Spinach Ravioli Stuffed with Goat Cheese

At the restaurant Mirabelle these delicious ravioli are used as a soup garnish, but, tossed with butter and salt and pepper, they are a wonderful first course on their own.

Dough

- 1 medium garlic clove, peeled
- 8 ounces spinach, washed well and stems removed
- 2 teaspoons olive oil
- 1½ cups unbleached all-purpose flour, or more as needed
- 2 large eggs
- 2 large egg yolks
- ½ teaspoon lemon juice
- ½ teaspoon salt
  Freshly grated nutmeg

Filling

- 4 medium garlic cloves, peeled
- 5 ounces goat cheese, such as Montrachet, crumbled
- ¼ cup fresh basil leaves, shredded

- 1 large egg, lightly beaten
  Unsalted butter as needed, for serving
  Salt and freshly ground black pepper, for serving

To make the dough, cook the garlic and spinach in the oil in a large skillet over moderately high heat until the spinach is wilted, 3 to 4 minutes, stirring. Drain and squeeze as dry as possible with a kitchen towel.

Chop the spinach fine in a food processor with the metal blade, about 5 seconds. Add the remaining ingredients for the dough and process until the dough forms a ball, about 15 seconds. (If the dough is too wet, add more flour by the tablespoon.) Process for 10 seconds more to knead it. Dust with flour, divide into 6 pieces, and cover with an inverted bowl.

To make the filling, drop the garlic through the processor feed tube with the motor running and chop fine, about 5 seconds. Combine in a bowl with the cheese and basil.

Roll out the dough, one piece at a time, with a pasta machine according to the manufacturer's instructions, down to the lowest setting, dusting well with flour to prevent sticking.

Place rounded ½ teaspoons of filling 2 inches apart down the center of a dough sheet. Brush the dough with the beaten egg and top with a second dough sheet. With a 2½-inch scalloped cutter, cut out circles around each mound of filling, sealing the edges well. Repeat with the remaining dough sheets and filling.

Cook the ravioli, in batches, in a saucepan of boiling salted water until tender, about 5 minutes per batch. Drain, then toss with butter and salt and pepper to serve.

Serves 6

[ELIZABETH PEARCE]

Spinach and Lobster Salad

4 small lobsters (about 1 pound each)
2 cups water
  Freshly ground white pepper
2 sprigs fresh thyme
2 medium celery ribs (about 4 ounces total), cut into 2-inch pieces
  Salt
3 tablespoons vegetable oil
3 tablespoons unsalted butter
1 tablespoon olive oil
2 teaspoons fresh lemon juice
  Cayenne pepper
4 ounces fresh spinach leaves, stems removed, washed, dried, and torn into bite-size pieces
3 tablespoons sour cream
8 cherry tomatoes (about 4 ounces total), cut into ¼-inch slices, for garnish
  Chopped celery leaves, for garnish

To prepare the lobsters, wipe the shells with a damp paper towel. Place each lobster right side up on a cutting board. Place the tip of a heavy chef's knife at the center of the lobster where the body joins the head. Plunge the tip of the knife straight down, then quickly push the blade completely through the head.

Sever the tail from the body and cut the tail segments crosswise into 5 medallions.

Remove and discard the sand sac from the body. Remove the greenish tomalley (liver) and, if present, the coral (roe) from 2 of the lobsters and reserve for the sauce (see note below). Scrape away and reserve any remaining flesh and liquid from the bodies and heads and set aside.

Sever and discard the small side legs.

Sever the large front claws from the body and at the first and second joints. Use a cleaver to crack the claws and joints to expose the flesh.

Combine the water, pepper, thyme, celery, and lobster heads and bodies in a large saucepan and bring to a boil. Reduce the heat to a simmer and cook, uncovered, until the liquid is reduced to ½ cup, about 30 minutes. Drain, reserving the liquid.

Sprinkle the exposed lobster meat on the tail and claw pieces with salt and pepper.

Preheat the oven to 150°F, or the lowest possible setting.

Heat 2 tablespoons each of the vegetable oil and butter in a large skillet. Place the large claws and joint sections from the lobsters in the skillet in a single layer. Cook until lightly browned on both sides and cooked through, 1½ minutes total for the joint sections and 2 minutes for the claws. Transfer to a warm platter and place in the preheated oven.

Add the remaining 1 tablespoon each butter and vegetable oil to the skillet and cook the lobster tail medallions until lightly browned on both sides, about 1½ minutes total. Transfer to the platter in the oven.

Discard any fat remaining in the skillet. Stir in the reserved reduced liquid, the olive oil, the reserved tomalley and coral, and the flesh and liquid from the heads and bodies. Cook, stirring, over moderately high heat for about 1 minute.

Process the contents of the skillet in a food processor with the metal blade for 10 seconds. Scrape down the sides of the workbowl and add the lemon juice, salt, and several good shakes of cayenne pepper. Continue processing until smooth, about 20 seconds.

Strain the sauce into a large bowl. Add the spinach and toss to mix well.

Divide the spinach among 4 luncheon plates. Brush the exposed lobster flesh with sour cream. Reassemble a lobster tail and 2 claws on each plate and garnish with cherry tomatoes and celery leaves.

Serves 4

NOTE: Purée the remaining livers and roe. Freeze and use in fish sauces.

[JEAN-LOUIS GERIN]

Spinach with Pine Nuts and Almonds

  3 tablespoons olive oil
  1 large garlic clove, peeled and minced
  ¼ cup pine nuts
  ¼ cup slivered almonds
  1 pound fresh spinach, washed and stems
       removed
  1 ounce ham, finely diced
  1 teaspoon salt

Heat the olive oil in a large skillet over moderate heat until a light haze forms. Add the minced garlic and cook 1 minute, stirring continuously. Add the pine nuts and almonds to the hot oil and cook 2 to 3 minutes until the nuts are slightly browned. Watch carefully so they do not burn. Add the spinach leaves, ham, and salt. Toss until all ingredients are mixed and thoroughly heated. Serve immediately.

Serves 4 as a side dish

[KATIE STAPLETON]

Squash
Summer and Winter Varieties

Squash is a species of the gourd family and can be divided into two groups, summer and winter. Summer squash are picked when they are immature and have very thin, edible skin and seeds. Varieties of summer squash include zucchini, crookneck, and pattypan. Winter squash—acorn, buttercup, butternut, golden nugget, Hubbard, pumpkin, spaghetti, and turban—thrive in winter months and are distinguished from summer squash by their hard, thick skins and seeds and their dark, sweet flesh.

When purchasing summer squash, look for those that are brightly colored, have no bruises, and are relatively heavy for their size. Their skin should be tender enough to prick with your fingernail. Summer squash will keep in the refrigerator for a few days. Choose winter squash that have hard skin and no blemishes or bruises. They can be stored whole in a cool place; they do not need to be refrigerated.

Zucchini Sticks

2 large eggs
2 tablespoons water
1½ cups unbleached all-purpose flour
  Salt and freshly ground black pepper
4 medium zucchini (about 9 ounces each), ends trimmed and cut into 3 × ⅜ × ⅜-inch pieces
  Vegetable oil, for frying

Beat the eggs and water lightly in a shallow bowl. Mix the flour with salt and pepper in another bowl. Dip about a dozen of the zucchini sticks in the egg mixture, then roll them in the flour to coat.

Deep fry the zucchini sticks without crowding in 2 inches of heated oil (375°F) until golden brown, about 1 minute. Remove with a slotted spoon and drain on paper towels. Repeat with the remaining zucchini sticks, dipping them first in the egg and flour before frying. Sprinkle with salt and serve immediately.

Serves 8

[N A O M I   B A R R Y]

Zucchini Galette

1 small zucchini (about 6½ ounces), ends trimmed, cut to fit the feed tube of a food processor vertically
½ teaspoon salt
1 tablespoon unsalted butter
2 large eggs
⅛ teaspoon freshly ground black pepper

Process the zucchini in a food processor with the fine slicing disc. Place the slices in a colander, sprinkle with the salt and toss to mix. Drain for 20 minutes, then rinse under cold water to remove the salt and pat dry on paper towels. Transfer the slices to a small bowl.

Use the butter to grease the bottom and partway up the sides of an ovenproof skillet with an 8½-inch-diameter bottom. Set aside.

Process the eggs and pepper in the processor with the metal blade for 10 seconds. Reserve 2 tablespoons and pour the remaining egg mixture over the zucchini slices. Toss to coat well.

Preheat the oven to 400°F.

Arrange the zucchini slices overlapping in a single layer in the buttered skillet. Drizzle the reserved egg evenly over the top.

Cook the zucchini over moderately high heat for about 1½ minutes, or until the bottom is lightly browned. Transfer the skillet to the preheated oven and bake for 1½ minutes, or until the top looks dry.

Loosen the edges of the galette with a spatula and invert onto a serving plate. Serve immediately.

Serves 4

[S U Z A N N E   S .   J O N E S]

Summer Squash with Lemon and Black Olives

10 brine-cured black olives, rinsed and patted dry

3 small zucchini (about 1 pound total) washed and ends trimmed

3 small yellow squashes (about 1 pound total), washed and ends trimmed

2 tablespoons unsalted butter
Salt and freshly ground black pepper

2 teaspoons grated lemon zest

Pit the olives and cut each one into 4 pieces. Set aside.

Cut each squash lengthwise into quarters and remove the seeds. Cut each strip on the diagonal into ¼-inch pieces.

Melt the butter in a large skillet over moderately high heat. Add the squash pieces, season with salt and pepper, and cook, stirring often, until just tender, about 4 minutes. Stir in the olives and heat through.

Remove from the heat, add the lemon zest, and toss well to mix. Taste for seasoning.

Serves 6

[DEIDRE DAVIS]

Butternut Squash Soup

2 large butternut squashes (2 pounds each)

2 medium onions (about 10 ounces total), ends cut flat, peeled, halved

¾ stick unsalted butter

6 cups chicken stock
Salt and freshly ground white pepper
Pinch freshly grated nutmeg
Croutons (recipe follows)

⅓ cup freshly grated Parmesan cheese
Chopped parsley

Preheat the oven to 400°F.

Bake the squashes in a shallow baking pan in the center of the oven until the tip of a knife easily penetrates the skin, about 1 hour.

Remove the squashes from the oven, cut them in half lengthwise, and cool to room temperature.

Process the onions in a food processor with the slicing disc. Cook the onions in the butter in a small skillet over low heat, partially covered, until soft, about 15 minutes, stirring often.

Remove the seeds from the squashes and scoop out the pulp. Purée the pulp and onions in the processor with the metal blade, about 1 minute. Whisk the purée into the stock and simmer, covered, for 10 minutes. Season to taste.

Serve hot topped with Croutons, Parmesan cheese, and chopped parsley.

Serves 8 to 10

[JOYCE GOLDSTEIN]

Croutons

2½ ounces French bread, cut into ½-inch
    cubes
2 tablespoons olive oil

Preheat the oven to 300°F.

    Bake the bread cubes in a single layer on a
baking sheet until lightly golden and dry,
about 10 minutes.

Heat the oil in a large skillet. Add the
bread cubes and sauté, stirring, until golden
brown. Remove to paper towels. Serve warm
or at room temperature.

Makes about 2½ cups

[JOYCE GOLDSTEIN]

Curried Ragout of Pork with Butternut Squash

2 large garlic cloves
2 large onions (about 14 ounces total),
    peeled and cut into eighths
3 pounds trimmed pork butt, cut into 1½-
    inch cubes
4 to 6 tablespoons unsalted butter
1 tablespoon vegetable oil
    Salt and freshly ground black pepper
1 tablespoon curry powder
2 tablespoons tomato paste
⅛ teaspoon ground cloves
2 dried hot red chili peppers (about 2 × ⅜
    inches each), cut in half
¼ teaspoon ground coriander
¼ teaspoon ground cinnamon
2 cups chicken stock, preferably home-
    made
1 butternut squash (about 2 pounds),
    peeled, seeded, and cut into 1-inch
    cubes
2 tablespoons dark brown sugar
1 tablespoon cornstarch mixed with
    2 tablespoons chicken stock
½ cup finely chopped fresh cilantro

Drop the garlic through the feed tube of a
food processor with the metal blade in place
and the motor running. Process until finely
chopped, about 10 seconds. Add the onion
pieces and pulse 7 times or until finely
chopped. Reserve.

    Preheat the oven to 350°F.

    Pat the pork dry with paper towels. Heat 2
tablespoons of the butter and the oil in a large
skillet over moderately high heat. Brown the
pork, in 3 batches, on all sides in the skillet,
adding more butter as necessary. Transfer the
pork to a large heatproof casserole and season
with salt and pepper. Set aside.

    Discard all but 3 tablespoons of fat from
the skillet (or add additional butter to equal 3
tablespoons fat) and cook the garlic-onion
mixture over medium-low heat until soft but
not browned, about 3 minutes. Stir in the
curry powder, tomato paste, cloves, chili peppers, coriander, and cinnamon. Add the
chicken stock and stir to combine. Pour the
onion-stock mixture into the casserole and
bring to a boil. Cover and place it in the cen-

ter of the preheated oven to cook for 1 hour 30 minutes, or until the meat is tender.

Meanwhile, bring about 2 inches of water to a boil in a medium saucepan and steam the squash in a vegetable steamer for 3 minutes. Remove. Melt 2 tablespoons butter in a medium skillet and add the brown sugar and squash. Cook, stirring, over high heat, until the brown sugar melts and the squash is caramelized, about 3 minutes.

Fifteen minutes before the pork is done, add the squash to the casserole, cover, and cook the mixture until the squash is tender but not too soft.

Remove the pork and squash with a slotted spoon to a bowl. Remove and discard the chili peppers. Degrease the pan juices and bring to a boil. Whisk in the cornstarch mixture. Return the pork and squash to the casserole and heat through. Adjust seasoning to taste. Sprinkle with the chopped cilantro and serve.

Serves 6

[P E R L A   M E Y E R S]

Pumpkin Cheesecake

Crust

2½ cups unbleached all-purpose flour
1 cup unsalted butter, chilled
½ cup sugar
½ teaspoon salt
½ cup blanched almonds, finely ground
½ teaspoon ground cinnamon
1 teaspoon pure vanilla extract
2 large eggs

Filling

5 packages (8 ounces each) cream cheese, at room temperature, cut into pieces
1¼ cups sugar
4 large eggs
3 large egg yolks
3 tablespoons unbleached all-purpose flour

1 teaspoon salt
1 cup heavy cream
1 can (16 ounces) pumpkin
2 teaspoons cinnamon
1 teaspoon ground cloves
1 teaspoon ground ginger
1 tablespoon pure vanilla extract

Place all the ingredients for the crust in a food processor fitted with the steel blade. Turn on and off until the mixture is mealy. Turn out onto a piece of wax paper and work into a ball. Wrap in the paper and refrigerate for about 1 hour.

Butter the bottom and sides of a 10-inch springform pan. Remove the sides and set aside.

Take one-third of the pastry. Roll it out ⅛ inch thick on a lightly floured board. Roll the pastry up on the rolling pin and center it on the bottom of the springform pan. Trim off all but ½ inch of the surplus that hangs over the edge. Fold the surplus edge over loosely; you will need it for sealing the pastry on the sides of the pan.

Roll out the remaining pastry ⅛ inch thick. Cut into strips to fit the sides of the pan. Fit the strips to the sides of the pan, joining the ends by pressing together. Trim the top edge of the pastry so only the bottom three-fourths of the sides are covered. Reassemble the pan, pressing the surplus pastry edge on the bottom against the pastry on the sides to seal. Refrigerate the pan while you make the filling.

Preheat the oven to 425°F.

Combine all the ingredients for the filling in a large bowl and beat with an electric mixer at medium speed until smooth and creamy. Pour into the prepared crust and bake in the preheated oven for 15 minutes. Reduce the oven heat to 275°F and bake 1 hour longer. Turn off the heat and leave the cake in the oven overnight. The following morning, remove the cake from the oven and refrigerate.

To serve, remove the sides of the pan but leave the cake on the base.

Serves up to 20

[HELEN McCULLY]

then pull back the breast and detach it, cutting down through the bones that still attach it to the back. Remove the skin from the breast. Working first on one side of the breastbone, cut the meat away in 1 piece. Repeat on the other side. Cut the back crosswise into 3 or 4 pieces and reserve with the wing tips and breastbone.

Heat the oil with the butter in a heavy medium skillet over moderate heat. Sauté the breast meat for 30 seconds on each side and remove to a platter. Sauté the chicken legs, thighs, and wings for about 15 minutes, turning occasionally, until they are evenly browned. Remove to the platter.

Sauté the back pieces, wing tips, and breastbones, turning occasionally, until they are browned, about 10 minutes. Remove to the platter and sprinkle ½ teaspoon of the salt and ⅛ teaspoon of the pepper over all of the chicken pieces.

In the same skillet sauté the turnips, onions, and unpeeled garlic cloves for about 15 minutes, stirring occasionally and taking care that the onions do not burn. When the vegetables are lightly browned and slightly tender, sprinkle with the remaining salt and pepper; return the chicken legs, thighs, wings and carcass pieces to the skillet, on top of the vegetables. Cover the pan loosely and cook over low heat for about 20 minutes, stirring gently once or twice so the vegetables do not stick to the pan.

Add the chicken breast and any juices that have accumulated. Cover and cook for 10 minutes more. Remove the carcass pieces and wing tips. Serve the chicken and vegetables directly from the skillet.

Serves 4

[LYDIE MARSHALL]

Gratin of Potatoes and Turnips

The turnips in this gratin add a mild background sweetness to the potato's flavor without really announcing their presence. This side dish is excellent with beef, lamb or chicken and can be assembled in advance, left unbaked, and refrigerated. Before baking allow the dish to come to room temperature, or increase the baking time 10 minutes.

1 large garlic clove, peeled
1 large Spanish onion (about 10 ounces), peeled and quartered
3 tablespoons unsalted butter
1 large baking potato (about 8 ounces), peeled
2 small white turnips (about 8 ounces), peeled
⅔ cup plus 3 tablespoons heavy cream
⅔ cup milk
1 teaspoon salt
    Freshly ground black pepper
    Freshly grated nutmeg

Drop the garlic through the feed tube of a food processor with the metal blade in place and the motor running. Process until minced.

Leaving the garlic in the bowl, remove the metal blade and insert the slicing disc. Process the onion using moderate pressure.

Melt the butter in a 2-quart heavy saucepan over moderate heat. Add the garlic and onions and cook for 5 minutes, until soft but not brown.

While the garlic and onions are cooking, use the thin slicing disc with firm pressure to process the potatoes and turnips. Put them in the pan with the garlic and onions. Add the ⅔ cup cream, the milk, salt, pepper, and nutmeg. Cook over moderately low heat, stirring frequently, for 25 minutes, until the vegetables are almost tender and the mixture is thick.

Preheat the oven to 325°F. Butter a 9-inch gratin dish.

Transfer the contents of the saucepan to the gratin dish. Smooth the surface with a spatula. Spoon the 3 tablespoons cream over the top. Bake for 20 minutes. Place the gratin dish under the broiler, 6 inches from the heat, and broil for 5 minutes, until the top is lightly browned.

Serves 6

[F R É D Y G I R A R D E T /
A B B Y M A N D E L]

Glazed Turnips

16 small white turnips (about 2¼ pounds total), peeled (see note below)
½ teaspoon salt
⅛ teaspoon freshly ground black pepper
4 tablespoons unsalted butter, cut into 4 pieces
1 tablespoon sugar

Place the turnips in a skillet just large enough to hold them comfortably in a single layer. Sprinkle the turnips with the salt and pepper and add enough water to almost cover them; they should not float. Add the butter and sprinkle in the sugar.

Bring quickly to a boil, then partially cover the pan, lower the heat, and cook at a moderate boil for 15 to 20 minutes, or until the turnips can be pierced easily with a fork. If the water has not completely evaporated by the time the turnips are done, remove the lid and boil the remaining liquid rapidly until it has evaporated. Gently shake the pan or use two spoons to roll the turnips in the glaze remaining in the pan.

Serves 4

NOTE: If small turnips are not available, cut large ones into halves or quarters.

[P H I L I P A N D M A R Y H Y M A N]

¼ teaspoon freshly ground pepper
¼ teaspoon dried thyme
  Flaky Pastry (recipe follows)
1 large egg yolk, beaten, for glaze

Place the potatoes in a small saucepan with enough water to cover. Add the salt and cook over moderate heat for about 12 minutes, or until potatoes are just tender. Drain and set aside.

Place the sausage meat in a large, heavy skillet over low heat. Break up the meat with a spoon as it cooks. When it is lightly browned, transfer it to a large sieve set over a bowl and let the fat drain off.

In the same skillet in which you browned the meat, melt the butter over medium heat. Add the onions and celery and cook for about 8 minutes, or until the onions are golden brown. Place the cooked onions and celery in a large bowl. Add the drained sausage meat, apples, and potatoes. Set aside to cool to room temperature.

When the mixture has cooled, stir in the eggs, parsley, pepper, and thyme. Gently blend all the ingredients.

Lightly butter a 9-inch pie or quiche pan.

Divide the Flaky Pastry dough in half. Roll out one half of the dough into a circle approximately 11 inches in diameter and ⅛ inch thick. Lift the dough onto a rolling pin and unroll it onto the pie or quiche pan. Gently drape the pastry to conform to the sides of the pan, allowing the excess pastry to overhang the rim of the pan. Mound the sausage mixture evenly into the shell. It will be very full.

Roll out the remaining pastry into the same shape as the bottom crust. Lift it onto the rolling pin and drape it over the pan. With a knife, trim off the excess pastry. Seal the two layers of pastry together by pressing them together with the tines of a fork.

With a pastry brush, spread the beaten egg yolk over the top of the pie. Place it in the refrigerator to rest for 20 minutes.

Adjust the oven rack to the bottom third and preheat the oven to 400°F. Bake the pie for 45 minutes, or until the crust is a deep golden brown.

Serves 6 to 8

[JOHN CLANCY]

Flaky Pastry

2¼ cups all-purpose flour
¼ teaspoon salt
10 tablespoons unsalted butter, very cold
2 tablespoons vegetable shortening, very cold
6 to 8 tablespoons ice water

Place the flour in a medium bowl. Scatter the salt over the flour. Add the butter and shortening to the bowl.

Quickly, rub the ingredients together between your thumbs and the tips of your fingers only. The mixture will turn into coarse separate pieces, then into granules.

One tablespoon at a time, sprinkle 6 tablespoons ice water over the granules. Combine the water and the granules. Now, cupping your hands, gather all the dough into a ball. If the ball crumbles, add more ice water.

Alternatively, to make the pastry in the food processor, cut the butter into about 10 pieces. Place it and the flour, salt, and shortening in the workbowl fitted with the steel blade. Process until the mixture has the consistency of coarse meal. With the machine running, pour the ice water in through the feed tube. Stop processing as soon as the dough starts to form a ball.

Flatten the dough slightly and wrap in plastic wrap. Chill in the refrigerator for 30 minutes.

Makes enough for one two-crust 9-inch pie

[J O H N   C L A N C Y]

Chicken Sautéed with Apples

- 1 frying chicken (about 2½ pounds) cut into 8 pieces
- ½ teaspoon salt
- ¼ teaspoon freshly ground pepper
- 8 tablespoons clarified butter (see note below)
- 1 cup coarsely chopped onion
- ¼ cup applejack or Calvados
- ½ cup chicken broth
- 1 apple
- 1 tablespoon sugar
- 1 teaspoon arrowroot
- 1 teaspoon water
- ¼ cup heavy cream
- 2 tablespoons chopped parsley, for garnish

Season the chicken with the salt and pepper. In a large heavy skillet, heat 6 tablespoons of the clarified butter until it is very hot. Brown the chicken pieces. When brown, transfer them to a platter. Place the chopped onions in the skillet and cook until they are lightly browned. Add the applejack and ignite by touching the edge of the pan with a long lighted match. The flame will be high, so avert your face.

When the flame has died, add the chicken broth and chicken. Bring to a boil, then reduce the heat, cover, and simmer for about 15 minutes, or until the juices of the chicken run clear. (Test by inserting the point of a paring knife deep into the thighs of the chicken.)

In the meantime, core the apple and slice it into 8 rings about ⅓ inch thick. Heat the remaining 2 tablespoons butter in another skillet, drop in the apple rings, and sprinkle with the sugar. Cook the apple rings about 4 minutes on each side. Remove from the skillet and keep warm.

When the chicken is done, remove it to a hot platter. Place the apple rings on top.

Mix the arrowroot and water. With a wire whisk, beat the arrowroot mixture into the chicken broth in the first skillet. Cook until it is thoroughly thickened. With the whisk, stir in the heavy cream and heat through. Taste for salt and pepper. Pour the sauce over the apple rings and chicken. Sprinkle with the chopped parsley to serve.

Serves 4

NOTE: When butter is clarified it loses about one-fourth of its original volume (use 10 tablespoons of butter to make 8 tablespoons of clarified butter). To make clarified butter, cut unsalted butter into 1-inch pieces. Melt the butter over low heat in a heavy saucepan. Remove from the heat, let stand for 3 minutes, and skim the froth. Strain the butter through a sieve lined with double cheesecloth, leaving the solids in the bottom of the pan. Pour the clarified butter into a jar and store, covered and chilled.

[J O H N   C L A N C Y]

Creeping Crust Apple Cobbler

As this cobbler bakes, the batter rises and literally "creeps" up through the apple slices, hence the name. It is a truly American dessert but also reminiscent of the classic French *clafoutis.* The amount of sugar in the batter creates an unusually enjoyable, chewily textured pastry. This dish is a delightful change from the more customary dry-textured cobblers. Try it warm or at room temperature. When you serve it topped with slightly softened vanilla ice cream, apple pie à la mode will become just a distant memory.

  5 large apples, peeled, halved, and cored
1½ cups sugar
  ½ teaspoon ground cinnamon
  ½ cup unsalted butter, melted and cooled
       to room temperature
  1 cup unbleached all-purpose flour
  1 teaspoon baking powder
  ¾ cup milk

Adjust the oven rack to the middle and preheat the oven to 375°F.

Slice the apple halves in a food processor with the medium slicing disc. Remove the apples to a large bowl. Add ½ cup of the sugar and the cinnamon and toss until well mixed.

With a pastry brush, coat the sides of a 12 × 9-inch shallow baking dish with some of the melted butter. Pour the remaining butter into the dish and tilt it back and forth until the bottom is completely covered with the butter.

Sift together the flour, remaining 1 cup sugar, and the baking powder into a medium bowl. With a wooden spoon, beat in the milk until you have a smooth batter. Pour the batter into the butter-coated dish. Sprinkle the apples, as well as the juice that will have accumulated, evenly over the batter.

Bake the cobbler 35 to 45 minutes, or until the top is a deep golden brown.

Serves 6 to 8

[J O H N   C L A N C Y]

Apple Pudding

5   slices dry firm white bread, untrimmed
1   medium lemon (about 6 ounces)
⅓   cup sugar
3   medium apples (about 7 ounces each),
      such as Golden Delicious or Granny
      Smith
      Freshly grated nutmeg
4   large eggs
2   teaspoons pure vanilla extract
1½ cups heavy cream
      Confectioners' sugar, for garnish

Generously butter the bottom and sides of a 9 × 2-inch pie plate or 9 × 2-inch round baking dish. Set aside. Preheat the oven to 350°F.

Tear the bread slices into quarters. Process them to medium-fine crumbs in a food processor with the metal blade. Pulse 4 times, then process for about 10 seconds. There should be about 1⅓ cups crumbs. Reserve.

Remove the yellow zest from half the lemon with a swivel-bladed vegetable peeler. Reserve the rest of the lemon for another use.

Process the zest and sugar in the processor with the metal blade until the peel is finely chopped, about 1 minute. Remove and reserve.

Core and peel the apples and process them, cored end down, in the processor with the medium slicing disc.

To assemble the pudding, sprinkle 2 tablespoons of the bread crumbs over the bottom of the buttered pie dish. Layer one-third of the apple slices over the crumbs and sprinkle with one-third of the sugar-lemon mixture, nutmeg to taste, and 2 tablespoons of bread crumbs. Repeat the layering twice more, and use the remaining crumbs to make a thick layer on top.

Process the eggs and vanilla in the processor with the metal blade for 5 seconds. With the motor running, pour 1 cup of the cream through the feed tube. Pour the egg-cream mixture slowly over the apples, letting it seep through the layers.

Bake in the center of the preheated oven for 30 minutes, then reduce the heat to 300°F and continue baking until the apples are tender, about 15 minutes more.

Cool in the baking dish set on a wire rack. Serve slightly warm or at room temperature, sprinkled with confectioners' sugar.

Just before serving, whip the remaining ½ cup cream, and serve in a separate bowl, sprinkled with nutmeg.

Serves 8

[S U Z A N N E   S .   J O N E S]

Spiced Apple Cake

This is the cake to have on hand for unexpected guests. Like fruitcake, it can be stored for weeks at a time in the refrigerator, tightly wrapped in foil or in an airtight container to retain its moisture. It has its place on the breakfast table and can be just the right snack before bedtime or whenever the urge for a sweet gets to you.

While not eye-appealing before they are mixed with the molasses and honey that this recipe calls for, the best dried apples are those found in health food stores because they are sun dried without preservatives, and their flavor is superior to the usual supermarket varieties.

- 1 cup dried apples
- 3 cups boiling water, or as needed
- ¼ cup dark unsulphured molasses
- ¼ cup honey
- 2 teaspoons unsalted butter, softened
- 2 cups unbleached all-purpose flour
- 2 teaspoons baking powder
- 1 teaspoon ground cinnamon
- ½ teaspoon ground cloves
- ½ teaspoon salt
- ½ cup sugar
- 1 large egg
- ½ cup plain yogurt

Place the dried apples in a 3- to 4-cup heatproof bowl. Add the boiling water to cover them in excess of about 2 inches. Let the apples soak for 3 hours.

Drain the apples in a colander, dry with paper towels, and chop into ¼-inch bits. (The chopping can be done in a food processor fitted with the metal blade.) In a large bowl, combine the chopped apples with the molasses and honey.

Adjust the oven rack to the middle and preheat the oven to 350°F. Coat a 9 × 5 × 3-inch loaf pan with the softened butter. Sift the flour, baking powder, cinnamon, cloves, and salt together onto a large piece of wax paper. Beat the sugar, egg, and yogurt into the apple, molasses, and honey mixture. Next add the flour mixture, ½ cup at a time, beating with each addition until the flour is well incorporated.

Scrape the batter into the buttered loaf pan, spreading it evenly. Bake for 1 hour, or until a toothpick inserted deep into the cake comes out clean. Allow the cake to cool in the pan for about 30 minutes. Turn it out onto a wire rack to cool to room temperature before serving.

Makes one 9 × 5 × 3-inch loaf

[J O H N   C L A N C Y]

Apricots

This small fruit is a lovely color both inside and out. The skin is soft and velvety and the flesh juicy, yet firmer than a peach. Apricots are one of the first stone fruits of the season, appearing on the market in late May and lasting until early August. Choose apricots with a warm, orange-reddish hue and store them at room temperature for no more than 2 days. Both fresh and dried, apricots are versatile and can be eaten raw or cooked.

Apricot Walnut Stuffing

1 cup dried apricots
1 tablespoon unbleached all-purpose flour
¾ cup golden raisins
2 tablespoons bourbon or dark rum
1 cup walnut pieces
1 medium garlic clove, peeled
2 medium onions (about 5 ounces each), peeled and quartered
4 medium celery ribs (about 14 ounces total), cut into 3-inch pieces
1 stick plus 1 tablespoon butter
⅔ cup condensed chicken stock
10 cups fresh white bread crumbs
Salt and freshly ground black pepper to taste

Process the apricots and flour in a food processor with the metal blade until the apricots are coarsely chopped, about 10 pulses.

Transfer to a large bowl and stir in the raisins and bourbon or rum. Set aside, at room temperature, for 1 hour.

Coarsely chop the walnuts in the processor with the metal blade, about 5 pulses. Add to the apricots and raisins.

Drop the garlic through the feed tube of the processor with the motor running and process for 5 seconds, or until finely chopped.

Add the onions and pulse 12 times or until finely chopped. Remove and reserve.

Insert the medium slicing disc in the processor. Stand the celery pieces in the feed tube vertically and process.

Melt 4 tablespoons of the butter in a medium skillet, over moderate heat. Add the garlic, onions, and celery and cook until tender, about 6 minutes. Transfer to the bowl with the fruit and nuts.

Melt the remaining butter and add with the remaining ingredients to the bowl. Toss to combine and season to taste.

Use to stuff, loosely, a 14-pound turkey.

Makes about 9¾ cups

[CARL JEROME]

Alsatian Apricot Tart

This tart is made in the style of fruit tarts popular in Alsace. The whole-wheat crust and cream cheese custard are Americanizations, however. Cooks who are not particularly adept with dough will find this crust easy to handle and patch. When baked, it has the consistency of a butter cookie—leftover dough makes lovely cookies.

Crust

¼ cup sugar
Ground cinnamon
Zest of 1 medium lemon
¼ cup cake flour
1¼ cups whole-wheat flour
2 large egg yolks, 1 hard-cooked and 1 raw
½ cup unsalted butter, chilled and cut into bits

Filling

- 3 quarts water
- 1 cup sugar
- 2-inch piece vanilla bean (optional)
- 1½ to 2 pounds fresh apricots
- 1 cup apricot preserves
- 2 teaspoons Grand Marnier or Cointreau
- ¼ cup cream cheese or Crème Fraîche, at room temperature
- Pinch ground cinnamon
- Dash freshly grated nutmeg
- ¾ cup heavy cream
- 1 large egg
- 1 large egg yolk

Make the crust: Add sugar and a pinch of cinnamon to a food processor fitted with the metal blade. Turn the machine on and add the lemon zest through the feed tube. Process until the zest is chopped, about 30 seconds. Add the cake flour, whole-wheat flour and hard-cooked yolk and process with about 8 quick on-and-off turns. Add the butter and raw egg yolk. Turn the processor on and run it for about 20 seconds, or until the mixture just forms a ball that makes no more than two revolutions around the bowl. Take care not to overprocess. Remove the dough, wrap it in plastic, and refrigerate 1 hour.

Cut 4 pieces of wax paper 20 inches long. Overlap two on work surface, place dough over it, and cover with the other two pieces of wax paper, also overlapping. Roll dough between the paper evenly to a circle 14 to 15 inches in diameter.

Have ready a 10-inch black loose-bottomed tart pan. Remove the top layer of wax paper. If the dough sticks, refrigerate for 15 minutes. Then in one swift motion—grasping the wax paper firmly—turn the dough face down over the pan. Take care that the sharp pan rim does not cut through the dough. The bottom sheets of wax paper should peel off easily. Press the dough into the pan. Once the dough lines the bottom and sides, press it against the pan rim with your fingers to remove excess dough. Patch where necessary with excess dough. Make sure the dough fits snugly around the bottom rim and that the fluted sides are the same thickness at the top rim as elsewhere.

Chill the crust 1 hour loosely wrapped or freeze until it is very hard.

Preheat oven to 375°F. Place a sheet of lightweight aluminum foil, shiny side down, over the hardened crust. Press the foil to fit all contours of the crust. Fill with rice, beans, or metal pie weights. Bake 15 minutes. Remove from the oven but leave the oven on. Let the crust cool for 5 minutes. Carefully remove the beans and foil. Return the crust to oven and bake an additional 5 minutes. Remove from the oven and let cool to room temperature. Do not remove the crust from the pan.

Prepare the filling: Place water, sugar and vanilla bean in a 5-quart Dutch oven. Bring to a boil. Turn the heat to low and simmer 20 minutes. Add the apricots and simmer, partially covered, for 5 to 6 minutes, or until a small knife inserted into the center of the fruit meets only slight resistance. If the apricots are very ripe, decrease poaching time to 4 minutes; if very hard, increase to 8 minutes. Uncover and cool the apricots in poaching liquid to room temperature. Peel, cut in half, and remove the pits. Drain. (If the apricots are very small and tender with thin skins, they need not be peeled.) The liquid may be re-used or discarded.

Preheat the oven to 375°F.

Heat the apricot preserves with 1 teaspoon Grand Marnier. Strain the preserves and brush 2 tablespoons over the bottom and sides of the cooled crust to seal. Reserve the remaining preserves for a glaze.

Fit the processor with the steel blade. Add the cream cheese, cinnamon, and nutmeg. Process about 15 seconds or until smooth. Stop and scrape down the sides of the work-bowl. With the processor on, immediately add the heavy cream through the feed tube. Stop the machine and add the egg, egg yolk, and remaining 1 teaspoon Grand Marnier. Mix with 2 or 3 quick on-and-off turns. Do not overprocess.

Pour half the cream mixture into the cooled crust. Arrange the apricot halves evenly around the shell, rounded sides up.

Top with remaining cream mixture. Bake for 35 minutes in the preheated oven or until custard is set. Cool thoroughly.

When tart is cool, reheat the remaining preserves and spoon over custard to make an even transparent layer. Chill.

To serve, place the pan on a wide jar and carefully remove the rim, letting it fall down.

Serves 8 to 10

NOTE: In an emergency or out of season, canned apricots may be substituted for fresh. Use a 28-ounce can of whole apricots. Drain them and discard the liquid. Cut in half and pit, then rinse with water. Pat dry before using. Since canned apricots are precooked, omit the poaching step.

[JANE SALZFASS FREIMAN]

Pecan Apricot Pound Cake

1¾ cups unbleached all-purpose flour
⅓ cup dried apricots
4 large eggs
1 cup sugar
1½ tablespoons dark rum
1 teaspoon pure vanilla extract
¼ teaspoon salt
1 cup unsalted butter, at room temperature, cut into pieces
½ cup pecans

Rum Glaze (recipe follows)

Lightly butter and flour a 6-cup ring mold or tube pan. Preheat the oven to 325°F.

Process the flour and apricots in a food processor with the metal blade until the apricots are finely chopped, about 45 seconds. Remove and reserve.

Still with the metal blade, process the eggs, sugar, rum, vanilla, and salt until well mixed. With the machine running, drop the softened pieces of butter through the feed tube and process until they are incorporated and the mixture is creamy, scraping down the sides of the workbowl when necessary. Add the nuts and turn the machine on and off 3 or 4 times. Then add the flour-apricot mixture and turn on and off just until the flour disappears. Do not overprocess.

Pour the batter into the prepared pan and tap the pan on the counter to settle. Bake for 55 to 60 minutes, or until the cake begins to pull away from the sides of the pan and a toothpick inserted in the middle comes out clean. Allow to cool in the pan for 5 minutes, then invert on a wire rack and let cool thoroughly. Drizzle with the Rum Glaze before the cake cools completely.

Serves 8 to 10

[S U Z A N N E S. J O N E S]

Rum Glaze

½ cup confectioners' sugar
1 tablespoon dark rum
½ teaspoon pure vanilla extract
2 tablespoons heavy cream

Process all ingredients in the food processor with the metal blade until smooth.

Makes about ¼ cup

Bananas

Many Americans cannot imagine starting their day without a banana sliced over a bowl of breakfast cereal, and they are not alone in their admiration; this perfect convenience food is internationally popular. Besides the familiar yellow banana (the Cavendish), you can sometimes find the smaller "finger bananas" and even a red-skinned variety. This very versatile fruit is available year-round. Choose evenly colored yellow bananas with specks of brown, which shows ripeness. Bananas will ripen at home in a couple of days if they are left at room temperature. To speed up ripening, place bananas in a brown paper bag with holes in it. To keep ripe bananas for later use, store them in the refrigerator; the color of their skin will turn brown, but the flesh will remain unchanged.

Oatmeal-Banana Muffins

1   cup plus 2 tablespoons quick-cooking
 rolled oats
1   cup buttermilk
1   teaspoon pure vanilla extract
1   cup unbleached all-purpose flour
½   teaspoon baking soda
1   tablespoon baking powder
1   teaspoon salt
¼   teaspoon ground cinnamon
½   teaspoon freshly grated nutmeg
¼   cup walnuts, coarsely chopped
1   large banana, peeled and chopped
1   large egg
¾   cup firmly packed light brown sugar
¼   cup unsalted butter, melted

Grease 18 muffin cups, ⅓-cup capacity. Preheat the oven to 400°F. Adjust the rack to the middle of the oven.

 Combine the rolled oats, buttermilk, and vanilla in a bowl. Set aside.

 In another bowl, stir together well the flour, baking soda, baking powder, salt, cinnamon, and nutmeg with a fork. Add the walnuts and bananas to the bowl with the flour mixture. Set aside.

 In a large bowl combine the egg and brown sugar. Add the melted butter and beat until thoroughly combined. Gradually add the oatmeal mixture, in batches, stirring after each addition. Add the flour mixture and stir until just combined. Do not overmix.

 Spoon the batter into muffin pans, filling cups ⅔ full. Sprinkle the top of batter with additional cinnamon. Bake in the preheated oven for 18 minutes. Remove the muffins from the pans and cool on wire racks.

Makes 18 muffins

Banana Ice Cream

3¾   pounds ripe bananas, peeled and cut
 into 2-inch pieces
1   tablespoon fresh lemon juice
½   cup plus 2 tablespoons heavy cream
2   tablespoons sugar
1½   tablespoons dark rum

Process the banana pieces in a food processor with the metal blade for 1 minute, or until they are puréed, stopping once to scrape down the sides of the workbowl. Add the remaining ingredients and process for 20 seconds. Transfer the mixture to a freezer container until it is partially frozen.

 Spoon the semifrozen banana mixture back into the processor bowl and turn the machine on and off about 8 times. Then process until it is completely blended, smooth, and fluffy, about 2 minutes. Place in a container and freeze. Before serving, let the ice cream soften slightly at room temperature.

Makes about 1 quart

Broiled Bananas with Vanilla Ice Cream

4 ripe bananas
½ lemon
  Dark brown sugar
2 tablespoons unsalted butter
1 pint vanilla ice cream

Peel the bananas and cut them in half lengthwise. Arrange on a foil-lined rack over a shallow roasting pan. Rub the cut side of each banana with the exposed part of the lemon. Sprinkle the bananas generously with a layer of brown sugar and dot with butter. Set aside until after you have finished the main course of your dinner (see note below).

Preheat the broiler.

Place the bananas on a shelf about 4 inches below the preheated broiling unit, leaving the door slightly ajar. Broil for 3 to 4 minutes, until the sugar is bubbly and the tops have begun to color. Watch carefully after the first 2 minutes. If the bananas look like they are going to burn before they are heated through, lower them another inch or two from the broiling unit.

Serve hot with vanilla ice cream.

Serves 4

NOTE: Broiling the bananas will require a few minutes of your time between courses to be certain the brown sugar glaze doesn't burn.

[CARL JEROME]

Blackberries and Blueberries

The blackberry, purplish-black and juicy, is the largest berry. Up to 1 inch in length, cultivated blackberries come to market in the summer, from June to August. Wild blackberries gathered in woodlands and fields tend to be smaller and have more seeds; they are wonderfully sweet yet tart. Buy plump blackberries with glossy black skin, with no green or red patches and without mold. Also, avoid ones with their hull still attached; these berries are immature and will be very tart. Do not keep blackberries for longer than a day or so, and hull them just before use. They can be stored in the refrigerator placed on a baking sheet lined with paper towels and covered lightly with plastic wrap.

Blueberries keep well and adapt well to many cooking preparations. These small round beauties can be made into jam or used in cheesecake, muffins, pancakes, and pie. The two varieties— wild and cultivated—are distinguishable by their size and taste. The wild lowbush produces tiny, intensely-flavored fruit while the cultivated highbush has larger, milder berries. When buying blueberries, look for deep blue berries with a hint of silver that are uniform in size without being shriveled. Keep them in the refrigerator in the carton they come in for up to 3 days.

Orange Blackberry Tarts

Pastry

- 1¼ cups all-purpose flour
- 6 strips orange zest (2 × ¾ inch each)
- 2 teaspoons sugar
- ½ cup unsalted butter, chilled and cut into 8 pieces
- ½ teaspoon salt
- ¼ cup ice water

Filling

- 2 strips orange zest (2 × ¾ inch each)
- ¼ cup sugar
- 1 tablespoon unbleached all-purpose flour
- 2 teaspoons cornstarch
- 1 large egg
- 1 cup milk
- 3 tablespoons unsalted butter
- ¼ teaspoon pure vanilla extract
- 1 pint fresh blackberries or raspberries
   Julienned orange zest, for garnish

To make the pastry, process ¼ cup of the flour, the zest, and the sugar in a food processor with the metal blade until the zest is as fine as the sugar, about 2 minutes. Add the remaining 1 cup flour, the butter, and salt and process until the mixture resembles coarse crumbs, about 10 seconds. Add the water and pulse until the pastry just begins to hold together, about 9 times. Turn out onto wax paper and form into a 6-inch circle. Wrap in the wax paper and chill for 30 minutes.

Roll out the chilled dough ⅛ inch thick on a lightly floured surface (see note below). Cut into shapes a little larger than individual 4-inch tart pans and fit into the pans, pressing gently without stretching the pastry. Trim off any excess. Chill for 20 minutes.

Preheat the oven to 400°F.

Line the shells with heavy-duty foil and prick with a fork. Bake on a baking sheet in the center of the preheated oven for 15 minutes, then remove the foil and bake until golden, 3 to 5 minutes more. Cool on a rack.

To make the filling, process the zest and sugar with the metal blade until the zest is as fine as the sugar, about 2 minutes. Add the flour, cornstarch, and egg and process until smooth, about 10 seconds.

Bring the milk to a boil in a saucepan, and with the motor running, pour through the feed tube. Return the mixture to the saucepan and cook over moderately high heat, stirring vigorously with a wire whisk, until very thick and bubbly in the center. Remove from the heat, stir in the butter and vanilla, and transfer to a bowl to cool. Chill, covered, until cold.

Spread the filling in the shells and top with the blackberries. Garnish with the julienned orange zest.

Serves 12

NOTE: To make a large tart, roll out the pastry to a 14-inch circle and fit into an 11-inch tart pan with removable fluted rim. Bake with the foil for 20 minutes and without for 10 to 15 minutes more.

[JIM DODGE/ELAINE RATNER]

Strawberry and Blackberry Strip

10 ounces Puff Pastry dough (recipe
    follows)
1 large egg yolk
1 teaspoon water
1 cup Crème Pâtissière (page 184)
3 cups fresh strawberries, hulled
3 cups fresh blackberries
½ cup Berry Glaze (page 184)

On a lightly floured surface roll the dough
into a 16 × 10-inch rectangle, about ⅟₁₆ inch
thick. Dampen a cookie sheet. Roll the
dough loosely onto the rolling pin and unroll
it onto the cookie sheet, floured side up.
Brush off excess flour. With a sharp knife trim
the edges of the rectangle. Brush with water
along the long edges to a width of about 1
inch, and then fold the edges over to make a
1¼-inch rim. With a sharp knife trim the
folded edge. Prick the dough all over with a
fork. With the back of the knife make vertical

impressions about ½ inch apart along the
side. Beat together with a fork the egg yolk
and the teaspoon of water and brush it over
the rim, taking care that it doesn't drip down
the sides. Put the strip in the freezer for 10 to
15 minutes.

Preheat the oven to 425°F. Bake the strip
for 15 to 20 minutes, until it is lightly
browned. Remove to a wire rack to cool completely.

Then transfer to a serving platter. Spread
the Crème Pâtissière over the pastry, inside
the rim, and arrange the berries in decorative
rows over it.

Spoon and brush the glaze over the berries. Serve within 2 hours.

Serves 8

[JACQUES PÉPIN]

Puff Pastry

1 cup unbleached all-purpose flour,
    chilled in the freezer for at least 4 hours
¾ cup cake flour, chilled in the freezer for
    at least 4 hours
⅛ teaspoon salt
½ cup plus 1 tablespoon ice water
1 cup unsalted butter, cut into ⅛-inch
    slices, well chilled

Stir together the flours with the salt in a large

bowl. Add the ice water and, with your hands,
mix lightly until the dough begins to hold together. Distribute the chilled butter over the
mixture. Gather the dough over the top of the
butter and pat together. Transfer to a smooth,
cool surface. Pat into a rectangle about 6 by 8
inches. Fold the dough in thirds. Flour the
surface lightly and rotate the dough so that a
short edge is toward you.

Roll the dough into a rectangle 12 × 6

183

inches and ½ inch thick. Then fold the short edges to meet in the center and fold in half along the line where the edges meet. This is one double turn.

Rotate the dough so that a short edge is toward you and make a second double turn.

Rotate the dough again and make the third and final double turn. If the dough is too elastic to roll, refrigerate for 30 minutes before making the final double turn.

Refrigerate the completed dough for at least 2 hours before using.

Makes about 20 ounces

[JACQUES PÉPIN]

Crème Pâtissière

1¼ cups milk
  2 large egg yolks
  ¼ cup sugar
  ½ teaspoon pure vanilla extract
  3 tablespoons unbleached all-purpose
       flour
  4 tablespoons unsalted butter, softened

Bring the milk to a boil in a 1-quart saucepan over moderate heat. Meanwhile, whisk together the egg yolks, sugar, and vanilla in a small bowl for about 1 minute and then whisk in the flour. Add to the boiling milk and, whisking continuously, bring to a boil.

Transfer to a bowl. When the mixture has cooled to lukewarm, stir in the softened butter. Cover and refrigerate until needed.

Makes about 1½ cups

[JACQUES PÉPIN]

Berry Glaze

⅔ cup raspberry preserves
 1 jar (10 ounces) red currant jelly

Using a sieve or the finest disc of a food mill, strain the raspberry preserves into a small saucepan. Add the currant jelly to the saucepan. Stir over moderate heat until the mixture comes to a boil. Cool to lukewarm before using.

Makes about 1¼ cups

[JACQUES PÉPIN]

Blueberry Streusel Muffins

Streusel Topping

¼ cup sugar

3 tablespoons unbleached all-purpose flour

1 tablespoon unsalted butter, chilled and cut into 2 pieces

½ teaspoon ground cinnamon
Pinch salt

Batter

1 cup unbleached all-purpose flour

½ cup whole-wheat flour

2 teaspoons baking powder

½ teaspoon baking soda

¼ teaspoon salt

¾ cup sugar

⅔ cup buttermilk

½ cup unsalted butter, melted and cooled

2 large eggs

1 teaspoon pure vanilla extract

1½ cups frozen, unthawed blueberries

Preheat the oven to 375°F. Oil twelve ½-cup muffin cups. Set aside.

Make the streusel topping by processing all the ingredients in a food processor with the metal blade until coarsely crumbled, 10 to 15 seconds. Set aside.

Process all the ingredients for the batter except the blueberries in the processor with the metal blade for 3 seconds. Scrape down the workbowl and pulse 2 times more. Transfer the batter to a medium bowl and stir in the blueberries.

Fill each muffin cup two-thirds full with batter and sprinkle each with 1 tablespoon of the streusel topping. Bake in the center of the preheated oven for 25 to 28 minutes, or until the muffins are firm to the touch and the tops are golden brown. Cool in the muffin cups for about 8 minutes, then remove to a wire rack. Serve warm.

Makes twelve muffins

[ABBY MANDEL]

Blueberry Carole

Crust

1 cup unsalted butter, very cold, preferably frozen

2⅔ cups plus 3 tablespoons all-purpose flour

2 teaspoons salt

2 teaspoons sugar

2 large egg yolks (reserve whites for filling)
Ice water

Crumb Topping

½ cup unsalted butter, very cold, preferably frozen

1 cup unbleached all-purpose flour

1 cup sugar

Filling

- 2 large egg whites
- 2 pints firm, ripe fresh blueberries, stems removed, washed, and patted dry

Preheat the oven to 400°F. Butter a 15½ × 10½ × 1-inch jelly-roll pan.

Cut the butter into 7 or 8 pieces. With the metal blade in place, add the butter, 2⅔ cups flour, the salt, and sugar to a food processor. Process, turning machine on and off, until the mixture is the consistency of coarse meal, 5 to 10 seconds.

Add the egg yolks to a 1-cup measure and bring the volume to ½ cup with ice water. Mix lightly with fork. With the processor motor running, pour the mixture through the feed tube in a steady stream. Stop the machine as soon as balls of dough start to form. This will ensure a tender, flaky crust. (The dough may be used immediately or wrapped in plastic wrap and chilled.)

Roll out the dough and press into the prepared jelly-roll pan. Sprinkle evenly with the 3 tablespoons flour. Refrigerate while you prepare the topping and filling.

To make the filling, process the egg whites in the food processor with the metal blade until stiff, about 50 seconds. Fold them gently and thoroughly into the blueberries.

Cut the butter for the topping into 8 pieces. With the metal blade in place, process the butter, flour, and sugar in the food processor to the consistency of fine crumbs, 25 to 30 seconds. Remove and reserve.

Spread the filling evenly over the pastry crust. Sprinkle the crumb topping uniformly over filling. Bake in the preheated oven for 35 minutes. Serve warm or at room temperature.

Serves 15 to 18

Blueberry Cheese Tart

Pastry

- 1½ cups unbleached all-purpose flour
- ¼ cup sugar
- ½ teaspoon baking powder
  Pinch salt
- ½ cup unsalted butter, cut into 8 pieces and chilled
- 1 large egg, beaten with 2 tablespoons cold water

Filling

- Zest of ½ medium lemon
- ¼ cup sugar
- 1 package (7½ ounces) farmer cheese
- 2 large eggs
- 1 tablespoon unbleached all-purpose flour
- 1¾ cups firm, ripe fresh blueberries, stems removed, washed, and patted dry

To make the pastry, process the flour, sugar, baking powder, and salt in a food processor with the metal blade until combined, about 5 seconds. Add the butter and pulse until the mixture resembles coarse meal, about 12 times. Add the egg mixture and pulse until the dough begins to clump together, about 10 times. Shape the pastry into a disc, wrap in plastic wrap, and refrigerate for 1 hour.

On a lightly floured surface, roll the pastry into a 14-inch circle. Fit the pastry into a 10-inch tart pan with removable bottom. Roll a rolling pin over the top edge to trim off the excess pastry. Refrigerate the pastry crust for 30 minutes.

Preheat the oven to 400°F.

Line the crust with foil, fill the foil with pie weights, dry beans, or rice, and bake in the preheated oven for 10 minutes. Remove the foil and its contents and bake the crust until golden brown, about 4 minutes more.

Reduce the oven temperature to 350°F.

To make the filling, process the lemon zest and sugar in the processor with the metal blade until the peel is as fine as the sugar, about 2 minutes. Add the cheese and process until smooth, about 30 seconds. Add the eggs and flour and process until smooth, about 10 seconds.

Spread the blueberries in the pastry crust. Pour the cheese filling evenly over them and bake in the center of the preheated oven until the filling is set, about 30 minutes. Cool in the pan on a wire rack.

Serves 8

[NICK MALGIERI]

Blueberry Liqueur

- 5 pints firm, ripe fresh blueberries
- 1 cup sugar
- 3 cups gin

Put the blueberries in a 2½-quart glass container with a tight lid. Add ½ cup of the sugar, cover, and shake. Add the remaining sugar in 2 batches, shaking after each addition. Pour in the gin, cover tightly, and shake well. Set aside in a dark place for 3 to 4 months, shaking occasionally. Strain liquid through a coffee filter into a decanter, reserving the berries for another use.

Makes about 4 cups

[JEHANE BENOIT]

Cherries

Deep red Bing cherries—with their sweet juices that stain teeth and T-shirts—are a true summertime treat. The two main types of cherries—sweet and sour—each have numerous varieties. Most cherries sold in the United States come from the Pacific Northwest and are available starting in May, with the height of their season in July. Sour cherries are smaller, rounder, and softer than sweet ones, and because they are so tart they are cooked rather than eaten raw. Whatever the variety, choose bright plump fruit with green and flexible stems. Keep cherries in a plastic bag in the refrigerator for no more than 2 or 3 days, and wash them just before using.

Medallions of Venison with Cherry Sauce and Chestnut Purée

If you have an entire back of venison, separate the rack from the saddle. If you are making the saddle of venison variation, you will need 2 cups of venison stock; or you may substitute beef stock.

  1   double rack of venison (about 3½ pounds)
       Stems from 1 bunch parsley
       Venison Marinade (page 191)
  2   tablespoons vegetable oil
  1   pound sweet red cherries, pitted
  1   cup ruby port
  6   tablespoons unsalted butter
  1   tablespoon unbleached all-purpose flour
10   cups water
1½ teaspoons salt
½   teaspoon freshly ground black pepper
  2   tablespoons currant jelly
½   teaspoon arrowroot or cornstarch mixed with 2 teaspoons water
16 fresh sage leaves or watercress sprigs, for garnish
       Chestnut Purée (page 191)

Place the rack, bone side down, on a cutting board. With a sharp knife, remove the loin of meat from each side in one piece. Trim excess skin, fat, and gristle from the meat and put the loins and trimmings into a large bowl. Cut the rack itself into 4 pieces and add to the bowl, along with the parsley stems.

Bring the Venison Marinade to a boil over moderate heat and pour it over the meat in the bowl (see note below). Turn the meat to coat it, then drizzle on the oil. Let stand for 2 hours, turning after 1 hour.

Remove the marinated loins and set them aside at room temperature. Strain the marinade and set aside separately the marinade liquid, the vegetables, and the marinated bones.

Put the cherries in a 1-quart bowl and pour in the port. Marinate for at least 2 hours while you make the stock.

To make the venison stock, first melt 3 tablespoons of the butter in a 10-quart stockpot over moderately high heat. Add the reserved marinated bones and brown them, stirring occasionally, for 10 to 12 minutes. Add the reserved marinade vegetables to the stockpot. Sprinkle on the flour and cook, stirring, for 2 to 3 minutes.

Add the reserved marinade liquid, the water, and ½ teaspoon of the salt. Bring to a boil, lower the heat, and simmer for 2 hours, uncovered and skimming as necessary during the first hour. Partially cover the pot for the second hour of simmering.

Remove and discard the bones. Strain the stock into a 3-quart saucepan, pressing on the vegetables with a spoon to extract the liquid. Discard the vegetables. Over high heat reduce the stock to 4 cups. Measure and set aside 2 cups. The remaining 2 cups may be frozen for up to 6 months.

Cut each reserved marinated loin crosswise into 8 equal medallions, each about ½ to ¾ inch thick. Sprinkle them on both sides with the pepper and the remaining 1 teaspoon salt.

Melt the remaining 3 tablespoons butter in a large skillet over high heat. When the butter is sizzling, put the medallions in the pan without crowding and sauté them for 1½ to 2 minutes on each side or until nicely browned on the outside but still rare. Remove to a platter and keep warm.

To make the cherry sauce, first deglaze the skillet, adding ½ cup of the reserved stock and stirring to release all of the brown bits from the bottom of the pan. Transfer to a 2-quart saucepan, add the remaining 1½ cups of reserved stock, and reduce over high heat for 3 to 4 minutes. Strain the port from the cherries into the saucepan, reserving the cherries. Stir in the currant jelly and cook for 2 to 3 minutes more. Add the reserved cher-ries and cook for 5 minutes, covering the saucepan after 2 minutes. Stir the arrowroot or cornstarch mixture briskly into the sauce. Simmer the sauce for 30 seconds more.

To serve, put about 3 tablespoons of the cherry sauce on each plate and divide the cherries evenly among the plates. Place 2 venison medallions on each plate and garnish with the sage leaves. Serve the Chestnut Purée separately.

Serves 8

NOTE: You may use cold marinade, but it will take longer to penetrate the meat. Put the meat, bones, trimmings and parsley stems in a double plastic bag, add the cold Venison Marinade and oil, and refrigerate overnight, turning occasionally.

[JACQUES PÉPIN]

Variation: Saddle of Venison with Cherry Sauce and Chestnut Purée

You will need 2 cups of venison stock.

Marinate the saddle as described in the recipe above. At the same time marinate the cherries in the port.

Preheat the oven to 450°F. Melt 4 table-spoons of butter in a 13 × 9 × 2-inch roasting pan over moderately high heat. When the butter is sizzling, add the saddle and brown it for about 1 minute on each side. Turn it bone side down and cook it in the center of the preheated oven for 30 minutes. It should be rare.

Remove to a platter and let stand at room temperature for 15 minutes to let the juices settle. Meanwhile, make the cherry sauce, first deglazing the roasting pan with the ½ cup of venison stock and then continuing as in the recipe above.

To carve, place the saddle bone side down and cut horizontally along the lower bones on each side. Then cut thin lengthwise slices parallel to the center bone. Turn the saddle over and remove the tenderloins from each side in one piece.

To serve, place the saddle bone on a large platter and drape the meat slices over the center. Pour the cherry sauce around the bot-

tom. Slice the tenderloins on a diagonal and arrange the slices at each end. Serve the Chestnut Purée separately.

Makes 8 servings

[JACQUES PÉPIN]

Venison Marinade

4 medium onions, peeled and halved
3 medium carrots, peeled, trimmed, and cut into 2-inch lengths
1½ cups dry white wine
1 cup red wine vinegar
12 juniper berries
1½ teaspoons whole black peppercorns
1½ teaspoons dried thyme
½ teaspoon coriander seeds

Slice the onions and carrots in a food processor with the thick or medium slicing disc. Transfer to a 3-quart nonreactive saucepan. Stir in the remaining ingredients.

Makes about 5 cups

[JACQUES PÉPIN]

Chestnut Purée

12 ounces (2 cups) dried chestnuts, covered with warm water and left to soak overnight at room temperature
4 cups water
1½ cups chicken stock, preferably homemade
5 celery leaves
1 teaspoon salt
Pinch sugar
Freshly ground black pepper
¾ cup heavy cream

Drain the soaked chestnuts and remove any brown skin remaining on them. Put the chestnuts into a 3-quart saucepan and add the water, chicken stock, celery leaves, and ½ teaspoon of the salt. Bring to a boil over high heat, reduce the heat, and simmer, uncovered, for about 1½ hours, or until the chestnuts are soft. Drain the chestnuts, reserving the liquid.

Purée the chestnuts with ⅓ cup of the cooking liquid in a food processor with the metal blade, processing for about 30 seconds and scraping down the workbowl as neces-

191

Cherries

sary. Add the remaining ½ teaspoon salt, the sugar, and pepper to taste. With the motor running, add ½ cup of the cream through the feed tube. The mixture should be smooth and have the consistency of mashed potatoes. If it is too thick, scrape down the workbowl and add more of the cooking liquid 1 tablespoon at a time, processing for 2 seconds after each addition.

Return the purée to the saucepan and cover with the remaining ¼ cup cream. Before serving, reheat over low heat, stirring in the cream.

Serves 8

[J A C Q U E S   P É P I N]

Danish Rice Cream with Almonds and Cherries

A traditional Danish dessert, served with a cold sour cherry jelly rather than the usual hot, sweet fruit sauce. This version is adapted from one served by Jean-Jacques Belin at Copenhagen's Plaza restaurant.

- ½ cup blanched almonds
- 3 tablespoons sugar, plus additional if necessary
- 1 quart milk
- 1 small piece vanilla bean (1 inch), split
- ½ cup short-grain rice
- 1 large egg, separated
- 1 cup heavy cream
- 1 can (16 ounces) sour cherries
- ¼ cup kirsch
- ½ teaspoon grated lemon zest
- 1 tablespoon cornstarch

Coarsely chop the almonds in a food processor with the metal blade, pulsing 8 to 10 times. Remove and reserve.

Stir the 3 tablespoons of sugar into the milk in a medium saucepan. Add the vanilla bean and bring slowly to a boil.

Remove the vanilla bean and stir in the rice. Reduce the heat and simmer the mixture, uncovered, for about 35 minutes, or until the rice is very tender and the milk is thick. Stir the mixture often with a wooden spoon to prevent it from sticking to the bottom of the saucepan.

Remove the rice from the heat and stir in the reserved almonds. Beat the egg yolk lightly and stir it into the rice. Transfer the rice to a large bowl and cool at room temperature for 30 minutes, stirring occaionally.

Beat the egg white and cream in separate bowls until stiff. Fold the egg white into the cream, then fold the cream mixture into the rice. Cover and refrigerate the rice mixture while making the topping.

Pour off and reserve ¼ cup of cherry juice from the can of cherries. Put the cherries and the remaining juice in a nonreactive saucepan. Stir in the kirsch, another teaspoon of sugar (if you think the cherries need sweetening), and the lemon zest. Bring to a boil, then lower the heat and simmer, stirring occasionally, for 5 minutes.

Stir the cornstarch into the reserved cherry juice and add to the mixture in the saucepan. Cook, stirring, until thickened, about 30 seconds. Cool for 10 minutes.

Transfer the rice to a serving bowl and pour the cherry mixture over the top. Refrigerate, covered with plastic wrap, for at least 4 hours or until well chilled.

Serves 6

[ELENE MARGOT KOLB]

Brioche and Butter Pudding with Dark Cherries

   6 stale brioche slices (each about ½ inch thick and 4 inches in diameter)
   4 tablespoons unsalted butter, softened
1¼ cups poached dark cherries with ¼ cup poaching liquid or frozen or canned dark cherries with ¼ cup liquid
1¼ cups milk
   2 large eggs
   2 large egg yolks
      Pinch salt
   2 tablespoons kirsch
      Granulated sugar
      Confectioners' sugar, for garnish
      Bowl of Crème Fraîche, homemade if desired (see page 30) or unsweetened whipped cream, for serving

Preheat the oven to 350°F. Toast the brioche slices and use the softened butter to butter both sides. Arrange half the slices, side by side, on the bottom of a lightly buttered 5-cup shallow baking dish. Place the cherries on top and cover with the remaining brioche cut into wedges.

In a large bowl combine the ¼ cup cherry liquid, milk, eggs, egg yolks, salt, and kirsch, beating to blend. Add granulated sugar to taste. Pour the mixture over the prepared brioche slices. Set in a larger pan of hot water on the middle shelf of the preheated oven. Bake 30 minutes. Twice while cooking, press the brioche down with a spatula so it remains moist and in place. Sprinkle the top with confectioners' sugar; transfer to the upper oven shelf, raise the oven heat, and allow the top to brown nicely.

Serve lukewarm or cold with a bowl of crème fraîche or whipped cream.

Serves 6

Sour Cherry Almond Squares

¾ cup blanched almonds
1 cup unbleached all-purpose flour
½ cup firmly packed light brown sugar
½ cup unsalted butter, chilled and cut into
      8 pieces
¼ teaspoon pure vanilla extract
¼ teaspoon almond extract
½ cup sour cherry preserves
      Confectioners' sugar, for garnish

Preheat the oven to 350°F.

Chop ¼ cup of the almonds coarsely in a food processor with the metal blade, about 10 pulses. Remove and reserve.

Process the remaining ½ cup almonds, the flour, sugar, butter, vanilla, and almond extract until the mixture resembles coarse crumbs, about 20 seconds.

Reserve ½ cup of the crumb mixture and press the remainder into an ungreased 9-inch square baking pan.

Process the preserves until smooth, about 15 seconds. Spread over the crust and sprinkle with the reserved crumb mixture and chopped almonds.

Bake in the preheated oven until golden, about 30 minutes. Cool overnight and cut into 2¼-inch squares. Dust with the confectioners' sugar.

Makes 16 squares

Coconuts

Coconuts are the fruit of the tropical palm tree and are available in markets year-round. Their hard shell is covered on the outside with brown fiber and inside with dense white flesh, and contained within is a thin, mildly sweet liquid (not the same as coconut milk). Choose a coconut that is heavy for its size and one with plenty of liquid. Shake the coconut close to your ear to hear the liquid inside. The coconut can be cracked by baking it for about 15 minutes in a 350°F oven for 15 minutes and then opening it with a hammer or heavy cleaver (see Rich Coconut Milk on page 198 for details on opening). Remove the coconut meat by levering it out carefully with the point of a strong knife or small screwdriver, making sure to shave off any brown fiber. Shred the coconut meat in a food processor or shave it with a vegetable peeler.

Fresh Spinach and Coconut Soup

1 pound fresh spinach, with stems, but
   roots trimmed
1 medium firm lemon, scored and ends
   cut flat
2 medium onions (8 ounces total), peeled
   and quartered
2 tablespoons unsalted butter
3 one-inch squares fresh coconut (2 ounces
   total), shelled and peeled
4 cups chicken broth
½ teaspoon freshly grated nutmeg
   Salt and freshly ground black pepper
   Plain yogurt, for serving

Wash the spinach thoroughly; do not dry. In a dry 3-quart saucepan over high heat, cook the spinach in the water clinging to its leaves. As soon as it wilts, put it in a colander and rinse with cold running water until completely cold. Press out the liquid and set aside.

Slice the lemon in a processor with the thin slicing disc, using firm pressure. Remove and reserve for garnish.

With the medium slicing disc, slice the onions using moderate pressure. Melt the butter in a 3-quart saucepan over moderate heat and cook the onions for 10 minutes, until soft but not brown.

Shred the coconut in the processor with the shredding disc, using firm pressure. Add it, along with the broth, to the onions. Simmer gently, covered, for 20 minutes.

Strain out the onions and coconut, reserving the liquid. Fit the processor with the metal blade and add the onions and coconut; process for 10 seconds. Add the spinach and ½ cup of the reserved liquid; process for 1 minute, stopping once to scrape down the sides of the workbowl. Return this mixture and the reserved liquid to the saucepan and heat thoroughly; then season. The soup can be served hot or cold. If you serve it cold, you can stir in 3 tablespoons of yogurt for every cup of soup. Garnish with the lemon slices.

Serves 6 to 12

[ROGER VERGÉ/
ABBY MANDEL]

Coconut Bread

In Guatemala, village women sell coconut bread from huge baskets balanced on their heads. Copeland Marks met a group of them and they gave him their recipe. It was the inspiration for this recipe.

½ cup Rich Coconut Milk (page 198)
2 tablespoons honey
1 package dry yeast
2 large eggs
3 cups unbleached all-purpose flour
¼ teaspoon salt

3 tablespoons unsalted butter, at room
temperature, cut into 3 pieces

In a small saucepan, warm ¼ cup of the Rich
Coconut Milk to 110°F. Stir in the honey and
yeast and leave for 10 minutes. In a 1-cup
measure, stir the remaining ¼ cup coconut
milk and the eggs briskly with a fork and set
aside.

Process the flour, salt, and butter in a food
processor with the metal blade just to mix, 10
seconds. With the motor running, add the
yeast mixture, then the coconut milk and egg
mixture, through the feed tube in a steady
stream as fast as the flour absorbs it. Continue
processing for 45 seconds more to knead the
dough.

With lightly floured hands, remove the
dough from the processor and form it into a
ball. Put it in a lightly floured 1-gallon plastic
bag and close the end with a wire twist, leaving space for the dough to rise. Leave in a
warm place (about 80°F) to rise until doubled, about 1½ hours.

Remove the twist and punch down the
dough in the bag. Remove from the bag,
shape into a loaf, and place in an oiled 9 × 5
× 3-inch bread pan. Cover with oiled plastic
wrap and leave to rise until doubled, about
1 hour.

Adjust the rack to the middle of the oven
and preheat the oven to 375°F. Bake the
bread for 35 to 40 minutes, or until it is nicely
browned and sounds hollow when tapped.
Remove from the pan and cool on a wire
rack.

Makes one 1½-pound loaf

[C O P E L A N D   M A R K S]

Striped Bass in Ginger-Green Chili Coconut Sauce

A dish from Kerala, in southern India, where
curry is called *moolee* and rice is a staple.
Serve with boiled rice or rice noodles and
spicy lemon or lime pickle.

2 large onions, peeled and quartered
6 tablespoons vegetable oil
2 tablespoons ground coriander
1 large garlic clove, peeled and minced
 Rich Coconut Milk (recipe follows)
 Salt

1 whole striped bass or sea bass (about 2 to
 2½ pounds), cleaned, with head and
 tail left on
6 to 8 red lettuce leaves (optional), washed
 and dried
4 fresh green chilies (serrano or jalapeño),
 stemmed and seeded
2 pieces fresh ginger (each about 2 × ¾
 inches), peeled and halved
¼ cup chopped fresh cilantro, for garnish
¼ cup shredded coconut, for garnish

Process the onions, in 2 batches, in a food processor with the metal blade, pulsing 12 to 14 times or until minced.

Heat the oil in a large skillet over moderately high heat. Add the minced onions and cook, stirring, until soft, about 5 minutes. Reduce the heat to moderate and stir in the ground coriander and minced garlic; cook for 1 minute more. Add the Rich Coconut Milk and salt to taste and bring to a boil over high heat. Reduce the heat and simmer, uncovered, for 15 minutes, stirring occasionally. The sauce should be thick and pulpy.

Meanwhile, cover one side of the fish with the lettuce leaves, if used. Bring water to a boil in a steamer; place the fish, with the lettuce leaves on top, in the steamer, cover, and cook for 15 minutes. Remove the steamer from the heat (see note below).

While the fish is cooking, chop the chilies and ginger in the processor with the metal blade, pulsing about 20 times or until finely chopped. When the coconut milk sauce has thickened, stir in the chilies and ginger and cook for 4 minutes (if the sauce seems too thin, raise the heat to high and boil for a few minutes before adding the chilies and ginger).

To serve, transfer the fish to a serving dish. Remove the lettuce leaves and discard. Pour the sauce over the fish and garnish with the cilantro and coconut.

Serves 4 to 6

NOTE: If you do not have a fish steamer, put a cake rack in a roasting pan large enough to hold the fish and add ¼ inch of water. Bring the water to a boil over high heat. Put the fish on the cake rack and cover the roasting pan tightly with aluminum foil.)

[J U L I E   S A H N I]

Rich Coconut Milk

1 coconut
1¾ cups hot water
1½ cups hot milk

Preheat the oven to 400°F.

Bake the coconut until the shell cracks, about 15 minutes; cool until easy to handle.

Put the coconut inside two plastic bags and seal them with a wire twist. With a hammer, crack the shell open. Discard the liquid and separate the meat from the shell. With a vegetable peeler, remove the brown skin from the meat; cut the meat into 1-inch pieces.

Process half the coconut in a food processor with the metal blade, pulsing 10 times or until the meat is coarsely chopped. With the motor running, add the hot water through the feed tube and process for 1 minute. Transfer to a mixing bowl and repeat with the remaining coconut meat and the milk.

Let the coconut mixture stand for 15 minutes, then strain it through a colander lined with dampened cheesecloth, pressing down to extract as much liquid as possible. The coconut milk may be refrigerated in a covered container for up to 4 days or frozen for up to 3 months.

Makes about 2½ cups

[JULIE SAHNI]

Coconut Flans

- 1 cup firmly packed light brown sugar
- 2 tablespoons water
- 4 large eggs
- 2 large egg yolks
- 2 teaspoons pure vanilla extract
- ¾ cup sugar
- 1 cup Fresh Coconut Milk (recipe follows)
- 1 cup heavy cream
- 1 cup finely chopped fresh coconut, reserved from making Fresh Coconut Milk

Preheat the oven to 350°F.

Combine the brown sugar and water in a saucepan and bring to a boil over high heat. Boil until caramel-colored, about 30 seconds, stirring constantly. Remove from the heat and divide among eight ½-cup custard cups or ramekins. Set aside.

Process the eggs, egg yolks, and vanilla in a food processor with the metal blade until blended, about 3 seconds. Add the sugar, Fresh Coconut Milk, and cream and pulse until combined, about 5 times. Transfer to a bowl and stir in the coconut.

Divide among the prepared cups, stirring to distribute the coconut evenly. Place the cups in a baking pan and add enough boiling water to the pan to reach halfway up the cups. Bake in the preheated oven until set, 45 to 50 minutes. Remove the cups from the pan and cool.

To unmold, run a sharp knife around the inside edge of each cup. Invert a serving plate over each cup and invert the flans onto the plates.

Serves 8

[GAYLE HENDERSON WILSON]

Fresh Coconut Milk

1 small coconut (about 1 pound)
1¼ cups boiling water

Preheat the oven to 400°F.

Punch a hole in each eye of the coconut with a hammer and ice pick. Drain out the liquid.

Bake the coconut on a baking sheet in the preheated oven until the coconut cracks, about 30 minutes. Wrap in a towel, crack the shell into pieces with a hammer, and separate the meat from the shell. Use a vegetable peeler to remove the brown skin from the meat.

Chop the meat fine in a food processor with the metal blade, about 15 seconds. Reserve 1 cup for the Coconut Flans. With the motor running, pour the boiling water through the feed tube and process with the remaining coconut for 30 seconds. Let stand for 10 minutes and strain, discarding the solids.

Makes about 1 cup

[GAYLE HENDERSON WILSON]

Cranberries

Cranberries grow on low vines in sandy bogs and are harvested by flooding the bogs with water—a scarlet sea of floating berries. Cranberries grow in the cooler northern climes of the United States, particularly in Massachusetts. Although available only for three months, from October to December, cranberries store well and can be frozen and enjoyed throughout the year. Look for cranberries that are firm and uniform in color, without any signs of shriveling. Because of their tartness, cranberries are usually cooked and combined with sweeter fruit. They are suitable in both sweet and savory dishes.

Yam Timbales with Cranberry Purée

1 pound fresh yams
2 large eggs
1 large egg yolk
1 cup heavy cream
1 tablespoon light brown sugar
½ teaspoon salt
½ teaspoon ground cinnamon
   Cranberry Purée (recipe follows)

Preheat the oven to 400°F.

Bake the yams for 30 to 40 minutes, or until tender. Cool until comfortable to handle, then peel and cut into 1-inch pieces. Reduce the oven temperature to 350°F.

Add the yams to a food processor fitted with the metal blade. Pulse 5 times, then process the yams continuously until smooth, about 1 minute, stopping once to scrape down the sides of the workbowl. Add the eggs, egg yolk, cream, brown sugar, salt, and cinnamon; turn the machine on and off 5 times, scrape down the workbowl, and then process for about 5 seconds.

Generously butter six ½-cup timbale molds and fill them with the yam mixture. In a baking pan large enough to hold the molds with a little space between them pour in boiling water to a depth of 1 inch. Put the timbales in the water, cover loosely with foil, and bake for 45 minutes or until a knife inserted in the center comes out clean.

Let stand for 10 minutes while you prepare the Cranberry Purée. Then run a knife around the inside edge of each mold and invert a serving plate over the mold. Invert the timbales onto the plate. Spoon the Cranberry Purée over the timbales.

Serves 6 as an appetizer or side dish

[MARLENE SOROSKY]

Cranberry Purée

1 can (8 ounces) whole cranberry sauce
¼ cup water
2 tablespoons fresh lemon juice

Process the cranberry sauce, water, and lemon juice in a food processor with the metal blade until thick and smooth, about 45 seconds. Transfer to a 1-quart saucepan and stir over moderate heat until warm.

Makes about 1½ cups

[MARLENE SOROSKY]

Turkey, Ham, and Cranberry Pie

Twenty-four hours must be allowed for chilling the pie, and 2 more hours for the Cranberry Port Topping to set.

    Raised Crust (recipe follows)
2   tablespoons whole-grain mustard

First Layer

1   small garlic clove
1   pound boneless pork loin, cut into 1-inch pieces, chilled
2   ounces smoked ham, cut into 1-inch pieces
1   large egg
1   teaspoon salt
½   teaspoon coarsely ground black pepper
⅛   teaspoon ground allspice
¼   teaspoon freshly grated nutmeg
3   tablespoons brandy
12 ounces thinly sliced raw dark turkey meat
1   tablespoon whole-grain mustard

Second Layer

¼   cup loosely packed parsley leaves
8   slices whole-wheat bread (3¾ × 3½ × ⅜ inches each), untrimmed, quartered
4   tablespoons unsalted butter
1   small onion, peeled and finely chopped
1   teaspoon dried thyme leaves
½   cup chicken stock, preferably homemade
1   large egg, lightly beaten

Third Layer

10 ounces thinly sliced smoked ham
1   pound thinly sliced raw turkey breast
1   tablespoon brandy
1   tablespoon whole-grain mustard

    Cranberry Port Topping (recipe follows)

Prepare the crust according to the directions for Raised Crust. After the dough has been kneaded into a ball, roll it into a 16-inch circle, ⅜ inch thick. Lightly flour the dough. Fold it in half; fold in half again, forming a triangular shape. Place in a 9 × 2¾-inch springform pan with the point of the dough in the center and the remaining dough draped up the side. Unfold the circle and press the dough onto the bottom and against the sides of the pan. Trim the overhang to ½ inch. Brush the bottom and sides of the crust with the 2 tablespoons mustard.

Preheat the oven to 300°F.

To make the first layer: Drop the garlic through the feed tube of a food processor with the metal blade in place and the motor running. Process until finely chopped, about 5 seconds. Add the pork and ham and finely chop, 8 to 10 pulses, scraping down the workbowl as necessary. Add the egg, salt, pepper, allspice, nutmeg, and 2 tablespoons of the brandy and process until the mixture is smooth, about 2 minutes. Spread it evenly on the bottom of the prepared crust. Cover with the dark turkey meat and brush with the mustard and remaining 1 tablespoon brandy.

To make the second layer: Process the parsley until finely chopped, about 10 seconds. Coarsely chop the bread in 2 batches, about 5 pulses for each batch. Transfer to a bowl.

Sauté the onion in the butter in a small skillet, until soft but not brown, about 3 minutes.

Add the onion, thyme, chicken stock, and egg to the bread crumbs and mix. Spread the mixture over the dark turkey meat.

To make the third layer: Arrange the sliced ham, then the sliced turkey breast over the bread layer. Brush with the brandy and mustard.

Turn the crust overhang to the inside and pinch to make a decorative edge. Place a circle of wax paper over the meat filling and cover with aluminum foil.

Bake in the center of the preheated oven until the filling is cooked, about 2¼ to 2½ hours (it should register 165°F on an instant reading thermometer).

To compress the filling, put a 3-pound weight in an 8-inch round cake pan and place it on top of the pie.

Cool the pie to room temperature, then refrigerate it for 24 hours.

Remove the weight, foil, and wax paper. Release the sides of the pan and slide the pie onto a serving plate. Spread the Cranberry Port Topping around the edge and chill the pie for 2 hours, or until the topping is firm.

Cut into wedges to serve.

Serves 10 as an entrée or 20 as an appetizer

[B E A T R I C E   O J A K A N G A S]

Raised Crust

3½ cups unbleached all-purpose flour
 1 teaspoon salt
 1 teaspoon sugar
 ¾ cup lard cut into 1-inch pieces, chilled
 1 large egg
 ⅔ cup cold water

Pulse the flour, salt, sugar, and lard in a food processor with the metal blade until the lard is coarsely chopped, about 6 pulses. Stir the egg into the water in a small glass measure, and with the motor running, pour the liquid through the feed tube. Process just until the dough holds together.

On a floured surface, knead the dough into a smooth ball.

[B E A T R I C E   O J A K A N G A S]

Cranberry Port Topping

⅓ cup water
⅓ cup sugar
1 cup fresh or frozen cranberries
1½ teaspoons unflavored gelatin
1½ tablespoons ruby port

Bring the water and sugar to a boil in a small saucepan. Add the cranberries and simmer, uncovered, for 10 minutes. Dissolve the gelatin in the port and stir into the cranberry mixture. Cool to room temperature.

Makes about 1 cup

[BEATRICE OJAKANGAS]

Cranberry Bread

This quick bread is not overly sweet and can accompany most meals. Fold the berries in carefully so that they are evenly distributed throughout the bread; avoid crushing them. The springform pan gives an unusual shape to the bread.

⅓ cup bran flakes
3¼ cups unbleached all-purpose flour
1 teaspoon salt
1 tablespoon sugar
1 teaspoon baking powder
1 teaspoon baking soda
4 tablespoons unsalted butter, cut into 6 pieces
1⅓ cups milk
2 large eggs
1½ cups fresh or frozen cranberries
½ cup chopped walnuts

Preheat the oven to 350°F. Butter an 8 × 2½-inch springform pan.

Combine the bran flakes, flour, salt, sugar, baking powder, and baking soda in a large bowl. Heat the butter and milk in a small saucepan, stirring, until the butter has melted. Pour the hot liquid over the dry ingredients and stir to mix. Beat the eggs with a fork and add to the contents of the bowl.

Fold in the cranberries and walnuts, being careful not to overmix. Scrape the batter into the prepared springform pan and place on a baking sheet.

Bake in the lower third of the preheated oven for 55 to 60 minutes. Cool the bread in the pan on a wire rack for about 20 minutes before removing the sides of the pan.

Serves 10 to 12

[JACQUES PÉPIN]

Grapes

There are grapes grown specifically for winemaking, and then there are grapes grown for the table. Winemaking grapes generally have a high acidity and are sharp tasting, which makes them too tart for eating out of hand, whereas table grapes have a low acidity and would produce bland wine. There are thousands of grape varieties, from those with seeds to those without, from those with slip-off skins to those that cling hard to their skins, from deep purple to green ones. Grapes grow in small clusters on bushes in temperate climates around the world and are available year-round. They are more often eaten raw than cooked. Choose those that are plump and firm with fresh stems.

Herb Cream from Zaragoza with Fried Croutons and White Grapes

3 slices firm white bread, about ⅜ inch thick, crusts removed and dried for 10 minutes in a 200°F oven
¼ cup fresh chives
¼ cup parsley leaves
½ teaspoon fresh thyme or ¼ teaspoon dried thyme
3 tablespoons fresh watercress leaves
½ teaspoon fresh sage leaves or ¼ teaspoon dried sage
4 small heads Bibb lettuce, cored, washed, and patted dry
6 tablespoons unsalted butter
4 cups chicken or veal stock, preferably homemade
¾ teaspoon salt
1 cup heavy cream
2 large egg yolks
1 teaspoon Cognac
Freshly ground white pepper
36 small green seedless grapes

Quarter the bread slices and process in a food processor with the metal blade until coarsely chopped, about 10 pulses. Remove and reserve.

Add the chives, parsley, thyme, watercress, and sage to the processor and process to a medium-fine chop, about 8 pulses. Remove and reserve.

Place each head of lettuce, cored side down, in the feed tube and process with the medium slicing disc, using light pressure. Empty the workbowl as necessary.

Melt 4 tablespoons of the butter in a large saucepot over moderate heat. Cook the lettuce, stirring, until just wilted, about 1 minute. Add the stock and chopped herbs and heat just to a boil, stirring frequently. Remove from the heat and let stand, covered, for 10 minutes.

Meanwhile, melt the remaining 2 tablespoons butter in a medium skillet over moderately low heat. Add the reserved bread crumbs and ¼ teaspoon salt and cook, stirring, until the crumbs are crisp and golden brown, about 2 minutes. Keep warm while finishing the soup.

Place the lettuce mixture back on the heat and bring to just below a boil. Whisk the cream, egg yolks, cognac, pepper, and remaining salt together in a medium bowl. Slowly whisk in 1 cup of the hot lettuce mixture. Whisk in 1 more cup, then stir the warmed cream-egg mixture back into the saucepot. Heat through, but do not boil.

Divide the soup among 6 individual serving bowls. Sprinkle about 2 teaspoons of the warm bread crumbs and 6 grapes over each portion. Serve immediately.

Serves 6

[ELENE MARGOT KOLB]

Lemon Rice with Grapes

This is an unexpected combination that is sensational as part of a cold buffet. It goes best with delicate foods, such as veal or cold poached chicken breasts in aspic.

3   tablespoons unsalted butter
2   cups long-grain white rice
4   cups boiling water
    Salt
2   large lemons
2   cups green seedless grapes, sliced in half
    lengthwise

Heat the butter in a 3-quart saucepan over medium heat. Add the rice and cook, stirring constantly, for 2 to 3 minutes, or until the rice becomes opaque. Stir in the boiling water and add salt to taste. When the liquid returns to the boil, cover the pan, reduce the heat to low, and cook for 18 minutes. Do not stir.

Remove the pan from the heat. Uncover, place 2 kitchen towels over the pot, replace the lid over the towels, and let stand for 20 minutes.

Fluff the rice with 2 forks and transfer to a 3-quart serving dish. Cover with a towel and let stand for 30 minutes. Meanwhile, grate the zest of the lemons and reserve. Juice both lemons. Combine the halved grapes and half of the lemon juice in a shallow bowl and let stand for 30 minutes.

Add the reserved lemon zest and the remaining lemon juice to the rice and toss. Add the grapes with the lemon juice and toss again.

Serves 10 to 12

[R U T H   S P E A R]

Mixed Fruit in Armagnac

2½ pounds fresh fruit (use a mixture of
    cherries, raspberries, strawberries,
    mirabelles, grapes, and green plums)
½   cup sugar
1   bottle (approximately ⅕ quart)
    Armagnac

Prepare the fruit as follows: stem, wash and dry cherries; pick over and rinse raspberries, discarding any that are damaged or moldy; wash, hull, and dry strawberries; stem, wash and dry mirabelles, grapes, and green plums. Mix the fruits together in a large bowl. Pack loosely into glass jars with tightly fitting covers.

Combine the sugar and Armagnac; stir until the sugar is completely dissolved. Fill the jars of fruit with the lightly sweetened Armagnac; cap and allow to ripen in a dark place for at least 2 weeks before serving. The fruit will keep for up to 3 months.

Makes 2 quarts

[J E A N - J A C Q U E S   J O U T E U X /
N A O M I   B A R R Y]

Grapefruit

This large yellow citrus fruit is loved for its tart yet sweet juicy flesh. The sharp refreshing juice is especially good at breakfast time. Available year-round—from Florida, California, Texas, and Arizona—grapefruit is grown in clusters like grapes, hence its name. Their flesh can range from pale white to a brilliant ruby red, which contains more vitamin A. Choose those that are thin-skinned without blemishes and are heavy for their size—a sure sign of juiciness. After 2 days at room temperature, store grapefruit in the refrigerator, where they ought to last a couple of days more.

Pico de Gallo
Grapefruit Medley

- 3 large grapefruits
- 1 small sweet red pepper, cored, seeded, and cut into ¼-inch dice
- 2 tablespoons minced parsley
- 2 teaspoons minced onion
- ½ teaspoon red pepper flakes
- ½ teaspoon salt

With a serrated knife, peel the grapefruits, taking care to remove all of the white pith.

With a small sharp knife, cut out the grapefruit segments, discarding the membranes.

Cut the segments into ½-inch pieces and put them into a 2-quart bowl. Add the remaining ingredients and stir gently to mix. Refrigerate for at least 1 hour before serving.

Serves 6 to 8

[C O P E L A N D   M A R K S]

Tangy Pink Grapefruit Marmalade

- 2 small pink grapefruits (1½ to 1¾ pounds), cut vertically into quarters
- 3½ cups sugar

Remove any visible grapefruit seeds with a paring knife.

Use a food processor fitted with the medium serrated slicing disc to process the grapefruit quarters, using light pressure. Empty the grapefruit into a plastic bag. Insert the metal blade, return the sliced fruit to the workbowl, and process for about 20 seconds until finely chopped. Return the processed grapefruit to the plastic bag and close bag tightly with a twist. Place the first bag in a second one to catch any leakage. Refrigerate 24 hours.

Stir together the grapefruit and sugar in a nonreactive 2-quart saucepan. Bring to a boil, stirring frequently, then reduce to a slow boil. Cook over moderately high heat for about 25 to 30 minutes, or until mixture reaches 220°F on a candy thermometer.

Remove from the heat. Place in half-pint jars, screw on covers, and store in the refrigerator. Opened jars of marmalade will keep for weeks without refrigeration.

Makes about 3½ cups

Kiwis

Egglike in shape and size with brown fuzzy skin, the kiwi's beautiful, brilliant green flesh with central tiny black edible seeds is delicious eaten raw. The flavor is sweet, with a touch of tartness. Kiwis are grown in both the Northern and Southern Hemispheres and therefore are available year-round. Look for somewhat firm fruit and avoid shriveled ones. They can be stored in the refrigerator for 2 weeks. Peel them before eating.

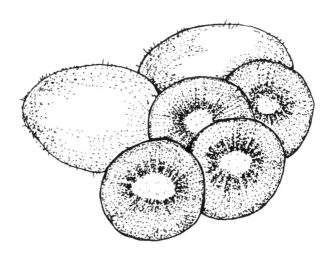

Kiwi Fluff

Please note: This recipe uses raw egg whites. If eggs are a problem in your area, do not prepare this recipe. Be sure to use salmonella-free eggs.

- 12 ounces frozen kiwi, peeled and cut into 1-inch pieces
- 2 large egg whites
- 1 tablespoon fresh lemon juice
- ¼ to ⅓ cup sugar (more or less depending on the sweetness of the fruit)
- 1 tablespoon fruit liqueur or spirits

Finely chop the frozen fruit in a food processor with the metal blade, scraping down the sides of the workbowl and top as necessary. The fruit should look somewhat like powdered ice.

If you have a whisk adaptor for your processor (see note below), remove the metal blade. Lock the whisk adaptor to the motor shaft of the food processor and add the remaining ingredients. Connect the power unit to the adaptor with the whisks in place, pushing down as far as the unit will go.

Let the motor run until the mixture is thick and fluffy and reaches the top of the beaters. Stop once to scrape the frozen fruit from the sides of the workbowl. This will take from 3 to 5 minutes.

The fluff can be served immediately or spooned into parfait glasses or serving dishes and placed in the freezer for up to 2 hours. It can also be frozen solid, covered, for up to 2 days. If frozen solid, remove from the freezer 10 to 15 minutes before serving to soften.

Serves 6

NOTE: Alternatively, the fluff can be made with a hand-held electric mixer: Chop the fruit with the metal blade as directed above, then transfer to a large flat-bottomed mixing bowl or the bowl of a stand mixer. Add the remaining ingredients and beat at high speed, scraping down the sides of the bowl with a spatula, if necessary, until the mixture is thick, fluffy, and has about tripled in volume, about 10 minutes.

[S U Z A N N E   S .   J O N E S]

Kiwi Fruit Soufflé

To achieve the best results, be sure to follow the cooking instructions to the letter.

⅓ cup plus 2 tablespoons puréed kiwi, strained of all seeds (from 3 kiwis weighing about 9 ounces total)
1 tablespoon fresh lime juice
2 large egg yolks
5 tablespoons plus 2 teaspoons granulated sugar
4 large egg whites, at room temperature
2 teaspoons confectioners' sugar

Set the oven rack in the lower third of the oven. Place a baking sheet on the rack. Preheat the oven to 400°F.

Prepare a flameproof baking pan large enough to hold four or five ½-cup soufflé dishes. Line the bottom of the pan with a folded kitchen towel to cushion the soufflé dishes. Pour in ¾ inch of water. Place the pan over moderately low heat: the water should be simmering when the soufflés are placed in it. Bring 2 quarts of water to a simmer in a tea kettle.

Generously butter the insides and rims of the soufflé dishes.

In a small nonreactive skillet over medium heat, cook the 2 tablespoons kiwi purée until it reduces to 1 tablespoon. Remove from the heat and add the lime juice.

In a 1-quart bowl, use a whisk to beat the egg yolks with 2 tablespoons plus 1 teaspoon of the granulated sugar until they are thick and light-colored. Whisk in 1 tablespoon of the kiwi and lime mixture. Set the mixture aside.

Put the egg whites with 2 tablespoons plus 1 teaspoon of the granulated sugar into another 1-quart bowl. Beat with a hand-held electric mixer until soft mounds form—neither stiff peaks nor foamy and runny. Carefully beat in the remaining kiwi and lime mixture. Gently but thoroughly fold a quarter of the yolk mixture into the whites, then fold in the remainder.

Working quickly, fill the soufflé dishes to the top. With the straight edge of a knife, smooth the surface of each dish. Run a finger around the inside of the rim to form a channel about ¼ inch deep.

Place the soufflé dishes in the simmering water in the baking pan; the water should come halfway up the sides of the dishes. If it doesn't, add more from the kettle. Simmer on top of the stove for 5 minutes: the soufflés will look poached and slightly puffy.

With a wide metal spatula, quickly transfer the dishes to the baking sheet in the preheated oven. Bake for about 5 minutes, until the soufflés are risen and a light golden brown.

While the soufflés bake, make the kiwi sauce by stirring together the ⅓ cup kiwi purée with the remaining 1 tablespoon sugar until the sugar dissolves.

Open the oven and pull out the baking sheet just far enough so you can shake the confectioners' sugar over each soufflé. Bake for 1 minute longer, until the edges of the soufflés are dark brown.

Serve the soufflés immediately, with a tablespoon of the sauce spooned into the center of each.

Serves 4 to 5

[FRÉDY GIRARDET/ ABBY MANDEL]

Kiwi Sherbet

2 pounds kiwis, peeled and quartered
½ cup sugar
   Lemon juice to taste
   Vitamin C powder (ascorbic acid powder), to prevent discoloration

Put all the ingredients in a food processor fitted with the metal blade. Process until the fruit is finely puréed, stopping as necessary to scrape down the bowl. The time required depends on the texture of the fruit. Sieve to remove the seeds.

Spread the purée in an 8-inch aluminum cake pan and freeze it until not quite firm. Scoop it back into the processor and process again until smooth and fluffy.

Transfer the sherbet to an airtight freezer container and freeze again for 1 to 2 hours, until almost firm, before serving. If the sherbet freezes solid, let it soften in the refrigerator for 30 to 45 minutes before you serve it.

Makes 3 to 4 servings

Lemons

Lemons are indispensable in the kitchen. They brighten sauces, salad dressings, fish and poultry dishes, beverages, and fruit desserts. Lemons are in the market year-round, though they're at their peak in the summer. Select fruit that is heavy for its size, with brightly colored smooth skin. Lemons don't need to be stored in the refrigerator and, in fact, you'll get more juice from a lemon at room temperature. Whenever possible, use fresh lemon juice rather than frozen and bottled juices—they may contain preservatives and can never match the flavor of fresh lemons.

Lemon and Egg Soup

4 cups chicken stock, preferably home-
    made
    Zest of 1 medium lemon
1½ ounces Parmesan cheese, cut into 1-inch
    pieces
1 slice dry Italian bread (about 1 inch
    thick), crust removed, quartered
4 large eggs
3 tablespoons fresh lemon juice
    Salt and freshly ground white pepper
¼ cup finely chopped parsley, for garnish

Bring the stock to a boil in a medium saucepan.

Process the lemon zest, Parmesan, and
bread in a food processor fitted with the metal blade by pulsing 4 times, then processing continuously for 1 minute until finely
chopped. Add the eggs and lemon juice and
process 5 seconds to combine.

With the motor running, pour 1 cup of the
boiling stock through the feed tube. Whisk the
contents of the workbowl into the remaining
stock in the saucepan and cook, whisking constantly, until the soup is hot but not boiling.

Season to taste and serve immediately, garnished with the chopped parsley.

Serves 6

[LORENZA DE MEDICI/
ABBY MANDEL]

Lemon Flavored Lamb Stew

2 medium lemons, peeled, ends cut flat
2 small green peppers, cored, seeded, and
    cut vertically into 3 pieces
3 large leeks, trimmed of all but 1 inch of
    greens, washed
1 piece fresh ginger (about 1 by ½-inch),
    peeled
2 medium onions (about 10 ounces total),
    peeled and quartered
2 tablespoons lard
2¼ pounds lean lamb, cut into 2-inch cubes
2½ cups beef broth, preferably homemade
    Salt and freshly ground black pepper
2½ tablespoons unsalted peanuts
1 tablespoon unsalted butter

Process the lemons in a food processor with
the medium slicing disc. Remove and reserve.

Stack the pepper pieces upright in the
feed tube and process. Cut the leeks into
3-inch pieces. Stack them vertically in the
feed tube and process. Remove the peppers
and leeks and set aside.

Insert the metal blade in the processor.
With the motor running, drop the ginger
through the feed tube and process until finely
chopped, about 5 seconds. Add the onion and
process until coarsely chopped, about 5
pulses.

Melt 1 tablespoon of the lard in a large
stockpot over moderately high heat. Add half

the lamb cubes and cook about 5 minutes, turning often, until browned on all sides. Remove the lamb cubes to a plate. Repeat with the remaining 1 tablespoon lard and lamb cubes.

Add the peppers, leeks, ginger, and onion to the stockpot and cook, stirring, until the vegetables are limp, about 5 minutes.

Add the cooked lamb, lemon slices, beef broth, salt, and pepper to the stockpot and simmer, covered, for 35 minutes. Remove the cover and simmer 10 minutes more.

While the mixture is simmering, drop the peanuts through the feed tube of the processor with the metal blade in place and the motor running. Process until the peanuts are finely chopped, about 15 seconds. Add the butter and process to mix. Five minutes before serving, stir the butter-peanut mixture into the lamb stew.

Serves 4 to 6

[SOLANGE HESS]

Greek Lemon Chicken

2 whole chickens (about 3 pounds each)
2 large lemons
4 garlic cloves, peeled
2 teaspoons salt
1 teaspoon freshly ground black pepper
1 tablespoon dried oregano
¾ cup olive oil
2 medium onions (about 10 ounces total), peeled and cut in half
4 medium carrots (about 12 ounces total), trimmed, peeled, and cut to fit the feed tube of a food processor vertically
4 medium celery ribs (12 ounces total), trimmed and sliced into ¼-inch diagonal pieces
6 medium all-purpose potatoes (about 2¼ pounds total), peeled and cut into 2-inch cubes
⅔ cup fresh lemon juice
⅔ cup chicken stock, preferably home-made

½ cup unsalted butter, melted
    Greek olives, for garnish (optional)

Rinse the chickens and pat them dry; discard excess fat. Pierce the lemons at ¼-inch intervals with a two-tined kitchen fork. Place a lemon in the cavity of each chicken and close the opening with metal skewers or a trussing needle and twine.

Preheat the oven to 500°F.

Drop the garlic through the feed tube of a food processor with the metal blade in place and the motor running. Process until finely chopped, about 10 seconds. Scrape down the workbowl, add the salt, pepper, oregano, and ½ cup of the oil and process 10 seconds. Rub the mixture over both chickens.

Insert the medium slicing disc. Place the onions cut side down in the feed tube and process. Stack the carrots vertically in the feed tube and process.

217

Lemons

Place the onion, carrots, celery, and potatoes in the bottom of a large roasting pan. Place the chickens, breast side up, over the vegetables. Stir together in a bowl the lemon juice, chicken broth, butter, and remaining ¼ cup olive oil and pour over the chicken and vegetables.

Bake the chickens, uncovered, in the center of the preheated oven for 20 minutes. Turn them over and bake 20 minutes more, basting the chickens and vegetables with the pan juices every 10 minutes. Reduce the oven heat to 450°F and turn the chickens breast side up. Bake 20 minutes more, basting twice.

Remove the pan from the oven and transfer the chickens to a cutting board. Keep the vegetables warm. Let the chickens rest for 10 minutes, then remove the lemons from the cavities.

Quarter the chickens, removing the backbone and keeping the wings attached to the breast pieces. Arrange the chicken and vegetables on a platter, and degrease the pan juices. Cut the lemons in half and squeeze the juice over the chicken and vegetables. Garnish with olives and pass the pan juices separately.

Serves 8

[M A R L E N E   S O R O S K Y]

Lemon Pecan Popovers with Lemon Honey Butter

2   cups unbleached all-purpose flour
¼   cup pecans
2   cups milk
4   large eggs
¾   teaspoon salt
2   teaspoons finely grated lemon zest
    Lemon Honey Butter (recipe follows)

Preheat the oven to 425°F.

Process the flour and pecans in a food processor with the metal blade until the nuts are finely chopped, about 30 seconds. Remove and reserve. Add the milk, eggs, and salt to the processor and process for about 5 seconds, or until well mixed. Add the reserved mixture and the lemon zest and turn the machine on and off 3 or 4 times, or until the flour just disappears.

Butter the bottoms of twelve 6-ounce muffin-tin cups. Divide the batter evenly among the cups, filling each about two-thirds full. Bake for 30 to 35 minutes, or until the popovers are puffed and browned. Serve immediately with the Lemon Honey Butter.

Makes 12 popovers

[M A R L E N E   S O R O S K Y]

Lemon Honey Butter

½ cup unsalted butter, softened
2 tablespoons honey
2 tablespoons finely grated lemon zest
2 teaspoons fresh lemon juice

Process all of the ingredients in a food processor with the metal blade until the mixture is smooth, about 15 seconds, scraping down the workbowl once or twice.

Makes about ½ cup

[MARLENE SOROSKY]

Lemon Soufflé Tart

4 large eggs, separated
6 tablespoons granulated sugar
⅔ cup fresh lemon juice
4 tablespoons unsalted butter, cut into
    4 pieces
⅛ teaspoon salt
½ cup superfine sugar
1 baked 11-inch Pâte Brisée Shell (recipe
    follows)
2 tablespoons confectioners' sugar

Beat the egg yolks and sugar together in a large bowl with an electric mixer until the mixture forms a ribbon, about 5 minutes. Stir in the lemon juice.

Pour the mixture into a medium saucepan and add the butter. Cook over moderately low heat, stirring constantly, until it thickens, about 6 to 8 minutes. Pour into a medium bowl, cover the top with a buttered round of wax paper, and refrigerate until cool, about 3 hours.

Place a baking sheet on a rack in the top third of the oven and preheat the oven to 375°F.

In a large bowl, beat the egg whites with the salt until soft peaks form. Add the superfine sugar, 2 tablespoons at a time. Continue to beat until the mixture is very firm and shiny.

Stir one fourth of the egg white mixture into the chilled egg yolk mixture. Fold in the remaining whites and pour into the baked pastry shell.

Bake the tart on the preheated baking sheet in the oven until it is puffed and golden, about 15 minutes. Remove the sides of the tart pan and place the tart on a wire rack until cool, about 1 hour.

Just before serving, sift the confectioners' sugar over the top of the tart.

Serves 12

[SALLY DARR]

Tangy Lime Marmalade

4 medium limes (about 14 ounces), cut crosswise in half

3¾ cups sugar

Remove any visible lime seeds with a paring knife.

Use medium serrated slicing disc to process lime halves, using light pressure. Empty fruit into a plastic bag. Insert metal blade, return sliced fruit to bowl and process for about 20 seconds until finely chopped. Return processed fruit to the plastic bag and close bag tightly with a twist. Place first bag in a second one to catch any leakage. Refrigerate 24 hours.

In a 2-quart saucepan, stir together processed fruit and sugar. Heat to a boil, stirring frequently, then reduce to a slow boil. Cook over moderately high heat for about 10 to 15 minutes, or until mixture reaches 220°F on a candy thermometer.

Remove from heat. Place in ½-pint jars, screw on covers, and store in refrigerator. Opened jars of marmalade will keep for weeks without refrigeration.

Makes about 3 cups

Broiled Fish Fillets with Ginger and Lime Sauce

Ginger Butter Mixture

1½ ounces fresh ginger, peeled and halved

1 teaspoon lime zest, removed with a zester

4 tablespoons unsalted butter, at room temperature

¼ teaspoon salt

1 teaspoon fresh lime juice

Fish Fillets

8 fillets of salmon or trout (about 6 ounces each), all the same shape

1 tablespoon vegetable oil

Coarse (kosher) salt

Freshly ground black pepper

1 lime, skin scored and ends trimmed, cut into 8 slices, for garnish

Lime Sauce (recipe follows)

To prepare the ginger butter mixture, drop the ginger and lime zest through the feed tube of a food processor with the metal blade in place and the motor running. Process until finely chopped. Add the butter, salt, and lime juice and process until smooth. Transfer the mixture to a small saucepan and cook over low heat for 5 minutes. Set aside until ready to use.

Preheat the broiler.

Wash the fish fillets and pat them dry with paper towels. Rub them with the oil and season generously with salt and pepper. Put the fillets on a greased broiler rack, skin side up, and broil 8 inches from the heat source for 3 minutes. Turn the fillets and brush them with the ginger butter mixture. Broil about 5 minutes, or until the fish is firm to the touch but not yet flaky.

Place the fillets on a serving platter and garnish each with a lime slice. Spoon the Lime Sauce sparingly over them.

Makes 8 servings

[FRÉDY GIRARDET/
ABBY MANDEL]

Lime Sauce

2 tablespoons fresh lime juice
¼ cup plus 3 tablespoons white port
¾ cup unsalted butter, chilled and cut into
   tablespoon-size pieces

In a 1-quart saucepan, cook the lime juice and port over moderately high heat until the liquid is reduced to 1 tablespoon. Add the butter, piece by piece, shaking the pan and stirring until each piece melts before adding the next. The sauce can be kept warm for 1 to 2 hours in a container set in warm water.

Makes about ¾ cup

Roast Capon with Green Peppercorns and Lime Sauce on a Bed of Endive

Quick roasting at a high temperature gives the capon very juicy meat and an exceptionally crisp skin. Admittedly, the method also makes a mess of splatterings in the oven; but the results are well worth the slight inconvenience. Lime juice and green peppercorns create a remarkably fresh tasting, slightly astringent sauce.

1 capon (5 to 6 pounds)
2 tablespoons vegetable oil
   Salt and freshly ground black pepper
   Sautéed Belgian Endive (recipe follows)
¾ cup ruby port

½ cup veal or beef stock, preferably homemade
½ cup chicken stock, preferably homemade
3 tablespoons green peppercorns, drained
2 tablespoons fresh lime juice
½ cup unsalted butter, chilled and cut into
   8 pieces
   Zest of 1 lime, in thin strips, for garnish

Set the rack in the middle of the oven and preheat to 475°F. Lightly grease a roasting pan with sides 2 to 3 inches high.

Rub the capon with the oil and season it

with salt and pepper. Place the capon on its side in the pan. Roast the capon 30 minutes in the preheated oven, turning the capon onto its other side after 15 minutes. After 30 minutes, remove the pan from the oven, spoon out the melted fat, and turn the capon back to the first side. Return it to the oven and lower the oven heat to 425°F. Cook 40 minutes, turning the bird over after 20 minutes.

While the capon finishes roasting, prepare the Sautéed Belgian Endive.

Remove the capon to a platter and pour out and discard the grease from the pan. Deglaze the pan with the port. Add the stocks and reduce them to ⅔ cup. Put the capon back in the pan and cook over high heat, spooning the juices over the capon until it is richly glazed. Spread out the Sautéed Belgian Endive on the serving platter and place the capon on top.

Strain the sauce into an 8-inch skillet. Add the green peppercorns and lime juice. Bring it to a boil; whisk in the butter a piece at a time, waiting until each piece is melted before adding the next. Pour the sauce over the capon and garnish with the lime zest.

Serves 6

[FRÉDY GIRARDET/ ABBY MANDEL]

Sautéed Belgian Endive

8 large heads Belgian endive (about 2 pounds total)
2 tablespoons fresh lemon juice
1 tablespoon plus 1 teaspoon sugar
1½ teaspoons salt
4 tablespoons unsalted butter
Freshly ground black pepper

Cut the endive crosswise into ½-inch thick slices. In a 10-inch sauté pan or skillet, combine the endive, lemon juice, the 1 tablespoon sugar, and 1 teaspoon of the salt. Toss the endive to mix with all the ingredients.

Cover the pan and cook over moderately high heat for 12 to 15 minutes, stirring occasionally. The endive should be cooked through but still retain some texture; there will be some liquid in the pan.

Lift the endive out with a slotted spoon, set it aside, and reduce the endive juices until the pan is almost dry. Return the cooked endive to the pan along with the 1 teaspoon sugar and the remaining ½ teaspoon salt, and the butter; stir over high heat until the butter is melted. Add the pepper, adjust the seasoning, and serve immediately.

Serves 6 to 8

[FRÉDY GIRARDET]

Mangoes

This luscious juicy fruit can be a mess to eat, but it's well worth it. When ripe, the skins of the many types (more than 500 varieties) turn red, yellow, orange, or purple and the flesh is soft to the touch. The exotically sweet fragrant flesh must be cut away from the large oval pit and skin. Native to India and Southeast Asia and grown throughout the tropics, the mango's peak season is May through August. At the market, choose fruit with unblemished yellow skin that has a tinge of red. They will ripen at home placed in a paper bag at room temperature. Once ripe, they can be stored in the refrigerator for a couple of days.

Glassy
Beef and Sweet Mango

The name "Glassy" is a mystery—the English-sounding word may be a mistranslation of a Hindustani name. Serve this warm, with Indian or French bread.

- 4 small new potatoes, peeled and halved
- 3 tablespoons vegetable oil
- 1 piece fresh ginger (½ × ½ inch), peeled
- 2 garlic cloves, peeled
- 1 small onion, peeled and quartered
- 1 teaspoon salt
- ¼ teaspoon freshly ground black pepper
- 1 pound boneless beef chuck, cut into strips about ¼ inch thick, 3 inches long, and 1 inch wide
- 1 cup water
- 1 ripe medium tomato, seeded and coarsely chopped
- 1 small whole fresh green chili, stem removed and a 1-inch slit cut horizontally in the side
- 2 tablespoons sweet mango chutney

Cook the potatoes in a saucepan with water to cover for 5 minutes. Drain well. Heat the oil in a large skillet over moderate heat. Add the potatoes and cook, stirring, until lightly browned, about 4 minutes. Remove the potatoes to paper towels with a slotted spoon and reserve.

Drop the ginger, garlic, and onion through the feed tube of a food processor with the metal blade in place and the motor running. Process until finely chopped, about 10 seconds, scraping down the workbowl as necessary.

Add the onion mixture, salt, and pepper to the skillet and cook, stirring, over moderate heat until the onions are browned, about 2 minutes.

Add the beef and cook, stirring, for 2 minutes. Stir in the water and bring to a boil.

Add the tomato, chili, chutney, and reserved potatoes to the skillet. Reduce the heat and simmer, partially covered, until the meat is tender and the sauce has reduced and thickened slightly, about 40 minutes. If necessary, remove the cover for the last 5 minutes of cooking to thicken the sauce. Serve warm.

Serves 4 to 6

[COPELAND MARKS]

Gingered Mangoes

- 2 large or 4 small ripe mangoes (3 pounds)
- 1 piece fresh ginger (1½ inches), peeled and grated
- 1 lime
- ¼ cup honey

Peel the mangoes and cut into bite-size pieces. Put into a 2-quart serving bowl; sprinkle with the ginger.

Use a zester to remove the zest from the lime, or remove it with a vegetable peeler and cut it into 1/16-inch strips. Squeeze the lime juice over the fruit, scatter on the zest and drizzle with honey. Mix gently with a rubber spatula, cover, and let stand at room temperature for at least 1 hour before serving.

Serves 8

[MARYS WRIGHT]

Mango Sherbet

1 can (20 ounces) mangoes, or 4 or 5 fresh, ripe mangoes and ½ cup sugar
½ cup heavy cream
1 teaspoon pure vanilla extract

Freeze the unopened can of mangoes until solid, about 6 to 8 hours. If you use fresh mangoes, peel, seed, and cut them into 1-inch chunks. Sprinkle with the sugar, seal in plastic bags, and freeze for 6 to 8 hours.

Run warm water over the frozen can of mangoes. Open both ends and push one end to slide out the contents. Cut the frozen mango with juices into 1-inch chunks.

Insert the metal blade in a food processor. With the machine running, drop the frozen chunks of canned or fresh mango, a few at a time, through the feed tube. If some pieces remain whole, turn the machine off and on a few times; continue processing until the mango is light and snowy, about 1 minute.

With the machine running, pour in the cream and vanilla through the feed tube until the mixture is of sherbet consistency; serve immediately, or store in the freezer (see note below).

Serves 6

NOTE: After 3 or 4 hours in the freezer, the sherbet becomes too hard to serve as is. Divide the mixture into two batches and cut each into chunks. Fit the processor with the metal blade; with the machine running, drop the chunks of one batch, a few at a time, through the feed tube and process until of sherbet consistency. Repeat with the second batch.

[ANNE LINDSAY GREER]

Nectarines and Peaches

Nectarines and peaches are closely related and come into market from May to October. Both need plenty of sun to ripen, and most are grown in California and southern states. Nectarines are smooth-skinned versions of peaches and have juicy flesh with a peachy, almondy flavor.

There are hundreds of varieties of peaches—from creamy white to golden yellow—but the two most basic types are clingstone and freestone. As the name suggests, clingstones cling stubbornly to the pit and freestones separate from the pit. Clingstones are rarely seen at the market because they are firmer and less juicy than freestones; they are predominantly used in commercial preparations such as canned poached peaches. When shopping for nectarines and peaches, choose those that are fragrant and give slightly to the touch. Avoid fruit with bruises and any with green spots. Underripe fruit will ripen if left at room temperature for a couple of days. Ripe fruit can be kept in the refrigerator, although it's best to use the fruit quickly, as their fresh flavor fades.

Nectarine Ice/Frozen Nectarine Yogurt

Either of these is a perfect cool treat for a hot summer day. Each recipe yields about 1 pint of ice or frozen yogurt. If you're having a large party and would like to double the recipe, you can as long as your food processor has a workbowl with an inside width greater than 6½ inches.

Nectarine Ice

5   small nectarines (about 18 ounces total)
¼   cup baking soda
1½ teaspoons fresh lemon juice
¼   cup confectioners' sugar
¼   teaspoon vitamin C powder (available at health food stores and drugstores)

Frozen Nectarine Yogurt

5   small nectarines (about 18 ounces total)
¼   cup baking soda
½   cup plain yogurt
⅓   cup confectioners' sugar
¼   teaspoon vitamin C powder (available at health food stores and drugstores)

At least 5 hours before serving, prepare the fruit.

For either the Nectarine Ice or Frozen Nectarine Yogurt, peel the nectarines by the following method: Bring 3 quarts water to a boil in a large saucepot. Add baking soda and the fruit and simmer for 1 to 2 minutes. (Don't be alarmed if the water turns dark; the fruit remains unaffected.) Rinse the fruit well under cold running water, drain, and strip off the skin. Pit the nectarines.

Cut the fruit into 1-inch pieces. For fruit ice, freeze three-quarters of the fruit in a single layer on a baking sheet, and place the remaining one-quarter in the refrigerator. For frozen yogurt, freeze all of the fruit in a single layer on a baking sheet.

A few minutes before serving, process the frozen fruit with the metal blade of a food processor. Pulse about 8 times, then process continuously, scraping down the workbowl and the cover as necessary, until the fruit is finely chopped.

Add the refrigerated fruit pieces (or the plain yogurt) and any additional ingredients called for in each list of ingredients. Process just until the mixture becomes smooth and creamy, scraping down the workbowl as necessary. Taste for sweetness; add more sugar if needed.

The ice and yogurt are at their best when served immediately, but they may also be frozen for later use. To prepare the frozen mixture for serving, cut it into 1-inch chunks. Process with the metal blade just until the mixture becomes smooth and creamy.

Each recipe makes about 1 pint

[P A M E L A   M U R T A U G H]

Peach and Pistachio Crumb Tart

¾ cup shelled pistachios, lightly toasted
2 cups unbleached all-purpose flour
1¼ cups sugar
1 teaspoon coarse (kosher) salt
1 cup unsalted butter, chilled and cut into
    16 pieces
3 tablespoons ice water
8 medium peaches (2½ pounds total)
½ cup fresh orange juice

Chop ¼ cup of the pistachios fine in a food processor with the metal blade, about 15 seconds. Add 1 cup of the flour, 2 tablespoons of the sugar, the salt, and ½ cup of the butter and process until the mixture resembles coarse crumbs, about 10 seconds. Add the water and pulse until the pastry just begins to hold together, about 9 times. Turn out onto wax paper and form in a 6-inch disc. Wrap in the wax paper and chill for 30 minutes.

Roll the pastry out to a 14-inch circle on a lightly floured surface and fit into an 11-inch fluted tart pan with removable bottom, gently pressing the pastry into the pan and up the sides without stretching it. Trim the edge, leaving a 1-inch overhang. Fold in the overhang and gently press against the sides. Chill for 20 minutes.

Preheat the oven to 375°F.

Line the tart shell with heavy-duty foil and prick with a fork. Bake in the center of the preheated oven until the edges are golden, about 30 minutes. Remove the foil and cool on a rack. Leave the oven on.

Chop the remaining ½ cup pistachios coarsely in the processor with the metal blade, about 8 pulses. Remove and reserve. Add 1 cup of the sugar, the remaining 1 cup flour, and the remaining ½ cup butter and process until large clumps begin to form, about 45 seconds. Combine with the pistachios in a bowl and chill.

Peel the peaches if desired and cut into eighths. Halve the sections crosswise, toss in a large bowl with the orange juice, and drain. Toss with the remaining 2 tablespoons sugar and mound in the pastry shell, pressing down gently. Cover evenly with the pistachio mixture.

Bake in the center of the preheated oven until the peaches are tender and the topping is golden brown, about 50 minutes. Cool on a rack; remove the sides of the pan before serving.

Serves 12

[JIM DODGE/
ELAINE RATNER]

Ginger-Peach Jam

Peach varieties today have such fuzz-free, tender skin that the fruit need not be peeled for making jam. The blush on the skin gives this jam a glowing amber color.

  6 pieces crystallized ginger, each about the
       size of a quarter but twice as thick
  ⅓ cup fresh lemon juice
  2½ pounds ripe peaches, or as needed to
       make 5 cups processed fruit
  2⅔ cups sugar

Drop the ginger pieces through the feed tube of a food processor with the metal blade in place and the motor running. Turning the machine on and off, process until the ginger is finely chopped. You should have 2 tablespoons packed ginger. Scrape it into a 4-quart saucepan.

Place lemon juice in a medium stainless-steel or glass bowl. Wash, drain, pit, and stem the peaches. Cut them into 1-inch chunks directly into the lemon juice, stirring to coat the cut edges with juice to prevent them from darkening. Process the peaches, in 4 batches, in the food processor with the steel blade, with on and off motions. Scrape the sides of the workbowl as necessary. You should have a mixture of pulp and coarse chunks. Measure each batch and empty it into the saucepan with the ginger. When you have 5 cups of peaches, bring the mixture quickly to a boil, stirring constantly with a long-handled wooden spoon. (This mixture tends to splatter, so stand well back as you work.) When the mixture reaches a boil, set a lid, tilted slightly, on the pan and reduce the heat to maintain a steady boil, stirring often to prevent scorching and sticking. Keep the lid askew throughout to reduce splattering. Boil for 25 minutes.

Measure the sugar into a bowl. Remove the cooked fruit from the heat; add sugar all at once, stirring to blend. Return the pan to high heat and bring to a boil, stirring often, for 15 minutes, or until mixture thickens.

Ladle the hot jam into hot half-pint jars. Process according to the jar manufacturer's directions. Use within 3 months for best quality and flavor.

Makes about 4 cups

[J E A N N E   L E S E M]

Low-Calorie Ginger-Peach Jam

Leaving the skin on the peaches helps the color without changing the flavor or texture of the jam. Even so, the color will not be as bright as jam made with sugar, and the fruit flavor will be blander. Although it uses half as much ginger as its sugar-sweetened version, the ginger flavor is stronger in this sugar-free jam. The texture is that of a firm jelly.

3 pieces crystallized ginger, each about the size of a quarter but twice as thick

2 pounds ripe peaches, or as needed to make 4 cups processed fruit

2 teaspoons vitamin C powder (available at health food stores and drugstores) or 2 tablespoons fresh lemon juice

1 package (1¾-ounce size) jelling mix
No-calorie sweetener equal to ¾ cup sugar, or more to taste

Fit the workbowl of a food processor with the steel blade; turn machine on. Drop the ginger pieces through the feed tube of a food processor with the metal blade in place and the motor running. Turning the machine on and off, process until the ginger is finely chopped. You should have 3 to 4 teaspoons ginger. Scrape it into a 4-quart saucepan.

Wash, drain, pit, and stem peaches. Cut them into 1-inch chunks and place in a bowl.

Mix well with the vitamin C powder or lemon juice to prevent darkening.

Process the peaches, in 3 or 4 batches, in a food processor with the steel blade, with on and off motions, scraping the sides of the bowl as necessary, until the mixture is coarse. Measure each batch and empty it into the saucepan with the ginger. You should have 4 cups of peaches.

Stir the jelling mix into the fruit and ginger with a wire whisk or long-handled wooden spoon. Bring the mixture quickly to a boil, stirring constantly to prevent scorching and splattering. Continue to stir constantly for 2 minutes. Remove from the heat and keep stirring until the bubbling stops. Quickly stir in the no-calorie sweetener and taste for sweetness, remembering that it will taste less sweet at room temperature and even less so at refrigerator temperature.

Ladle the hot jam into sterilized half-pint jars and cover tightly. When cool, store in the refrigerator or at room temperature. If stored at room temperature below 70°F, use within 3 months.

Makes about 4 cups

[J E A N N E   L E S E M]

Fresh Peaches Poached in Fresh Raspberries

Poached together, the peaches and raspberries take well to either rum or brandy. Rum is more immediately wedded to the two fruits, and makes a smoother tasting effect. But brandy makes for a more spirited dish, and is superb. You may have to try both.

Either version is excellent with heavy cream added. But only offer the cream, and do not make it mandatory, because cream changes the direction of the dish. And people should get to taste first without it.

Simple and pure sponge cake slices are excellent accompaniments.

4 cups fresh red raspberries (see note below), rinsed and gently dried
6 medium peaches, blanched, peeled, halved, and pitted
1 cup sugar
3 tablespoons golden (medium) rum or
    4 tablespoons brandy
    Heavy cream, for serving (optional)

Gently turn the raspberries, peaches, and sugar in a saucepan to mix well. Cover and simmer 6 to 7 minutes, turning once or twice. Remove from the heat. Add rum or brandy and gently mix.

Turn the mixture into a glass serving bowl. Cover with plastic wrap and chill thoroughly, about 5 hours. Pass the cream separately if serving.

Serves 6

NOTE: 2 cups frozen unsweetened raspberries, thawed, may be substituted for fresh berries.

[SHIRLEY SARVIS]

Peach Lemon Tart

Pastry

1½ cups unbleached all-purpose flour
¾ cup unsalted butter, chilled and cut into 12 pieces
1 tablespoon sugar
    Pinch salt
3 tablespoons ice water

Filling

4 medium peaches (about 1¼ pounds total)
1 medium lemon (about 4 ounces)
¾ cup sugar
2 large eggs
2 tablespoons unbleached all-purpose flour

To make the pastry, pulse the flour, butter, sugar, and salt in a food processor with the metal blade until the mixture resembles coarse meal, about 12 times. Add the water and pulse until the dough begins to clump to-

233

gether, about 10 times. Turn the pastry out onto a lightly floured surface and, with the heel of your hand, press it away from you in 4 or 5 firm, quick motions a few times to distribute the fat evenly. Shape the pastry into a ball. Flatten the ball into a disc, wrap in plastic, and refrigerate for about 45 minutes.

On a lightly floured surface, roll the pastry into a 15-inch circle. Fit the pastry into an 11-inch fluted tart pan with removable bottom, pressing it against the sides. Run the rolling pin over the top of the pan to trim the edge, and prick the shell all over with a fork. Freeze for 1 hour.

Preheat the oven to 400°F.

Line the shell with foil, fill the foil with dried beans or rice, and bake in the preheated oven for 15 minutes. Remove the foil and beans or rice and bake the shell until golden brown, about 4 minutes more. Set aside.

Blanch the peaches in a saucepan of boiling water for 30 seconds. Peel and pit the peaches and cut them in ½-inch slices.

Remove half the zest from the lemon with a swivel-bladed vegetable peeler. Squeeze enough juice from the lemon to yield 2 tablespoons. Process the zest and sugar with the metal blade until the zest is as fine as the sugar, about 2 minutes. Add the juice, eggs, and flour and process for 10 seconds. Arrange the peach slices in the pastry shell and pour the lemon mixture over them.

Bake on a baking sheet in the center of the preheated oven until the filling is golden brown and set, about 30 minutes. Cool on a rack for 30 minutes. Serve warm or at room temperature, removing the sides of the pan before serving.

Serves 8

Oranges and Tangerines

Oranges, first brought to the United States in the fifteenth century, have become a very important crop in Florida and California. They can be divided into three groups—tight-skinned, loose-skinned, and bitter. Tight-skinned oranges are more difficult to peel than loose-skinned and include such varieties as the familiar navel, the Valencia, and red-fleshed blood orange. Belonging to the loose-skinned variety are all members of the mandarin orange family. Bitter oranges, too sour and tart to eat raw, are candied or crystallized and made into marmalade. Oranges are available year-round depending on the variety and where they are grown. Choose those that are heavy for their size, without any soft spots or mold. Store oranges in the refrigerator, where they will keep for up to 2 weeks.

The tangerine—a small, sweet fruit with seeds and easy-to-peel skin—is the most popular member of the mandarin orange family. Its proper botanical name is Dancy. One theory for how the tangerine got its name is that an entrepreneur, maybe as far back as 1842, attached the exotic name tangerine (derived from the city of Tangier, where tangerines were first exported from) to this kind of mandarin in order to boost sales. Tangerines can be found at the market from November through May.

Spicy Orange Pot Stickers

"Pot sticker" is a jocular reference to the fact that the dumplings can indeed stick to the bottom of the frying pan. To eliminate this, use a nonstick skillet.

- 4 dried black mushrooms
- 1 piece (1½ × 1½ × ⅓-inch) fresh ginger, peeled
- 1 garlic clove, peeled
- 1 medium carrot (about 3 ounces), peeled, trimmed, and cut into ½-inch pieces
- 1 bunch fresh spinach (about 10 ounces), stems removed, washed
- 2 medium scallions (about 1½ ounces total), trimmed and cut into 1-inch pieces
- 5 ounces trimmed veal, cut into 1-inch cubes and chilled
- 8 ounces shrimp, shelled and deveined
- 1 large egg white
- ½ teaspoon grated orange zest
- 1 tablespoon light soy sauce
- 2 teaspoons dry sherry
- 1 teaspoon sesame oil
- ½ teaspoon salt
  Pinch sugar
  Cornstarch, for dusting
- 30 round Dumpling Skins (recipe follows)
- 3 tablespoons vegetable oil

Spicy Orange Sauce

- ½ cup chicken stock, preferably home-made
- 2 tablespoons dry sherry
- 1 tablespoon oyster sauce
- 1 teaspoon finely chopped orange zest
- 1 teaspoon hoisin sauce
- ½ teaspoon chili sauce or paste
- ½ teaspoon sugar

Soak the mushrooms in hot water to cover until soft, about 30 minutes.

Drop the ginger and garlic through the feed tube of a food processor with the metal blade in place and the motor running. Process until finely chopped, about 10 seconds. Add the carrot pieces and pulse until finely chopped, about 7 times.

Cook the spinach in a large saucepan with 4 quarts simmering water for 15 seconds. Drain and rinse under cold running water. Squeeze out all the water.

Drain the mushrooms and pat them dry. Remove any tough stems and discard them; cut the caps in half. Add the mushrooms, spinach, and scallions to the processor bowl and pulse until finely chopped, about 8 times. Place in a large bowl.

Process the veal until finely chopped, 12 to 14 pulses; add to the spinach mixture.

Pulse the shrimp and egg white until finely chopped but not smooth, 7 to 8 times. Stir them and the next 6 ingredients into the mixture in the large bowl.

Line a baking sheet with wax paper and lightly dust it with cornstarch.

Place a scant tablespoon of the shrimp-veal filling on the center of a dumpling skin; moisten the edges with water and pleat one side with your fingers. Press this side against the opposite side.

Place on the prepared baking sheet and cover with plastic wrap. Repeat the process with the remaining filling and skins.

Heat the oil in a large nonstick skillet. Add the dumplings, and cook until dark brown on the bottom, about 5 minutes. Meanwhile, make the spicy orange sauce by stirring together all the sauce ingredients in a small bowl.

Remove the dumplings from the skillet and pour off the oil. Add the sauce to the pan, return the dumplings, browned side down, and cook, covered, until they are translucent, about 1½ minutes. Uncover and cook until the sauce reduces to a glaze, 2 minutes more. Transfer to large platter to serve.

Makes 30 dumplings

[H U G H   C A R P E N T E R]

Dumpling Skins

The dough is made in a food processor, rolled out into thin sheets, and then cut into squares or circles. The well-wrapped skins can be kept for several days in the refrigerator, or frozen for up to 3 months.

- 2 cups unbleached all-purpose flour
- ½ teaspoon salt
- ½ cup cold water
  Cornstarch, for dusting

Put the flour and salt in a food processor with the metal blade in place. With the motor running, slowly add the water through the feed tube and process just until the mixture resembles cornmeal. Do not overprocess or the dough will be tough. Transfer to a bowl and press into a ball.

To make the dumpling skins with a pasta machine (see note below), divide the dough into 6 equal pieces. Flatten one piece of dough into a 2 × 1-inch rectangle. Cover the remaining pieces. Dust the flattened dough with flour. Run the dough through the widest setting of a pasta machine, then fold it in thirds. Repeat until the dough is smooth and silky, about 8 times in all. (Fold the dough in half instead of in thirds the final time through.) Next, run the dough twice through each additional setting. Lightly brush both sides of the dough with cornstarch and cut it into 4-inch circles or squares. Stack the skins on a plate, wrap, with plastic wrap, and refrigerate. Repeat the rolling procedure with the remaining pieces of dough.

Makes about 60 dumpling skins

NOTE: To make the dumpling skins by hand, knead the dough on a lightly floured surface until smooth. Divide it in half. Work with one piece at a time, keeping the other portion covered with plastic wrap. Form each piece into a log. Cut each log into 30 pieces. Roll each piece out as thin as possible and cut into 4-inch circles or squares.

Oranges and Tangerines

Veal Stew with Orange

3 navel oranges, washed

7 tablespoons unsalted butter

1½ tablespoons vegetable oil

3 pounds veal stew meat (shoulder, round, or shank), cut into 1-inch cubes

1 pound fresh pork (butt or breast), cut into ½-inch cubes

¼ cup bourbon or Cognac

2 medium onions, peeled and sliced

1 bottle (25 ounces) dry white wine

3 garlic cloves, flattened with the side of a heavy knife or cleaver and peeled

2 cups chicken stock, preferably home-made, or as needed

Bouquet garni (tops from 1 celery rib, 1 teaspoon dried thyme, 1 bay leaf, and 2 sprigs parsley tied together in rinsed cheesecloth)

Salt and freshly ground black pepper

1½ teaspoons cornstarch (optional)

1 tablespoon water (optional)

1 tablespoon minced parsley, for garnish

Preheat the oven to 325°F. Grate the rind from the oranges. Set aside the grated rind and the oranges.

Heat 2 tablespoons of the butter with the oil in a large straight-sided skillet or ovenproof casserole over moderately high heat until almost smoking. Add as many pieces of veal as will fit in a single layer without crowding and brown them lightly on all sides. Transfer to a bowl and repeat for the remaining veal. When all of the veal has been browned, add the pork to the skillet. Brown it lightly, stirring often. Return the veal to the skillet and lower the heat to moderate. Pour the bourbon over the meat, set it aflame, and shake the skillet until the flames die.

Add 1 tablespoon of the butter and the onions and cook for 5 minutes, shaking the skillet often. Add the wine, bring to a boil, and simmer for 5 minutes more. Add the garlic and the reserved grated orange zest. If necessary, add chicken stock until the meat is about two-thirds covered with liquid. Bury the bouquet garni in the center, cover the skillet tightly, and bring to a simmer. Cook in the preheated oven for 45 to 55 minutes, or until the meat is very tender. After about 25 minutes, add salt and pepper to taste.

Meanwhile, with a sharp knife peel the reserved oranges, removing all of the white pith and the clear outer membrane. Cut the orange segments out from between the membranes, and set them aside.

With a slotted spoon, transfer the cooked meat to a warm serving dish and keep it warm while you prepare the sauce. Strain the liquid from the skillet into a 3-quart saucepan and skim off the fat. Over moderate heat reduce the liquid to 2½ cups. If desired, thicken the sauce slightly; stir together the cornstarch and water and whisk the mixture into the boiling liquid. Remove from the heat; whisk in the remaining 4 tablespoons butter, 1 tablespoon at a time.

Spoon the sauce over the meat, garnish with the reserved orange segments, and sprinkle with parsley.

Serves 6

[S I M O N E   B E C K]

Ambrosia

- 4 navel oranges
- ½ lemon
- 3 tablespoons Grand Marnier or Cognac
- ¼ cup superfine granulated sugar, or a little less depending on the sweetness of the oranges
- 1 cup lightly packed shredded sweetened coconut

Cut a slice off the top and bottom of each orange to expose the flesh. With a sharp paring knife, score the oranges in 5 or 6 places by cutting just through the peel from the top of the orange to the bottom. Pull off the peel. Using a serrated knife, cut the oranges crosswise into ¼-inch-thick slices. Reserve any juices that accumulate under the oranges; remove any seeds.

Layer the orange slices with the reserved juices in a decorative serving bowl. Sprinkle each layer with a few drops of lemon juice, some of the Grand Marnier or Cognac, a little sugar, and a generous amount of coconut.

Cover and chill before serving.

Serves 4 to 6

[CARL JEROME]

Orange and Cocoa Custard

Note that this needs to chill for at least a day to be completely firm.

Caramel

- ½ cup sugar
- 3 tablespoons water
- Drop fresh lemon juice

Custard

- 4 cups milk
- Zest of 4 medium oranges, removed with a zester
- ½ cup sugar
- Pinch salt
- 2 tablespoons unsweetened cocoa powder
- 1 teaspoon ground cinnamon
- 6 large eggs
- 4 large egg yolks
- Whipped cream sprinkled with cocoa, for serving

To make the caramel, boil the sugar, water, and lemon juice in a small saucepan over moderate heat, without stirring, until the mixture is a deep golden color, about 12 minutes. Carefully pour the caramel into a 2-quart soufflé dish. Tip the dish to coat the bottom and sides, then invert it onto a rack with foil underneath to let the excess run off. Let cool completely.

To make the custard, heat the milk in a medium saucepan just until small bubbles begin to form around the edge of the pan. Stir in the orange zest, then remove from the heat and let steep, uncovered, for 2 hours.

Preheat the oven to 300°F.

Strain the milk into a large saucepan, discarding the orange zest, and reheat it. Stir in the sugar and salt until dissolved. Remove from the heat. Whisk together the cocoa, cinnamon, and 3 tablespoons of the milk, then stir the mixture into the saucepan. Taste for sweetness.

Process the eggs and egg yolks in a food processor with the metal blade until mixed, about 3 pulses. With the motor running, add 1 cup of the milk mixture through the feed tube and process just until combined. Add to the remaining mixture in the saucepan, stir, and let cool for about 10 minutes.

Set the caramel-lined mold in a large pan and strain the custard mixture into the mold. Pour enough boiling water into the large pan to come halfway up the side of the mold. Tightly cover both mold and pan with foil. Bake until the custard is soft in the center but a skewer inserted comes out clean, 50 to 55 minutes.

Let the custard cool completely in the water bath, uncovered. Remove from the water bath and refrigerate, covered, until chilled, at least 24 hours. Unmold onto a serving plate and serve with whipped cream sprinkled with cocoa.

Serves 12

[DEIDRE DAVIS]

Orange Wine Cake

1 medium thick-skinned orange, washed and dried
2 cups unbleached all-purpose flour
1 cup seedless raisins
1 teaspoon baking soda
½ teaspoon salt
1 cup sugar
½ cup unsalted butter, at room temperature
2 large eggs
1 cup buttermilk
1 teaspoon pure vanilla extract
½ cup walnuts
Orange Glaze (recipe follows) or Wine Icing (recipe follows)

With a sharp knife, score the orange with 8 equally spaced vertical cuts. Slip your thumb under the peel at the top and pull off the peel in 8 sections; set aside. The pulp will not be used in this recipe. Preheat the oven to 350°F. Generously butter a 9- × 9- by 2-inch square baking pan.

If you are using the Wine Icing, line the bottom of the pan with wax paper and butter the paper; set aside 1 section of the orange peel for the icing, reserving the remaining 7 for the cake. (If you are using the Orange Glaze, do not line the pan with wax paper, and use all 8 of the orange peel sections in the cake.)

Process the flour, raisins, baking soda, and salt in a food processor with the metal blade, turning the machine on and off about 10 times, until the raisins are coarsely chopped. Transfer to a medium bowl.

Use the metal blade to process the orange peel sections with ½ cup of the sugar until the peel is minced, about 60 seconds. Add to the flour mixture.

Use the metal blade to process the remaining sugar with the butter until smooth and light in color, about 60 seconds, stopping once to scrape down the workbowl. Add the eggs, one at a time, processing for 15 seconds after each addition. With the machine running, add the buttermilk and vanilla through the feed tube. Process for 5 seconds, scrape down the workbowl, and process for 10 seconds more.

Add the walnuts and turn the machine on and off 2 or 3 times to break them up. Add the flour mixture and turn the machine on and off 4 or 5 times, until the flour just disappears.

Scrape the batter into the prepared pan and bake in the preheated oven for 30 to 35 minutes or until a cake tester inserted in the center comes out clean.

If you are using the Orange Glaze, prepare it while the cake is baking and spoon it evenly over the baked cake. Return the cake to the oven for 5 minutes. Cool in the pan on a wire rack. Cut into squares to serve.

If you are using the Wine Icing, cool the cake in the pan on a wire rack for 10 minutes. Turn out onto the rack and let cool completely before icing. Spread the icing evenly over the top and sides.

Makes one 9-inch cake

Orange Glaze

½ cup sugar
3 tablespoons fresh orange juice

In a small bowl, stir together the sugar and orange juice.

Makes about ½ cup

Wine Icing

2 cups confectioners' sugar
   Reserved section of orange peel from
   Orange Wine Cake recipe
5 tablespoons unsalted butter, at room
   temperature

1 large egg white
3 to 4 teaspoons dry sherry

Process the sugar with the orange peel in a food processor with the metal blade until the peel is minced, about 60 seconds. Add the butter and process for 20 seconds, stopping once to scrape down the workbowl. Add the egg white and process for 15 seconds. Scrape the sides of the workbowl, add 3 teaspoons sherry and process for 10 seconds more. If the icing is too thick to be spread easily, add up to 1 teaspoon more sherry, little by little, until it is of the proper consistency.

Makes about 1¼ cups

Scallop Brochettes with Tangerine Sauce

1½ pounds fresh sea scallops
 2 tablespoons olive oil
      Leaves of 1 celery rib, roughly chopped
1½ teaspoons finely chopped parsley
      Pinch of crumbled dried thyme
      Salt and freshly ground black pepper
 4 large heavy tangerines
 ¼ cup glace de homard (available in specialty food shops)
 2 tablespoons demiglace
 ½ cup heavy cream
      Fresh lemon juice (optional)
1½ tablespoons salted butter

Rinse the scallops and pat dry. Marinate in a mixture of the oil, celery leaves, parsley, thyme, salt, and pepper for 2 to 3 hours.

Squeeze the tangerines and strain the juice. You should have 1 cup juice. In an enameled or stainless-steel saucepan, boil down the tangerine juice to ⅓ cup. Add the glace de homard and the demiglace. Allow to melt over low heat. Stir in the cream and cook down to a good consistency—thick enough to coat a wooden spoon. Correct the seasoning of the sauce. If it is too sweet, adjust with a few drops of lemon juice. Keep the sauce hot, and just before serving, whisk in the butter, bit by bit.

Preheat the broiler.

Thread the scallops on skewers or saté sticks. Place on a baking sheet and broil 4 inches from the heat source for 2 to 3 minutes on a side. Spoon 2 tablespoons of the sauce onto individual serving plates and set the scallop brochettes on top. Serve immediately.

Serves 4

[JEAN-LOUIS PALLADIN]

Tangerine Waffles with Fruit

2 tangerines
2 cups fresh strawberries, hulled and sliced
2 tablespoons sugar
1 cup cake flour
1 teaspoon baking powder
½ teaspoon salt
2 large eggs
1 cup heavy cream
½ teaspoon pure vanilla extract

Syrup

Peel of ½ tangerine
¼ cup sugar
6 tablespoons unsalted butter
½ cup tangerine juice

Peel the tangerines, reserving the peels. Discard the pith and section the fruit. Halve the sections and seed them. Combine with the strawberries in a bowl.

To make the batter, process the peel from 1 tangerine with the sugar in a food processor with the metal blade until the peel is as fine as the sugar, about 1 minute.

Add the flour, baking powder, and salt and process until combined, about 15 seconds. Add the eggs, cream, and vanilla and process until combined, about 6 seconds, scraping down the workbowl as necessary. Transfer to a bowl.

To make the syrup, process the peel and sugar until the peel is as fine as the sugar, about 1 minute. Heat the butter and juice in a small nonreactive saucepan over moderate heat until the butter is melted, about 2 minutes. Add the peel mixture and cook over low heat, stirring, until the sugar is dissolved, about 2 minutes.

Preheat the waffle iron. Add 1 cup batter or enough to make a full waffle and bake according to the manufacturer's instructions until golden and crisp, 5 to 6 minutes. Keep warm in a low oven. Make 1 more waffle with the remaining batter.

Separate each waffle into 4 sections and place 2 sections on each plate. Top with the fruit and syrup.

Makes 4 servings

Tangerine Sherbet

1¼ cups water
1 cup sugar
    Zest of 4 medium lemons, cut into strips
1½ cups fresh tangerine juice (about 6 medium tangerines), strained
1 cup ice water
2 tablespoons fresh lemon juice
    Grated zest of 2 medium tangerines
    Mint leaves, for garnish
    Iced kirsch, for serving

Bring the water, sugar, and lemon zest to a boil in a 2-quart saucepan over moderately high heat. Reduce the heat to low and simmer, uncovered, for 5 minutes, stirring occasionally. Pour the syrup into a small bowl and refrigerate until well chilled, at least 2 hours.

Strain the syrup into a large bowl and discard the lemon zest. Stir in the tangerine juice, ice water, lemon juice, and grated tangerine zest.

Use an ice-cream maker, in accordance with the manufacturer's directions, to make the sherbet.

To serve, put 2 scoops of the sherbet in a serving dish and garnish with mint leaves. Sprinkle iced kirsch over the top.

Serves 6 to 8

[SALLY DARR]

Papayas

This elongated pear-shaped fruit grows in clusters on tall trees native to North America. As the fruit ripens, the inedible skin turns from green to yellowy-orange. When halved, a beautiful, deep peach-colored flesh is revealed that strikes a dramatic contrast to the black seeds that fill the center cavity. The peppery-flavored small seeds are edible, but usually removed before eating. Papayas have an exotic, sweet flesh that lacks acidity, so they are usually drizzled with lime juice when eaten raw. Look for bright-colored papayas without bruises that give slightly to the touch. If underripe, keep the fruit in a paper bag. Refrigerate when ripe and eat within 2 days. Papaya juice is often used as a meat tenderizer, as it contains an enzyme — papain — that breaks down protein.

Papaya and Shrimp Salad

1½ pounds medium raw shrimp (35 to 40 shrimp)
3 lemon slices
4 black peppercorns
1 bay leaf
1 teaspoon salt
2 ripe papayas
1 sweet red pepper, roasted, peeled, stemmed, and seeded or 1½ tablespoons diced pimiento
1 head Boston lettuce
2 ripe avocados
  Orange Vinaigrette (recipe follows)
1 medium lemon, juiced

Put the shrimp in a 3-quart saucepan and add the lemon slices, peppercorns, bay leaf, salt, and cold water to cover. Bring to a boil and continue boiling for 1 minute. Drain, rinse the shrimp under cold water, and then peel and devein. Set the shrimp aside.

Peel and seed the papayas and cut them vertically into thin slices. Slice the red pepper into thin strips 1 inch long. Separate the lettuce leaves from the core and rinse and dry them well. Place the papaya, shrimp, and pepper in separate bowls and refrigerate, along with the whole avocados and lettuce, for at least 1 hour.

Meanwhile, prepare the Orange Vinaigrette.

To serve, divide the lettuce leaves among 8 salad plates. Halve the avocados, discard the pits, peel, and cut vertically into thin slices. Arrange some of the avocado, papaya, shrimp, and pepper on each plate. Sprinkle the avocado slices lightly with lemon juice to prevent their discoloring. Spoon the Orange Vinaigrette over each serving.

Serves 8

[A N N E   L I N D S A Y   G R E E R]

Orange Vinaigrette

1 tablespoon parsley leaves
1 garlic clove
⅔ cup oil
3 tablespoons red wine vinegar
1 tablespoon fresh orange juice
1 egg white
1 teaspoon salt
¼ teaspoon freshly ground pepper
  Pinch sugar

Drop the parsley and garlic through the feed tube of a food processor with the metal blade in place and the motor running. Process until minced, then scrape down the bowl, add the remaining ingredients, and process until well blended, about 10 to 15 seconds.

Makes about 1 cup

NOTE: This recipe contains raw egg white. Please see note on page 119.

Warm Chicken and Papaya Salad

Orange-Ginger Vinaigrette

- 1 small shallot, peeled and halved
- 1 piece (1 × ¼ inch) fresh ginger, peeled
- ½ teaspoon Dijon mustard
- ¼ teaspoon salt
- ⅛ teaspoon freshly ground white pepper
- 3 tablespoons white wine vinegar
- ½ cup plus 2 tablespoons vegetable oil
- ½ small orange (about 2 ounces), peeled, seeded and sectioned

Salad

- 2 firm, ripe medium avocados (about 7 ounces each), halved lengthwise, pitted, and peeled
- ¼ cup fresh lemon juice
- 3 firm, ripe medium papayas (about 12 ounces each), halved lengthwise, seeded, and peeled
- 2 medium sweet red peppers (about 6 ounces each)
- 4 whole boneless, skinless chicken breasts (about 8 ounces each), trimmed and halved
- 2 small heads Bibb lettuce (about 9 ounces total), cored, washed, and chilled
- 6 tablespoons vegetable oil
- 2 tablespoons light soy sauce
- 2 tablespoons sesame seeds, toasted

Make the Orange-Ginger Vinaigrette: Drop the shallot and ginger through the feed tube of a food processor with the metal blade in place and the motor running. Process until finely chopped, about 10 seconds. Scrape down the workbowl, then add the remaining ingredients. Pulse about 6 times to mix. Remove and reserve.

Cut the avocado pieces in half crosswise. Stand the pieces cut side down in the feed tube of the food processor and process with the thick slicing disc. Line a baking sheet with wax paper, lay the avocado slices flat on the paper, and brush them with the lemon juice. Cover with more wax paper and refrigerate until ready to assemble the salad. Repeat with the papayas.

Place the red peppers stem side up on a cutting board. With a sharp knife, cut 3 or 4 vertical slices from each pepper, leaving only the core and stem. Remove any seeds and ribs from the slices.

Stack the slices upright in the feed tube and process with the fine slicing disc. Set aside.

Slice the chicken diagonally into ½-inch strips. Reserve.

When ready to assemble the salad, divide the lettuce leaves among 6 dinner plates. Arrange the avocado and papaya slices over the lettuce. Refrigerate the plates while you cook the red pepper and chicken.

Heat 2 tablespoons of the oil in a small skillet. Cook the reserved red pepper strips over moderately high heat, stirring constantly, for 1 minute. Reserve the peppers in a small bowl.

Wipe the skillet with paper towels, then heat 2 more tablespoons of the oil in it. Cook half the reserved sliced chicken, stirring constantly, until just cooked through, about 3 minutes. Transfer to paper towels with a slotted spoon. Repeat with the remaining oil and chicken.

Return all the chicken and peppers to the skillet. Add the soy sauce and the vinaigrette and just heat through.

To serve, mound an equal portion of the chicken mixture in the center of each prepared plate, using a slotted spoon. Strain any liquid remaining in the skillet and drizzle it over the chicken and fruit. Sprinkle each salad with sesame seeds to serve.

Serves 6

[A N N E L I N D S A Y G R E E R]

Chocolate Pecan Cake with Papaya Sauce

¾ cup pecan pieces
1 cup heavy cream
4 tablespoons unsalted butter
10½ ounces semisweet chocolate, such as Lindt or Tobler, cut into ½-inch pieces
2 ounces unsweetened chocolate, cut into ½-inch pieces
5 large eggs
⅓ cup sugar
1 teaspoon pure vanilla extract
Papaya Sauce (recipe follows)

Preheat the oven to 325°F.

Place a round of parchment or wax paper on the bottom of a 9 × 2-inch cake pan. Butter and flour the pan and paper.

Toast the pecans on a baking sheet in the preheated oven until fragrant, 8 to 10 minutes. When cool, process the toasted pecans with the metal blade of a food processor until finely chopped; pulse 8 times, then process continuously for 10 seconds. Remove and reserve.

Bring the cream and butter just to a boil in a small saucepan. Meanwhile, chop the chocolate very fine in the processor with the metal blade; pulse 6 times, then process continuously for 1 minute. With the motor running, pour the hot liquid through the feed tube and process until the chocolate is completely melted, about 15 seconds. Leave the mixture in the workbowl.

In a large bowl set over simmering water, beat the eggs, sugar, and vanilla with a handheld electric mixer on medium speed until the mixture is warm to the touch, 2 to 3 minutes. Take the bowl from the water and beat the egg mixture at high speed until tripled in volume, 7 to 10 minutes.

Add one-quarter of the egg mixture to the chocolate in the workbowl and pulse to combine, about 4 times. Transfer to a large bowl, stir in the chopped pecans, then gently and gradually fold in the remaining egg mixture until just blended.

Pour the batter into the prepared cake pan; it will completely fill the pan. Place the pan in a larger pan and pour in boiling water to come halfway up the sides of the cake pan.

Bake in the center of the preheated oven until a skewer inserted in the center comes out clean, about 40 minutes. The cake may rise over the rim of the pan, but it will deflate as it cools. Remove from the oven and let cool in the water bath for 30 minutes. Remove the cake from the water bath and let cool completely in the pan on a wire rack. Invert the cake onto a serving platter and remove the paper. Serve with Papaya Sauce.

Serves 16

[STEPHAN PYLES]

Papaya Sauce

- 1 very ripe papaya (about 14 ounces), peeled, seeded, and cut into 1-inch pieces
- 1 cup milk
- 1 piece vanilla bean (about 3 inches long)
- 3 large egg yolks
- ⅓ cup sugar
- ⅓ cup heavy cream

Process the papaya in a food processor with the metal blade until smooth, about 1 minute, scraping down the workbowl twice. Remove and push through a fine sieve, then reserve.

Heat the milk and vanilla bean in a small saucepan until small bubbles appear around the side of the pan.

Meanwhile, process the egg yolks and sugar until pale yellow in color, about 10 seconds. Remove the vanilla bean from the heated milk and, with the motor running, pour the milk quickly through the feed tube, then stop the motor.

Return the egg-milk mixture to the saucepan and cook over low heat until thick enough to coat the back of a spoon, about 15 minutes. Add the cream and transfer to a medium bowl. Place plastic wrap directly on the surface of the sauce and refrigerate until thoroughly chilled. Just before serving, stir in the papaya purée.

Makes 1¾ cup

[STEPHAN PYLES]

Pears

Meltingly sweet and fragrant, ripe pears are intoxicating. Not all types have the same qualities, however—their flavor can range from sweet to tart, their texture from firm to mealy and juicy to dry, their shape from resembling a bell to a ball, and their color from yellow to green to red. The most common varieties include: the sweet and juicy bell-shaped yellow-green Bartlett; the firm-fleshed sweet Anjou pear which tends to have yellow-green skin with blushes of red; and the slender-necked Bosc pear which is sweet-tart in flavor and is more of a cooking pear as it holds its shape when baked or poached. The majority of pears sold in the United States come from Oregon and Washington and are generally in season from August through mid-winter. Pears are delicious both cooked and raw. Look for ones that are firm and without bruises or soft spots. Pears will ripen after they're picked, so it's fine to purchase hard ones and let them ripen at room temperature. A pear is ripe when the flesh around the stem yields to gentle pressure. Once ripe, store pears in the refrigerator.

Baked Pears Stuffed with Chèvre, Leeks, and Walnuts

¼ cup walnut pieces, toasted
1 small leek (about 3 ounces), trimmed of all but 2 inches of green, well washed, and cut into 1-inch pieces
4 firm medium pears (about 7 ounces each), preferably Red Bartlett, halved and cored
6 tablespoons water
2 tablespoons lemon juice
1 tablespoon unsalted butter
4 ounces chèvre (goat cheese)
  Freshly ground black pepper
2 tablespoons walnut oil
1 tablespoon sherry wine vinegar
  Salt
1 medium head red leaf lettuce (about 8 ounces), torn into bite-size pieces

Preheat the oven to 350°F.

Process the walnuts in a food processor with the metal blade until coarsely chopped, about 6 pulses. Remove and reserve. Process the leek until finely chopped, about 10 pulses.

Place the pears cut side down in a 13 × 9 × 2-inch baking pan and add the water and lemon juice. Bake the pears in the preheated oven until they are tender but still firm, about 12 minutes. Pour off the liquid.

Meanwhile, cook the leek in the butter in a small skillet over low heat until softened, about 8 minutes. Remove from the heat and stir in the walnuts, chèvre, and pepper. Turn the pears cut side up and divide the chèvre mixture among the cavities, spreading it slightly. Bake 5 minutes more.

To make a dressing, whisk together the oil, vinegar, salt, and pepper in a small bowl. Toss the dressing with the lettuce and arrange on individual serving plates. Top the lettuce with the pears.

Serves 8

[E L I Z A B E T H   R I E L Y]

Duck Braised with Pears and Port

1 duck (about 5 pounds)
  Salt and freshly ground black pepper
4 cups chicken or veal stock, preferably homemade
1 medium onion, peeled and quartered
1 tablespoon unsalted butter
2 parsley sprigs
1 medium bay leaf
¼ teaspoon dried thyme
1 cup port wine
¼ teaspoon coarsely ground black pepper
2 firm medium pears, preferably Bosc, peeled, halved, and cored
  Watercress sprigs, for garnish

Preheat the oven to 450°F.

Remove the giblets, neck, and liver from the duck. Cut the giblets into pieces and set aside with the neck. Reserve the liver for another use.

Place the duck breast side up in a roasting pan and add ½ cup water. Prick the skin with a fork. Sprinkle lightly with salt and pepper and roast in the center of the preheated oven for 30 minutes. Pour off the fat and add the giblets and neck.

Reduce the temperature to 400°F and roast until the skin is crisp and brown but the flesh is still pink, 20 to 30 minutes more. Set aside the duck, giblets, and neck. Pour off the fat from the pan and deglaze the pan over moderate heat with 1 cup of the stock, scraping up the brown bits.

Cut off the duck legs at the hip sockets, leaving each leg in one piece. Remove the wings at the shoulders. Cut along the center of the breast, lifting the meat from the rib cage on either side with your fingers. Remove each breast half in one piece. Reserve the leg pieces and breasts, covered. Cut the wings and remaining carcass into pieces, discarding the skin and fat.

Process the onion with the metal blade of a food processor until chopped, about 6 pulses. Sauté the onion in the butter in a large saucepan over moderately high heat until it begins to color, about 4 minutes.

Reduce the heat and add the giblets, neck, carcass pieces, remaining 3 cups stock, herbs, and deglazed pan juices. Simmer, covered, for 1 hour.

Strain the stock into a large skillet. Discard the solids and skim off as much fat as possible.

To make a sauce, boil the strained stock over high heat until reduced to ½ cup, about 10 minutes, skimming the fat as necessary. Stir in the port and coarsely ground pepper.

Add the duck pieces skin side up and the pears cored side up. Simmer, partially covered, for 10 minutes. Turn the pears and simmer, uncovered, until just tender, about 10 minutes more, basting with the sauce. Remove the duck and pears. Thinly slice the pear halves without cutting through the stem end and fan them. Keep warm.

Skim off the fat and boil the sauce over medium-high heat until thick and syrupy and reduced to ¾ cup, about 4 minutes.

Divide the duck and pears among serving plates and nap with the sauce. Garnish with the watercress.

Serves 4

[ELIZABETH RIELY]

Pear Clafoutis

- 4 large eggs
- ¼ cup unbleached all-purpose flour
- 6 tablespoons sugar
- 3 tablespoons butter, melted
- 1 cup milk
- 1 pound (about 3 medium) pears, peeled, halved, cored and sliced

Preheat the oven to 350°F. Butter a 9-inch fluted quiche dish or pie plate.

Process the eggs, flour, sugar, melted butter, and milk in a food processor with the steel blade until well blended, about 1 minute.

Pour a thin layer of batter in the bottom of the quiche dish. Arrange the pears attractively on top and pour the remaining batter over the pears. Bake for 25 to 30 minutes.

Serves 8

[JEAN-JACQUES JOUTEUX/ NAOMI BARRY]

Puffy Pear Pancake

- 4 firm ripe medium pears (about 2 pounds total), peeled, cored, and cut into 1- to 2-inch pieces
- 4 tablespoons unsalted butter
- ½ cup plus 2 tablespoons granulated sugar
- 1 cup unbleached all-purpose flour
- 1 cup milk
- 4 large eggs
- ¼ teaspoon salt
- 1 teaspoon pure vanilla extract
  Confectioners' sugar

Chop the pears coarsely, in 2 batches, in a food processor with the metal blade, pulsing 6 to 8 times.

Melt the butter in a 10-inch ovenproof skillet or gratin pan over moderate heat. Add the chopped pears and ½ cup of the granulated sugar. Cook, stirring often, until most of the liquid has evaporated and the pears are beginning to caramelize, about 20 minutes.

Meanwhile, preheat the oven to 425°F.

Process the flour, milk, eggs, salt, and the 2 tablespoons granulated sugar with the metal blade until smooth, about 10 seconds, stopping once to scrape the workbowl.

When the pears begin to caramelize, stir in the vanilla. Pour the batter over the hot pears and bake in the center of the preheated oven for 20 minutes. Lower the heat to 350°F and bake for 15 minutes more, or until puffed and nicely browned.

Remove to a serving trivet, sprinkle with confectioners' sugar, and serve immediately.

Serves 8

Chocolate and Pear Tart

2½ cups unbleached all-purpose flour
⅓ cup unsweetened cocoa powder
1 cup unsalted butter, cut into 16 pieces, chilled
½ cup granulated sugar
   Pinch salt
1 large egg
5 tablespoons water
5 firm ripe medium pears (about 7 ounces each)
   Confectioners' sugar, for dusting

Pulse the flour, cocoa, butter, granulated sugar, and salt in a food processor with the metal blade until combined, about 6 times. Add the egg and pulse twice. With the motor running, add the water by the tablespoon through the feed tube until the dough forms a ball.

Remove the dough and divide it in half. Flatten each half into a 1-inch-thick disc, cover with foil, and refrigerate until firm enough to roll, about 1 hour.

Preheat the oven to 350°F.

On a lightly floured surface, roll out one half of the dough into a ¼-inch-thick circle. Press the dough into a buttered 9-inch tart pan with removable bottom, leaving a 1-inch overhang.

Cut the pears in half lengthwise. Core and peel each half and process them with the all-purpose slicing disc; arrange in the tart shell.

Roll out the remaining dough to a ¼-inch-thick circle. Place it over the pears and trim it, leaving a 1-inch overhang. Press the top and bottom crusts together and crimp the edges to seal. Cut a ½-inch hole in the center of the top crust to allow steam to escape.

Bake the tart in the center of the pre-heated oven until the pears are tender and the crust is crisp, 50 minutes to 1 hour. Remove from the oven and cool on a wire rack. Remove the sides of the pan and dust the tart with confectioners' sugar to serve.

Serves 8

VARIATION: For a richer chocolate flavor, sprinkle the bottom crust with 1½ ounces finely chopped semisweet chocolate before adding the pears. To finely chop chocolate, process chilled pieces in the processor with the metal blade for about 30 seconds.

[ADA PARASILITI, MICHI AMBROSI, ANGELA PARLINGIERI, AND GIULIANA VICINANZA]

Pineapples

Named for its pinecone appearance, the pineapple is a tropical delight. This juicy, sweet-tart fruit has characteristic bumpy diamond-patterned skin with a greenish-gray plume of leaves. A sign of a perfect pineapple is a distinctive fragrance, as well as easy-to-remove leaves. Pineapples are available year-round and at their best from March to July. Store fresh pineapple in the refrigerator for up to 3 days.

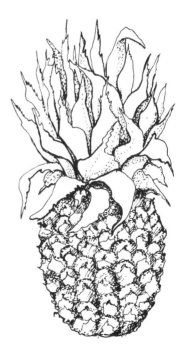

Traditional Pineapple Upside-Down Cake

In measuring the flour for this cake, sift it onto a sheet of wax paper; with a tablespoon, lightly drop enough of the sifted flour into a 1-cup and a fractional ⅓-cup measure to overflow slightly; with a small metal spatula, sweep off the excess flour.

1   can (20 ounces) unsweetened sliced pineapple
8   tablespoons unsalted butter, chilled and cut into 16 pieces
½   cup firmly packed light brown sugar
1⅓   cups sifted cake flour
2   teaspoons baking powder
¾   cup granulated sugar
1   large egg
½   cup milk
1   teaspoon pure vanilla extract
    Candied red cherries, for garnish
1   cup heavy cream (whipped until stiff and flavored with vanilla and a suspicion of sugar), for serving

Preheat the oven to 350°F. Drain 8 slices of the pineapple; 2 slices and the juice are not used in this recipe.

In a 9-inch round cake pan over very low heat, with a metal spoon stir 4 tablespoons (8 pieces) of the butter until melted but still creamy. Off heat, thoroughly stir in the brown sugar. With the back of the spoon, spread the mixture evenly over the bottom of the pan. Closely fit the 8 pineapple slices (one in the center) over the butter-sugar mixture. Let stand at room temperature while you prepare the batter.

In a food processor with the metal blade, pulse together the flour, baking powder, granulated sugar, remaining 4 tablespoons (8 pieces) butter, egg, milk, and vanilla until almost smooth, 10 to 12 times. Allow the metal blade to come to a stop after each pulse. Scrape down the workbowl, then pulse just until smooth, 10 to 12 times.

Insert a finger in the outer bottom opening of the workbowl to hold the blade in place; pour the batter over the pineapple. With the spatula, scrape the remaining batter in the bowl and on the blade into the pan; spread evenly.

Bake in the preheated oven until a deep golden brown and a cake tester inserted in the center comes out free of batter, 40 minutes. Let stand on a wire rack for 5 minutes. Place a serving plate upside down over the pan; holding the rack and the plate, invert. Remove rack and pan. If any sugar mixture drips onto the plate, remove it with a damp paper towel. Garnish the center of each pineapple slice with a cherry and serve hot or warm. Pass whipped cream.

Serves 8

[CECILY BROWNSTONE]

Fresh Pineapple Upside-Down Cake

Use the ingredients for Traditional Pineapple Upside-Down Cake but substitute 14 ounces peeled and cored fresh pineapple for the pineapple slices and 12 pecan halves for the candied red cherries. Cut the fresh pineapple into 1-inch pieces. Chop the pineapple, in 2 batches, in a food processor with the metal blade, pulsing 10 to 12 times or until coarsely chopped, scraping down the workbowl as necessary. (You should have 1½ cups.)

Preheat the oven to 350°F.

In a large skillet melt 4 tablespoons (8 pieces) of the butter over moderate heat. Add the pineapple and cook, stirring occasionally, until the liquid has evaporated, about 10 minutes. Remove the pan from the heat and thoroughly stir in the brown sugar.

Spread the pineapple mixture into a 9 × 1½-inch round cake pan. Press the pecan halves through the mixture to the bottom of the pan, forming a decorative pattern. Continue with the recipe for Traditional Pineapple Upside-Down Cake.

Serves 8

[CECILY BROWNSTONE]

Caramelized Pineapple Flans

  1 fresh pineapple (about 5 pounds)
  2 tablespoons cherry liqueur, such as kirsch
  1 cup sugar
  ¼ cup water
     Pinch cream of tartar
  4 large eggs

Peel and quarter the pineapple. Remove the core and wrap it and the peel in dampened cheesecloth. Squeeze over a bowl to extract as much juice as possible. There should be about ⅓ cup.

Cut the pineapple pulp into 1-inch cubes. Sprinkle half of the pineapple cubes with 1½ teaspoons of the liqueur and refrigerate, covered.

Combine ½ cup of the sugar, the water, and cream of tartar in a small saucepan. Bring to a simmer and cook without stirring until caramel in color, about 6 minutes. Divide among four 1-cup ramekins and swirl each so the caramel coats the bottom and part of the sides.

Purée the remaining pineapple in a food processor with the metal blade until smooth, about 1 minute, scraping down the workbowl as necessary. Combine with the pineapple juice and remaining ½ cup sugar in a large saucepan and bring to a boil over moderate heat. Reduce the heat and simmer for 5 minutes. Remove from the heat and stir in the remaining 1½ tablespoons liqueur. Let sit for about 5 minutes.

Preheat the oven to 350°F.

Whisk the eggs lightly in a large bowl. Gradually whisk in the pineapple purée. Divide the mixture among the ramekins.

Place the ramekins in a baking pan and add enough hot water to the pan to come two-thirds of the way up the sides of the ramekins. Bake in the center of the preheated oven until the flans are firm to the touch, 45 to 50 minutes. Remove the ramekins from the baking pan and cool for 30 minutes. Refrigerate, loosely covered, overnight.

Unmold the flans onto dessert plates and garnish with the chilled pineapple cubes.

Serves 4

Pineapple Boats with Yogurt Sauce

1   fresh medium pineapple (about 2½ pounds)
1   cup plain yogurt
1   cup sour cream
1   teaspoon pure vanilla extract
½   cup firmly packed light brown sugar

Quarter the pineapple lengthwise with a sharp knife and core the quarters, leaving the leaves intact. Cut the fruit from the peel, leaving the peel intact and the fruit spear in one piece. Halve the fruit lengthwise and cut it crosswise into bite-size pieces. Arrange the pineapple pieces back in the peel "boats."

Process the yogurt, sour cream, and vanilla in a food processor with the metal blade until smooth, about 3 seconds. Ladle over the pineapple and sprinkle with the sugar.

Serves 4

[GAYLE HENDERSON WILSON]

Plums

At the height of summer, markets spill over with nearly 150 varieties of California plums in hues of black, purple, blue, red, and green. A treat for the eye and the palate.

Vivid Red Beauts are usually the first plums of the season and are harvested in mid-May. June brings four more varieties: the Black Beaut, whose juicy, sweet flesh intensifies when cooked; the crimson-purple Santa Rosa, with its tart, winelike flavor; the Queen Rosa, whose mild flesh improves with cooking; and the dark red El Dorado, equally good cooked or raw.

The cream of the crop arrives in July. The Laroda may have the most desirable qualities of all—thin, tender red skin shielding very sweet yellow flesh that turns brilliant red when cooked. A close second is the juicy purple-skinned Simka.

September ends the plum season with the sturdy purple-blue Angeleno and the yellow-red Roysum, whose sweetness increases when cooked.

Plums should be bought when they are still firm, giving slightly with gentle pressure. Let them ripen for a few days at room temperature or place them in a paper bag to speed up the process. Cooking further brings out their sweet flavor.

Any unpeeled firm plum can be used in the following recipes, which range from succulent main dishes to delectable desserts.

Barbecued Plum and Chicken Kebabs

Plum Barbecue Sauce

- 4 firm plums (about 1 pound), quartered and pitted
- ¼ cup water
- 2 tablespoons firmly packed dark brown sugar
- 1 tablespoon vegetable oil
- 1 small onion (3 ounces), peeled and chopped
- 1 large garlic clove, peeled and finely chopped
- 2 tablespoons red wine vinegar
- 1 teaspoon dry mustard
- 1 teaspoon fresh lemon juice
- ½ teaspoon hot red pepper flakes
- ½ teaspoon salt
- ⅛ teaspoon freshly ground black pepper

- 1 whole boneless chicken breast (about 12 ounces) cut into 1-inch cubes
- 1 large firm plum (4 ounces), pitted and cut into 1-inch cubes

Make the Plum Barbecue Sauce: Bring the plums, water, and sugar to a boil in a large saucepan, reduce the heat to moderately low, and simmer, covered, until soft, 15 to 20 minutes, stirring often. Purée in 2 batches in a food processor with the metal blade, about 20 seconds per batch. Strain. There should be 1½ cups.

Sauté the onion in the oil in a saucepan over moderate heat until soft, about 3 minutes. Add the garlic and sauté for 1 minute. Add the plum purée and remaining ingredients and simmer over medium-low heat, stirring, until thickened, about 15 minutes.

Combine the chicken and ¼ cup of the barbecue sauce in a bowl and let stand for 30 minutes.

Prepare a charcoal grill or preheat the oven broiler.

Thread the chicken and plums on 5-inch metal skewers. Grill or broil until cooked through, 2 to 2½ minutes per side, basting with some sauce. Serve with the remaining sauce.

Serves 6

Rustic Fruit Tart

You can make this tart with soft fruit such as cherries, rhubarb, or the plums used in the recipe below. Because of the mixture of nuts, sugar, and flour that lines the bottom of the tart, the fruit's juice will not turn the crust soggy.

Pie Dough (recipe follows)
- ½ cup walnuts or any other nut
- ½ cup sugar
- ¼ cup unbleached all-purpose flour
- 1½ pounds (about 30) small dark plums, halved and stoned

5 tablespoons unsalted butter
1 tablespoon plum brandy, such as quetsch or slivovitz
1 cup apricot jam

Preheat the oven to 400°F.

Prepare the Pie Dough as directed.

Put the walnuts and ¼ cup of the sugar in a processor fitted with the metal blade. Turn the machine on and off twice and then process for 10 seconds. Add the flour and process 10 seconds more to make a fine powder.

On a lightly floured surface, roll out the dough into a rough rectangle about ⅛ inch thick. Wrap it loosely around the rolling pin and unroll onto a 16 × 12-inch baking sheet. Spread the nut mixture evenly on top of the dough, leaving a 1-inch border.

Neatly arrange the plum halves cut side down on the nut mixture. Fold the rim of dough up over the outermost fruit; pinch together any tears or gaps in the rim so that the juices cannot leak out during baking.

Cut the butter into small pieces and distribute them on top of the fruit. Sprinkle the remaining ¼ cup sugar evenly over the fruit and the rim.

Bake on the middle shelf of the preheated oven for about 1 hour, until the crust is golden. Remove from the oven and let the tart cool to lukewarm.

Stir the plum brandy into the apricot jam to dilute it slightly. Spoon and spread this glaze evenly over the fruit and crust. Serve the tart at room temperature.

Serves 8 to 10

[JACQUES PÉPIN]

Pie Dough

2 cups unbleached all-purpose flour (dip the cup into the flour and then level it)
½ cup unsalted butter, cut into small pieces
1 teaspoon sugar
½ teaspoon salt
1 large egg yolk
⅓ cup cold water

Combine the flour, butter pieces, sugar, and salt in a large bowl. With your fingers, loosely blend them to make a coarse mixture, leaving the butter in distinct pieces.

Add the egg yolk and the water, and mix by hand, just until the dough comes together into a ball: pieces of butter will still show distinctly on the surface. Refrigerate the dough until ready to use.

[JACQUES PÉPIN]

Plum Bread Pudding

    6   firm plums (1½ pounds total), quartered
        and pitted
    ¾   cup plus 2½ tablespoons sugar
    ¾   cup unsalted butter
    ¼   cup fresh orange juice
    ¼   cup water
    2   strips orange zest (each 2 × 1 inch)
    2   cinnamon sticks (3 inches each)
    1   loaf stale challah, cut into ½-inch slices
        and crusts trimmed
    1   cup milk
    4   large eggs
    1   teaspoon pure vanilla extract
    ¼   teaspoon salt
    1⅓ cups heavy cream
        Confectioners' sugar, for garnish

Slice the plums lengthwise in a food processor with the thick slicing disc. Remove and
reserve. Combine 6 tablespoons of the sugar,
4 tablespoons of the butter, the orange juice,
water, orange zest, and cinnamon sticks in a
saucepan and cook over moderately high
heat until the sugar is dissolved, about 5 minutes. Add the plums and cook until tender,
about 4 minutes. Cool.

Cover the bottom of a buttered 9-inch
square baking pan with a layer of bread slices.

Top with overlapping rows of plums and
cover with another bread layer. Reserve the
remaining plum mixture.

Cream the remaining ½ cup butter with
½ cup of the sugar in the processor with the
metal blade, about 1 minute. Add the milk,
eggs, vanilla, and salt and process until combined, about 30 seconds. Pour into the baking
pan, coating the bread evenly, and top with 1
cup of the cream.

Cover loosely with plastic wrap, place a
smaller pan on top, and put cans or weights
inside the pan. Set aside for 1 hour.

Preheat the oven to 350°F.

Remove the small pan, weights, and plastic wrap. Pour the remaining ⅓ cup cream
over the bread and sprinkle with the remaining ½ tablespoon sugar. Bake in the preheated oven until golden, about 1 hour. Cool
for 15 minutes.

To make a sauce, purée the remaining
plums and juice with the metal blade, about
30 seconds. Strain.

Cut the pudding into squares and sprinkle
with the confectioners' sugar. Serves with the
sauce.

Serves 8

Prunes

Prunes are plums that have been dried—either by the sun or by commercial dehydration. They have an intense sweetness and are a great source of dietary fiber. Look for those that are still plump and soft and not too leathery. Store them in a dry, airy place for up to 6 months. Prunes go particularly well with meat dishes and also are delicious in baked goods.

Roast Loin of Pork with Prunes

1 boneless pork loin (about 2½ pounds)
12 whole moist, pitted prunes
    Salt and freshly ground black pepper
4 tablespoons unsalted butter
1 teaspoon vegetable oil
½ cup water
    Bouquet garni: ½ teaspoon dried thyme,
       1 sprig fresh parsley, 1 crumbled bay
       leaf, tied in rinsed cheesecloth
6 medium potatoes (about 2½ pounds
       total), peeled and cut crosswise in half

Preheat the oven to 350°F.

With a sharp knife, make a lengthwise cut down the side of the pork loin and about halfway though the meat. Open the meat out and arrange the prunes in a layer down the center. Fold the meat over the prunes and tie it into a compact roll with kitchen string. Season with salt and pepper.

Heat the butter and oil in a large flameproof casserole over moderately high heat and brown the roast on all sides. Add the water and bouquet garni and bring to a boil. Transfer the casserole to the preheated oven and cook for 30 minutes, basting twice with the pan juices.

While the meat is roasting, cook the potatoes in water to cover for 15 minutes or until just tender. Drain the potatoes and add them to the casserole. Continue cooking for 30 to 35 minutes more, until the internal temperature of the meat reaches 160°F. Baste the meat and potatoes occasionally. Add more water if the pan begins to run dry.

Transfer the meat to a cutting board and let it rest for 10 minutes. Remove the string and cut the meat into ⅜-inch slices. Arrange on a warm platter with the potatoes. Remove the bouquet garni, then degrease the pan juices and pass separately.

Serves 6

[SUZANNE S. JONES]

Prune-Nut Filled Cookies

    Zest of 1 medium lemon, removed with a
       swivel-bladed vegetable peeler
½ cup plus 2 tablespoons granulated sugar
½ cup unsalted butter, cut into 8 pieces
1 tablespoon fresh lemon juice
1 large egg
2 cups unbleached all-purpose flour
¼ teaspoon baking powder

    Pinch salt
    Prune-Nut Filling (recipe follows)
    Confectioners' sugar, for garnish

Process the zest and the sugar in a food processor with the metal blade until the zest is finely chopped, about 1½ minutes. Remove 2 tablespoons of the lemon-sugar mixture and reserve for the filling. Add the butter to the workbowl and process until the mixture is smooth, about 20 seconds. Add the lemon juice and egg and process until blended, about 10 seconds. Add the flour, baking powder, and salt and pulse just until mixed, 8 to 10 times, scraping down the workbowl as necessary.

Transfer the dough to a medium bowl and cover the surface with plastic wrap. Refrigerate for up to 2 hours or until firm enough to shape. Make the Prune-Nut Filling.

Preheat the oven to 350°F. Butter a large baking sheet.

To make the cookies, roll a small piece of dough with your hands into a 1-inch ball. Flatten it with your fingers and palm to form a flat circle about 3 inches in diameter. Place about ½ teaspoon of the filling in the center and lift the sides of the dough up and over the filling, pinching the dough together at the top. Gently reshape into a ball and place the cookie seam side down on the baking sheet. Repeat with the remaining dough and filling, placing each cookie about 1 inch apart on the baking sheet.

Bake the cookies in the center of the preheated oven for about 10 minutes, or until they are firm to the touch but not brown. Remove to a wire rack and sprinkle with confectioners' sugar while still warm.

Makes about 3½ dozen cookies

[S U Z A N N E   S .   J O N E S]

Prune-Nut Filling

   2 tablespoons lemon-sugar reserved from
         preceding recipe
  ¼   cup walnut pieces
   5 whole moist, pitted prunes
 1½ teaspoons Armagnac (optional)

Pulse the lemon-sugar, walnuts, and prunes in a food processor with the metal blade until the mixture is finely chopped, about 12 times. Add the optional Armagnac and pulse 2 times more.

Makes about ½ cup

[S U Z A N N E   S .   J O N E S]

Prune Pudding

1 cup pitted prunes (about 8 ounces)
1 cup dried apricots (about 6 ounces)
¾ cup dry red wine
¾ cup orange juice
1½ cups milk (approximately)
¾ cup unbleached all-purpose flour
Pinch of salt
5 large eggs
¾ cup sugar
¼ cup Armagnac

Marinate the prunes and apricots overnight in the wine and orange juice. Drain the liquid from the fruits into a 2-cup measure and add enough milk to make 2 cups. Set aside the fruits and the liquid.

Preheat the oven to 400°F.

Use the metal blade of a food processor to process the flour, salt, and 1 egg, turning the machine on and off about 10 times, until you have a crumbly mixture. With the machine running, add the remaining eggs, one at a time, through the feed tube; then gradually add the sugar, then the milk mixture and the Armagnac. Continue processing until smooth, about 15 seconds, stopping once to scrape down the bowl.

Arrange the fruits in a buttered 2-quart casserole or soufflé dish. Pour the batter evenly over the fruits. Bake for 40 to 50 minutes, until puffed and nicely browned.

Serves 4 to 6

[JULES BOND/
GLADYS SANDERS]

Raisins and Currants

Raisins and currants are grapes that have been dried mechanically or in the sun. Their shapes and size depend on the grape type. Currants are dried Zante grapes, golden raisins are dried green grapes, and dark raisins are either dried Muscat or Thompson grapes. Raisins and currants hold an important place in the pantry, as they can be kept for several months.

Holiday Raisin Bread

Dough

- 1 package dry yeast
- 2 tablespoons granulated sugar
- ¼ cup warm water (105° to 115°F)
- ⅓ cup sour cream
- ¼ cup cold milk
- 1 large egg
- 1 teaspoon pure vanilla extract
- ¼ teaspoon pure almond extract
- 3 cups unbleached all-purpose flour
- 4 tablespoons unsalted butter, cut into 4 pieces
- ½ teaspoon salt

- 3 tablespoons unsalted butter, melted
- ¾ cup seedless dark raisins
- ¼ cup granulated sugar
- ¼ teaspoon ground cardamom or cinnamon
- 1 large egg beaten with 1 tablespoon water
  Confectioners' Sugar Glaze (recipe follows), if desired

To make the dough, dissolve the yeast and 1 tablespoon of the sugar in the warm water in a 2-cup liquid measure. Let stand until foamy. Whisk together the sour cream, milk, egg, and vanilla and almond extracts and add to the yeast mixture.

Process the flour, butter, salt, and remaining 1 tablespoon sugar in a food processor with the metal blade for 10 seconds. With the motor running, add the liquid ingredients through the feed tube in a steady stream as fast as the flour absorbs them. After the dough cleans the side of the workbowl, process for 40 seconds more to knead it.

Shape the dough into a ball and place in a lightly floured 1-gallon plastic bag. Squeeze out the air and close the top with a wire twist. Let rise in a warm place until double, about 1 hour.

Punch down the dough, remove it from the bag, and divide it into thirds. Roll each piece into an 18 × 4½-inch rectangle. Brush the rectangles with the butter and sprinkle with the raisins. Combine the granulated sugar and cardamom. Reserve 1 tablespoon and sprinkle the remainder over the raisins.

Starting with a long side, roll up the rectangles tightly and seal the seams. Place the rolls, side by side and seam side down, on a lightly buttered baking sheet. Braid the rolls without stretching them and keeping the seam side down, starting from the center and braiding toward each end. Tuck the ends under. Cover with buttered plastic wrap and let rise in a warm place until double, about 40 minutes.

Preheat the oven to 375°F.

Brush the braid with the egg wash and sprinkle with the remaining cardamom-sugar mixture. Bake in the center of the preheated oven until browned, about 25 minutes. Cool on a wire rack. While still slightly warm, drizzle with the Confectioners' Sugar Glaze.

Makes 1 braided loaf

[SUZANNE S. JONES]

Confectioners' Sugar Glaze

¾ cup confectioners' sugar
1½ tablespoons milk
½ teaspoon pure vanilla extract

Process all the ingredients until combined, about 15 seconds, scraping down the workbowl as necessary.

Makes ½ cup

[S U Z A N N E S. J O N E S]

Raisin Squares

2½ cups seedless dark raisins
½ cup granulated sugar
2 tablespoons cornstarch
¾ cup water
3 tablespoons fresh lemon juice
¾ cup unsalted butter, cut into 12 equal
  pieces
1 cup firmly packed dark brown sugar
½ teaspoon baking soda
1½ cups quick-cooking rolled oats
1½ cups unbleached all-purpose flour
½ teaspoon salt

Combine the raisins, sugar, cornstarch, water, and lemon juice in a nonreactive 2-quart saucepan. Cook gently, stirring constantly, until thick, about 5 minutes. Remove from heat and let cool.

Process the butter and brown sugar in a food processor with the metal blade until smooth and creamy, about 20 seconds, stopping to scrape down the workbowl as necessary. Add the remaining ingredients and pulse 6 to 8 times or until just combined.

Preheat the oven to 400°F.

Grease a 13 × 9 × 2-inch baking pan. Press half the oatmeal mixture evenly over the bottom of the pan. Spread the raisin filling over the oatmeal. Sprinkle the remaining oatmeal mixture evenly over the filling and press it lightly with your fingers.

Bake the cookies in the preheated oven until lightly browned, 20 to 30 minutes. When cool, cut into 1½-inch squares.

Makes about 4½ dozen cookies

[S U Z A N N E S. J O N E S]

Saffron Rice with Currants

Saffron is a spice best used sparingly. Just a pinch adds flavor and color to a mild food like rice; too much can leave a medicinal aftertaste. If you use thread saffron, dissolve it in a couple of tablespoons of hot water before you add it to the rice.

½ cup unsalted butter
1½ cups converted long-grain rice
1 teaspoon salt
1 teaspoon dried basil, finely crumbled
¼ teaspoon freshly ground black pepper
Large pinch of powdered saffron or crumbled thread saffron
3 cups beef or chicken broth, heated to boiling
⅓ cup currants

Heat the butter to bubbling in a heavy 2½-quart saucepan. Add the rice and sauté over moderate heat, stirring, until the rice is unbearably hot to the top of your hand, about 3 minutes.

Add the salt, basil, pepper, and saffron to the boiling broth. Pour the broth onto the rice and stir to mix.

Cover with several layers of paper towels and a tight-fitting lid and cook over moderately low heat for 15 minutes. Add the currants, stir briefly to mix, and then cover the pot again. Turn off the heat and let stand for 10 minutes, or until the rice is tender. Correct the seasoning and serve.

Serves 6

[MADELEINE KAMMAN]

Apple Currant Bread

2 cups unbleached all-purpose flour
1 teaspoon baking soda
1 tablespoon baking powder
1 teaspoon salt
1 teaspoon ground cinnamon
¼ teaspoon freshly grated nutmeg
⅔ cup dried currants
2 tart apples (10 ounces total), peeled, cored, and quartered
2 teaspoons lemon zest, in strips
1¼ cups sugar
3 large eggs

½ cup unsalted butter, at room temperature, cut into 4 pieces
1 tablespoon fresh lemon juice
1 teaspoon pure vanilla extract

Adjust the oven rack to the middle and preheat the oven to 350°F. Generously butter and lightly flour two 4-cup bread pans.

Combine the flour, baking soda, baking powder, salt, cinnamon, nutmeg, and currants in a bowl and stir to mix. Reserve.

Process the apples and lemon zest in a

food processor with the metal blade, turning the machine on and off until coarsely chopped. Then process until puréed, about 30 seconds, scraping the sides of the workbowl as necessary. (There should be about 1½ cups purée.)

Add the sugar and process for 30 seconds. Add the eggs and process for 1 minute. Add the butter, lemon juice, and vanilla extract. Process for 1 minute until fluffy. Add the reserved dry ingredients. Process, turning the machine on and off just until flour disappears, about 5 times. Do not overprocess.

Spoon the batter into the prepared pans and spread evenly with a spatula.

Bake for 40 to 45 minutes in the preheated oven until brown. Cool in the pans for 10 minutes, then turn out onto a wire rack and allow to cool completely.

Makes 2 small loaves

Raspberries

Raspberries grow most happily where summers are relatively cool. They come into market from May through November with a peak in June and July. There are three main varieties, including golden, black, and red—the most widely available. This exquisite summer fruit is wonderful both on its own and cooked into tarts and jams. Choose berries that look fresh: fully colored, plump, dry, free of bruising and mold, and with no signs of leakage in containers. As with all berries, do not buy more than you need for immediate use, as they are highly perishable. Spread them in a single layer on a plate lined with paper towels, cover, and store in the refrigerator. Rinse lightly before using.

Raspberry Bowl with Coffee Cream

2 cups fresh raspberries, rinsed and gently dried
½ cup plus 1 tablespoon sugar
½ cup heavy cream
½ teaspoon pure vanilla extract
1 pint coffee ice cream
4 tablespoons golden (medium) rum

Toss the berries with the ½ cup sugar and crush slightly. Let stand at room temperature until the sugar dissolves, about 15 minutes.

With a hand-held electric mixer, beat the heavy cream with the 1 tablespoon sugar and the vanilla extract until soft peaks form.

To assemble, put shallow scoops of ice cream into a serving bowl. Drizzle with rum and top with whipped cream. Spoon berries over all. Serve immediately.

Serves 4

[SHIRLEY SARVIS]

Raspberry Riches

1 cup sifted unbleached all-purpose flour
¾ cup sugar
½ teaspoon baking powder
¼ teaspoon baking soda
¼ teaspoon salt
1 large egg
⅓ cup buttermilk
½ teaspoon pure vanilla extract
⅓ cup unsalted butter, melted and cooled to room temperature
1¼ cups fresh red raspberries

Sugar-Crumb Topping

½ cup firmly packed light brown sugar
2 tablespoons flour
1 tablespoon unsalted butter, cut into small pieces
1½ teaspoons (½ ounce) semisweet chocolate, finely grated

Preheat oven to 375°F. Butter a 9-inch round or 8-inch square baking pan.

Sift together the flour, sugar, baking powder, soda, and salt into a large bowl. In another bowl, beat together the egg, buttermilk, and vanilla extract until smooth. Stir in the melted butter. Pour the liquid mixture into the flour mixture. Beat with a wooden spoon until nearly smooth.

Spread the batter evenly in the prepared pan. Sprinkle with the raspberries and set aside while you prepare the topping.

Add all the topping ingredients to a food processor fitted with the metal blade. Process to a fine consistency. Sprinkle the topping evenly over the berries.

Bake in the preheated oven until richly browned, about 40 to 45 minutes. Let cake cool on a rack. Serve warm.

Serves 10

[SHIRLEY SARVIS]

Raspberry and Peach Trifle Hotel Utah

A properly made trifle is meant to charm the eye as well as the palate. Assemble the trifle so that each layer is clearly visible through the side of the glass bowl.

  6 ripe peaches (about 1¾ pounds total)
1½ cups water
  ½ cup sugar
  1 teaspoon pure vanilla extract
      Custard Cream (recipe follows)
      Sponge Cake (recipe follows)
  ½ cup framboise liqueur
  2 pints fresh raspberries
  ⅓ cup sliced blanched almonds, toasted and cooled
  1 cup heavy cream, whipped
  2 sprigs fresh mint leaves, for garnish

Blanch the peaches in a saucepan of boiling water for 20 seconds. Rinse them under cold running water, drain, and peel.

Bring the water, sugar, and vanilla to a boil in a large saucepan over high heat. Boil rapidly for about 5 minutes. Reduce the heat and simmer the peaches in the syrup, covered, until they are still firm yet a knife can easily penetrate the fruit, about 4 minutes. (If the syrup does not cover the peaches, turn them as they cook.) Remove the peaches with a slotted spoon. Refrigerate 4 of the peaches. Reserve ½ cup of the poaching syrup in a medium saucepan.

Pit and coarsely chop the 2 remaining peaches. Simmer the chopped peaches in the ½ cup syrup, stirring, until the syrup reduces and thickens and the peaches are almost transparent, about 6 minutes. Transfer to a bowl and chill for at least 2 hours. Meanwhile, make the Custard Cream and Sponge Cake.

When ready to assemble the trifle, slice each Sponge Cake in half horizontally; you will have 4 layers. Pit and thinly slice the chilled peaches. Reserve 12 slices for garnish.

Assemble the trifle in a 2½ quart glass serving bowl in the following order:

1.   ½ cup Custard Cream
2.   1 Sponge Cake layer drizzled with 2 tablespoons framboise
3.   Half the chopped peaches in syrup
4.   Half the remaining sliced peaches (some arranged against the side of the bowl to display the fruit)
5.   ½ cup Custard Cream
6.   1 Sponge Cake layer drizzled with 2 tablespoons framboise
7.   1 pint raspberries (some arranged against the side of the bowl to display the fruit)
8.   ½ cup Custard Cream
9.   One-third of the toasted almonds

Repeat steps 2 through 9, but reserve 10 raspberries for garnish and spread the remaining Custard Cream over the raspberry layer.

Chill for 4 hours or overnight. Cover with whipped cream and garnish with the reserved peach slices, raspberries, and mint leaves. Sprinkle with the remaining almonds.

Serves 10 to 12

Custard Cream

2 cups light cream
6 large egg yolks
⅔ cup sugar
½ teaspoon pure vanilla extract
2 tablespoons framboise liqueur

Bring the cream to a boil in a medium sauce-pan. Process the egg yolks and sugar in a food processor with the metal blade until combined, about 20 seconds. Scrape down the side of the workbowl. With the motor running, add half the boiling cream through the feed tube. Whisk the cream–egg yolk mixture into the remaining cream in the saucepan and cook over low heat, stirring constantly, until thick enough to coat a spoon. Do not boil. Stir in the vanilla and framboise. Chill at least 2 hours.

Makes about 3 cups

Sponge Cake

6 large eggs, at room temperature
¾ cup sugar
1 cup unbleached all-purpose flour
6 tablespoons clarified butter (see page 000)
½ teaspoon pure vanilla extract

Preheat the oven to 350°F. Butter two 8-inch round cake pans and line them with wax paper. Butter and flour the paper.

Beat the eggs and sugar together in a large bowl with a hand-held electric mixer, about 20 seconds. Set the bowl over hot water and stir until the egg-sugar mixture is lukewarm, about 2 minutes. Beat with the mixer on high speed until the mixture is light, pale yellow and tripled in volume, about 12 minutes.

Sift the flour over the batter, and gently fold it in. Carefully fold in the butter and vanilla.

Divide the batter between the prepared pans and smooth the surface. Bake in the center of the preheated oven until a cake tester inserted in the center of the cake comes out clean, about 25 minutes.

Cool the cakes for 10 minutes in the pans. Then invert them onto wire racks and cool completely.

Makes two 8-inch sponge cake layers

[E L E N E   M A R G O T   K O L B]

Rhubarb

Although technically a vegetable (a member of the buckwheat family), rhubarb is eaten as a fruit. Available from April to June, the rhubarb plant has stalks that look like red celery and has small green leaves that are toxic; only the stalks are used. Rhubarb has such an intensely tart flavor that it is cooked and never eaten raw. Look for thin, firm stalks that have fresh-looking leaves.

Cranberry and Rhubarb Relish

This tangy, spicy relish is a wonderful accompaniment for game, but it serves equally well with any cold meat or pâté.

1 cup fresh rhubarb, diced into ½-inch pieces (if fresh rhubarb is not available, substitute frozen)
3 cups fresh cranberries (if fresh cranberries are not available, substitute frozen)
½ teaspoon mustard seed, crushed
1 teaspoon whole allspice, crushed
1 small onion (3 ounces), peeled and grated to almost a liquid consistency
¼ cup distilled white vinegar
½ cup maple syrup
½ teaspoon salt
½ teaspoon freshly ground black pepper

Combine all the ingredients in a medium saucepan, preferably stainless steel. Cover and bring to a boil. Boil gently for 4 to 5 minutes, or until the mixture has the consistency of a purée. Refrigerate and serve cold.

The relish will keep, refrigerated, for several weeks.

Makes about 2½ cups

[J A C Q U E S   P É P I N]

Rhubarb Jam

2 medium oranges (about 1 pound total)
3 cups sugar
½ cup water
2½ pounds fresh rhubarb, washed, trimmed, and cut into 1-inch pieces

Remove the zest from the oranges with a swivel-bladed peeler. Process the zest and 1 cup of the sugar in a food processor with the metal blade until the zest is finely chopped, about 1 minute.

Squeeze the juice from the oranges and strain into a large nonreactive saucepan. Add the contents of the workbowl and the remaining ingredients and stir to mix. Bring slowly to a boil, stirring occasionally. Reduce the heat and simmer, uncovered, until the mixture is very thick, about 1 hour.

Ladle the hot jam into hot half-pint jars, leaving about ½ inch of headspace, and vacuum seal according to the jar manufacturer's directions.

Place the jars in a boiling water bath for 10 minutes. Remove with tongs and cool to room temperature on wire racks covered with kitchen towels.

Makes about 4 cups

[S U Z A N N E   S .   J O N E S]

Strawberries

Cultivated strawberries come in several varieties: small, large, round, conical, some hollow, some dense, some with more seeds than others, some pale, and some deep red. A member of the rose family, strawberries also grow wild from April to June. Choose bright, firm, unblemished small strawberries and eat them on the same day if possible. Wash the fruit very quickly with their green tops still attached to avoid water getting into the fruit. Strawberries can be stored in the refrigerator, spread out in a single layer on a baking sheet, for 2 to 3 days.

Strawberry Sorbet

3 pints fresh, ripe strawberries or 3 pack-
　ages (10 ounces each) frozen strawber-
　ries in syrup
2 cups sugar or 1 cup sugar if using frozen
　berries
1½ cups fresh orange juice
¾ cup fresh lemon juice
⅓ cup Grand Marnier

Wash and hull the fresh strawberries or
slightly thaw the frozen strawberries. Combine in a bowl the fresh or frozen strawberries, sugar, and orange and lemon juices, and
let stand 2 to 3 hours. Put the mixture
through a sieve or a food mill, or purée in an
electric blender. Stir in the Grand Marnier
and pour into 2 large freezing trays. Freeze
until about 1 inch of the mixture is frozen on
all sides of the tray. Remove and beat the mixture until mushy. Return to the trays and
freeze until firm. For a more delicate sorbet,
beat the mixture up twice, freezing slightly in
between. You may also freeze it in an ice-
cream freezer.

Serves 8

[JAMES BEARD]

New England Strawberry Shortcake

2 cups unbleached all-purpose flour
2 teaspoons baking powder
2 teaspoons sugar, plus additional to
　sweeten the berries
½ teaspoon cream of tartar
¼ teaspoon salt
¾ cup unsalted butter, chilled
½ cup cold milk
2 pints fresh, ripe strawberries, hulled
1½ cups heavy cream

Preheat the oven to 400°F. Lightly butter an
8-inch round cake pan.

Mix the flour, baking powder, sugar,
cream of tartar, and salt in a food processor
with the metal blade, turning the machine
on and off 2 or 3 times.

Add ½ cup of the butter, in 8 pieces, and
process, turning the machine on and off 10 to
12 times, or until the mixture resembles very
coarse meal. Remove the cover and pour the
milk over the mixture. Replace the cover and
turn the machine on and off 4 to 6 times, or
until the dough just holds together.

Carefully remove the dough from the
workbowl and divide it in half. Pat or roll out
each portion into an 8-inch circle. Melt the
remaining ¼ cup butter. Press one circle into
the bottom of the prepared pan and brush
with about 1½ tablespoons of melted butter.
Place the second circle on top and press
down lightly.

Bake in the preheated oven for 15 to 17
minutes, or until lightly browned. Remove

the pan to a rack and let cool for 15 minutes. Meanwhile use the metal blade to process the strawberries, about 1 cup at a time, turning the machine on and off 4 or 5 times or until coarsely chopped. Sweeten to taste and set aside.

Run a knife around the edge of the shortcake; place a wire rack over the pan and invert. With a broad spatula gently lift the top layer and invert it onto a serving dish. Brush with the remaining melted butter and cover with some of the sweetened strawberries. Invert the second layer on top and cover with more strawberries. Pass a bowl of the remaining berries and the heavy cream in a pitcher.

Makes one 8-inch shortcake

Strawberry Glaze Pie

Crust

1¼ cups unbleached all-purpose flour, plus additional for rolling out
½ cup cake flour
2 tablespoons sugar
⅔ cup vegetable shortening
1 teaspoon salt
½ cup cold milk

Filling

4 pints fresh, ripe strawberries
2 tablespoons strained apricot jam
1 to 2 teaspoons confectioners' sugar
⅔ cup granulated sugar
2 tablespoons cornstarch
¼ cup water
2 tablespoons lightly salted butter
1 tablespoon kirsch

Topping

1 cup chilled heavy (whipping) cream
3 tablespoons Crème Fraîche (optional)
2 tablespoons confectioners' sugar
1 tablespoon vanilla extract

Process both flours, sugar, shortening, and salt in a food processor with the steel blade 10 seconds. With the motor running, quickly pour the milk through the feed tube. Process about 12 seconds longer until the dough forms a ball that makes no more than one or two revolutions around the bowl. Gather together any stray pieces. The dough will be soft and sticky. Wrap it in plastic and refrigerate for at least 3 hours, preferably overnight.

Generously flour a work surface (about ¼ cup flour). Sprinkle the dough liberally with flour and roll into a rectangle, about 14 × 7 inches. The mixture will be very crumbly and may break. Fold the dough in three (like a letter). Reflour the work surface and roll the dough into a 14-inch circle. The dough is sometimes troublesome. If it breaks apart or is difficult to roll, gather it into a ball; chill 30 minutes; then roll again, this time between double overlapping sheets of wax paper. Turn the crust into an 11-inch metal pie plate. Trim the dough to overlap the pan rim by ¾ inch. Turn the excess dough under. Do not worry if the crust cracks when folded under. Finger-flute the rim by pressing the dough between both index fingers to form a ridge, simultaneously exerting pressure with your thumb to keep the edges even.

Use the tines of a fork to prick the crust at 1-inch intervals over the bottom and sloping sides. Use a trussing needle or skewer to prick the ridges of each flute. Chill 30 minutes.

Preheat the oven to 450°F.

Bake the crust for 10 minutes until puffy; reduce the heat to 300°F and bake 10 minutes longer until evenly browned. Cool.

While the crust cools, prepare the strawberries for the filling.

Rinse strawberries under running water. Hull with a paring knife to remove stem and white core. Reserve 2 cups berries for the glaze and 8 good berries for garnish.

Melt the apricot jam and use it to brush the bottom and sides of the cooled crust.

Pile the remaining berries into the crust, points up. Fill in spaces by cutting as necessary. Arrange berry halves, points facing out in a decorative ring, around the sloping inner rim. Dust with confectioners' sugar.

Purée the reserved 2 cups strawberries in the food processor with the steel blade 10 to 20 seconds, until liquid. Pass purée through a very fine strainer to remove seeds. Place the purée and sugar in a 2-quart saucepan and bring to a boil, stirring to dissolve the sugar. Dissolve the cornstarch in the water and add to the purée. Add the butter; bring mixture back to a bubble; simmer, stirring, for 1 minute. While the mixture is hot, stir in the kirsch. Pour the hot glaze over the berries and set the pie aside for 30 minutes to cool while you prepare the topping.

Chill the steel blade of the food processor for 15 minutes, then fit it into the workbowl. Add the cream and the Crème Fraîche, if using. Process 10 seconds. Add the sugar and vanilla and process until the cream is very thick, about 30 seconds. Be careful not to overprocess (see note below). Use a #9 cannellated pastry tube to pipe cream decoratively on top of the pie. Garnish with the reserved strawberries. Chill.

Serves 10 to 12

NOTE: While the food processor will not whip cream to great volume, it does an excellent job of whipping cream for piping.

[J A N E   S A L Z F A S S   F R E I M A N]

Strawberries with Lichee Nuts

3 pints fresh, ripe strawberries, washed and hulled

2 cans (10 ounces each) lichee nuts in heavy syrup, drained

8 pieces ginger, preserved in syrup, each about ½ inch in diameter, finely chopped

¼ cup preserved ginger syrup

Combine the strawberries and lichee nuts in a large serving bowl. Toss gently with the ginger and syrup and refrigerate until serving time.

Serves 8

[CARL JEROME]

Strawberry Tart with Peppermint Cream

Pastry

1 cup plus 2 tablespoons unbleached all-purpose flour

1½ teaspoons sugar

⅛ teaspoon salt

½ cup unsalted butter, chilled and cut into 8 pieces

¼ cup ice water

Filling

1 peppermint herbal tea bag

1 cup milk

¼ cup sugar

1 tablespoon unbleached all-purpose flour

2 teaspoons cornstarch

1 large egg

3 tablespoons unsalted butter

½ cup heavy cream, chilled

2 pints fresh, ripe strawberries, hulled and halved lengthwise

½ cup pure strawberry jelly
Fresh mint leaves, for garnish

To make the pastry, process the flour, sugar, salt, and butter in a food processor with the metal blade until the mixture resembles coarse crumbs, about 10 seconds. Add the water and pulse until the pastry just begins to hold together, about 9 times. Turn out onto wax paper and form into a 6-inch disc. Wrap in the wax paper and chill for 30 minutes.

Roll the pastry out to a 14-inch square on a lightly floured surface and fit into a 9-inch fluted square tart pan with a removable bottom (see note below), gently pressing the pastry into the pan and up the sides without stretching it. Trim the edge, leaving a 1-inch overhang. Fold in the overhang and gently press against the pan sides. Chill for 20 minutes.

Preheat the oven to 400°F.

Line the tart shell with heavy-duty foil and prick with a fork. Bake in the center of the preheated oven for 20 minutes, then remove the foil and bake until golden brown, 10 to 15 minutes more. Cool on a rack.

To make the filling, immerse the tea bag in the milk in a heavy saucepan and bring just to a simmer over moderately high heat. Remove from the heat and let steep for 2 minutes. Squeeze the tea bag and discard it.

Process the sugar, flour, and cornstarch in the processor with the metal blade until combined, about 2 seconds. With the motor running, add the egg through the feed tube and process until smooth, about 4 seconds. Scrape down the workbowl, and with the motor running add the peppermint milk.

Return to the saucepan and cook over moderately high heat, stirring constantly with a wire whisk, until very thick and bubbly, about 2 minutes. Remove from the heat and stir in the butter. Transfer to a bowl and cool, stirring occasionally.

Beat the cream with the processor whisk attachment or an electric mixer until soft peaks form and fold it into the peppermint mixture. Spread the filling in the tart shell and chill for 30 minutes.

Arrange the strawberries on the filling in rows, cut side down. Melt the jelly in a small saucepan over low heat, stirring. Brush over the strawberries and garnish with the mint. Remove the sides of the pan before serving.

Serves 12

NOTE: The pastry may be rolled out to a 14-inch circle and fitted into an 11-inch fluted round tart pan with a removable bottom. Bake as directed. Arrange the strawberries on the filling in concentric circles with the points toward the center.

[JIM DODGE AND ELAINE RATNER]

Recipe Index

Contributor Index

About the Editors

MARIA KOUREBANAS was an associate editor at *Gourmet* magazine. She was the main writer and researcher for the magazine's "Cook's Corner" monthly column.

CARL SONTHEIMER started a cooking revolution when he introduced the Cuisinart® food processor to America in 1973. Shortly thereafter he founded the highly acclaimed magazine *The Pleasures of Cooking*. Sontheimer is the author of *Classic Cakes and Other Great Cuisinart® Desserts*. He is on the National Advisory Board for the James Beard Foundation and lives in Greenwich, Connecticut.